Critical Praise for
Rattiner's Financial Planner's Bible: The Advisor's Advisor

"Indispensable advice from an industry leader. Jeff Rattiner, one of the foremost financial planning educators in the country, has written a book that belongs in every planner's library."

> —Richard J. Koreto
> Executive Editor
> Financial Planning Magazine

"A one-stop shopping resource for setting up and running your financial planning practice. This is a comprehensive guide for beginners as well as advanced planners. I wish this bible had been available when we started our investment advisory firm 5 years ago."

> —Steven I. Levey, CPA/PFS
> Principal
> GHP Investment Advisors, Inc.

"Jeff Rattiner knows this business. For rookies just starting out or mid-career advisors refocusing their practices, this book offers sage advice on marketing and practice management. As the financial services industry continues to reinvent itself, all advisors can benefit from his experience."

> —Mitch Rose
> Executive Editor
> Horsesmouth

"Jeff Rattiner's Financial Planner's Bible is an indispensable tool for any advisor interested in meeting the competitive challenges in today's environment."

> —E. Clark Griggs
> Vice President-Financial Consultant
> A National Financial Services Firm

Rattiner's Financial Planner's Bible

Rattiner's Financial Planner's Bible

The Advisor's Advisor

Jeffrey H. Rattiner, CPA, CFP, MBA, RFC

John Wiley & Sons, Inc.

ISBN 0-471-22034-5

Printed in the United States of America.

10 9 8 7 6 5 4 3 2 1

To my children, Brandon, Keri, and Matthew, who everyday provide me with my greatest inspiration.

To my wife, Rochele, for her continued love and support.

To my parents, Esther and Ronald, who, when the going gets tough, never give up!

Preface

Through all the training I provide to companies, the one central theme everyone always seems to ask questions around is: "Jeff, we've been practicing for 20 years and we're still not sold on how we can create the optimum practice. We try this, that, and the other thing; yet we always seem to be going in circles. I'd like to establish a prototype model on what's required to develop the model practice. How can we be the best financial planners we can be? How do we learn to think outside the box, and not get caught up in the fads of today?"

Well, that got me thinking. I said to myself, if I were starting out today, what kind of tool would I like to see that would put me on the path to success? Or, if I was an experienced practitioner, what could I learn from other successful planners that would enable me to benefit from their experiences? At which point I said to myself, wouldn't it be great to develop a model of how practicing financial advisors can achieve these dreams and their lifelong ambitions of providing the ultimate in services to their existing clients and a model framework for acquiring new ones? And then, wouldn't it be great to write these ideas down for a practical book so other financial advisors can have the benefit of these ideas when they can still make a difference in their clients' lives? And wouldn't it be great to educate existing financial advisors on how they can make that happen, while showing them the pitfalls to avoid, the issues to contemplate, the steps to consider, and the hard decisions to make, while remaining focused in their quest to take their practices to unforeseen levels? What it came down to, in essence, is a book about being a strong, competent, and ethical financial advisor.

When I think about what makes a strong financial advisor, the one characteristic I see repeatedly is "doing what's best for the client" in an ethical, practical, and professional manner. How can you make your clients' lives better? How can you get them to where they want and need to be down the road, versus where they are today? In essence, how can you make their lives better? When you think about it, nothing else really matters, not the image you bestow, the type of office you have, or even the way you are paid. It all boils down to client honor and advisor integrity. And that is when I decided to take John Wiley & Sons up on their offer to write a book that shows advisors how to do the things necessary to build this successful practice. "Successful" being defined as what to do for your clients as well as what to do for yourself, or, in other words, creating the ultimate balance in your practice so you can have your cake and eat it, too!

The purpose of this book is to provide you with the logical and tested steps necessary to achieve this mission, all the while saving you time and resources, and avoiding any unnecessary mishaps and heartache experienced throughout the years by leading practitioners. It takes a consortium of approaches from various financial planning practitioners emphasizing the good, the bad, and the ugly, while telling you about the do's and don'ts of each. This book does not follow the sequence of a traditional book on financial planning or the way some of my other books are laid out. I describe to you things the way they are, not the way you would like them to be. I provide a reality check to help you distinguish fact from fiction. I delve into 50 insightful ways of marketing your practice that many practitioners do not currently use, as well as 25 intriguing ways to build up the infrastructure of your practice to support the things you want to do but cannot. We show you how to work with external alliances to create true win-win scenarios, because there really is enough money out there for everyone.

To help you visualize where you are in your practice, I have developed a self-assessment system that allows you to quantify exactly where your practice is today and what you can do to make improvements to match the objectives you have set for yourself. I have developed worksheets and audit-type programs to give you a true picture of where you stand today and what you need to do to practice successfully. All these practical ideas, along with a model for capturing the technical aspects of our business for planning in the areas of insurance, investment, income tax, retirement, estate, and other disciplines, are provided. By reading this book, when meeting with clients, you will ultimately acquire the skills necessary to look for specific issues, and digest, comprehend, and resolve common client critical concerns when performing comprehensive financial planning services by incorporating these matters into a model financial planning practice. This prototype practice details the kinds of questions you encounter from clients, and all the things you need to be as a competent financial advisor; it will ultimately tell you how to take your practice to the next level.

I wish to acknowledge the many planners I have interviewed who provided me with the guidance, passion, and insight into what makes their practices successful, and Judy Horwarth of John Wiley & Sons, Inc., as my editor, Sujin Hong as my associate managing editor, and John DeRemigis, as my project manager, who wanted to see a financial planning book that would turn upside down the conventional thinking of the industry and tell it the way it really is.

Jeffrey H. Rattiner, CPA, CFP, MBA, RFC
Englewood, CO
February 14, 2002

Contents

Rattiner's Financial Planner's Bible

1

Rattiner on the State of the Financial Services Industry

The financial services industry will never be the same! Well, that may be an exaggeration, but the truth of the matter is that 2001 brought us much ado about change. September 11, 2001, was the biggest blow. For the first time, it made people think more financially and the results have been disconcerting. People are not as free-spending, businesses have begun massive layoffs in greater numbers than prior to the 11th, and rates of return are being looked at more closely because we have our second down year in a row. That's a first in almost 20 years!

YOUR ROLE

So where do you fit in? Clearly, as a financial advisor your role has changed, too. No longer can you count on the automatic double-digit returns that have become commonplace within the past few years. In fact, since August 1982, the market has had its most un-paralleled upswing in history. While I am not an advocate of down markets, I can tell you that this prolonged bear market may be the best thing to happen to us in a long time. Just think of it in these terms: Many of the financial advisors in the marketplace were not around before 1982. Therefore, they have never seen a true bear market. Many advisors interpreted a bear market to mean "wait a few weeks until we get back on course." Clearly that

**Ten Changes to the Current Financial
Planning Environment and Why Financial Planners
Will Reap the Benefits**

1. Changing society
2. Raising the bar: The trend toward expertise in delivering quality financial planning advice
3. Repeal of Glass-Steagall and the formation of true financial services supermarkets
4. The need to become process oriented rather than transaction oriented
5. Trend toward fee-based rather than commission-based planning
6. Trend toward specialization, leveraging, and developing alliances in other areas
7. Trend toward technological advances and becoming more reliant on technology and less on the personal touch
8. Trend toward a revamped individual marketing approach: It is a different ballgame now
9. Trend toward building from within: It is cheaper and more effective to develop your infrastructure right the first time
10. Trend toward commoditization of services

did not happen during the 1970s! In fact, it looked like the stock market took a vacation until the 1980s. In any event, this market will finally enable people to look at a complete diversification strategy rather than diversifying through equities alone. The importance of bonds and other non-sexy investments in a portfolio will finally be recognized. Investors can once again begin to look at the entire picture.

CHANGING SOCIETY

We are living in a different world from the one in which we were raised. In essence, we have transformed into a market-oriented rather than a producer-oriented society. No longer do companies manufacture products in the hope that consumers will buy them. Nowadays, companies survey and test-market products long before they are available to the consumer. Sometimes, these products never make it to the consumer.

And to help make things more simple, we're now able to employ technology. (I'm still not convinced that it's entirely a good thing!) We got used to using technology to assist us in our daily tasks. Relationships were a stronghold then, whereby advisors would get back to the client relatively soon, but not instantaneously as is required in today's marketplace. Now, we as advisors require it, to gather as much information as possible because the consumer demands it. The bottom line is this: if we don't provide information to the consumer ASAP and as accurately as possible, someone else will. And that is the dilemma we face in this business. As a result, we have to gear up our staff to be politically correct, to appease the client at all times, to learn to use a variety of software programs and other sources of data, to interpret various studies, and to plan strategies in the likelihood that our clients will demand this from us immediately.

A major study was performed on the future of the financial advisory business and the delivery of advice to the semiaffluent investor in September 1999 by Mark Hurley of Undiscovered Managers™ ((214) 999-7205). The study, which can be found on the company's web site (*undiscoveredmanagers.com*), is fascinating and some of the results are appropriate for a discussion of the future of the financial planning profession. This book incorporates many of these findings and shows planners how they can grow their existing businesses to reflect a changing, dynamic environment.

The study reveals that the financial advisory business is on the verge of a major revolution, and that the staggering growth of the late 1990s is unsustainable. Therefore, going forward, competition will be fierce and the cost of acquiring clients will grow significantly. Technology is commoditizing many of the services we currently perform, which means we need to bring additional value to the table (something most of us are not doing now). Because of the tremendous success and prospects of this business, other financial services companies, including brokerage companies, large investment banks, and private banking companies, accounting firms, and money management companies, are joining the ranks in record numbers. In fact, brokerages have shifted their businesses from traditional transaction-based compensation systems to fee-based programs in order to compete for semiaffluent clients. All these companies are foregoing short-term profits to capture long-term intrinsic value, posing a serious threat to current smaller advisory firms. The financial advisory business will continue to evolve in a manner similar to that of the institutional money management business. In order to win over the long term, many of these advisory firms will build alliances with those companies that can help them succeed.

The effects of these issues will appear throughout the book.

RAISING THE BAR: THE TREND TOWARD EXPERTISE IN DELIVERING QUALITY FINANCIAL PLANNING ADVICE

As you can see, financial services companies are looking to improve the quality of their field forces in the financial advice arena. Many of these companies have enrolled their reps or even mandated that they earn a financial planning designation. The overwhelming choice of designation is the Certified Financial Planner™ (CFP)™. With some of the companies I provide this type of training for (as mentioned below), each has its own specific purpose. In fact, Merrill Lynch has instituted a new educational requirement. According to a company spokesperson, Merrill's new Financial Advisor training program requires new and existing advisors to get their CFP™ certification within five years. A nice bonus system has been installed to reward those reps who achieve this designation. First Tennessee Bank would like to have a CFP™ licensee in each branch. Wells Fargo's Private Client Services (PCS) wants its high-net-worth clients to be in the capable hands of CFP™ licensees. SunAmerica Securities and Sentra Spelman want their reps to have a competitive advantage. They are bringing an educational program leading to the CFP™ designation (Financial Planning Fast Track™ or

FPFT™, to be discussed later on) to various offices around the country. Many other companies are wait-listed for FPFT. The goal at all these companies I train for is to provide their staff with the highest level of training so that they can then compete with other practitioners in this arena and provide competent financial planning advice when working with clients. With this "rise to quality" occurring rapidly, many firms see the competition as too steep and are trying to differentiate themselves from their peers. Having your reps work with their customers at the highest level goes a long way toward accomplishing that goal. With over 39,000 CFP™ licensees in the United States, the CFP™ appears to be the designation of choice for financial advisors.

To earn the CFP™ designation, you must complete a course of study including general personal financial planning topics, insurance planning, investment planning, income tax planning, employee benefit and retirement planning, and estate planning. Each class is approximately 30 hours and includes various forms of testing. However, if you have a CPA, ChFC (Chartered Financial Consultant), PFS (Personal Financial Specialist), or PhD in Finance, you may be eligible to opt out of a registered educational program and proceed directly to the examination. If not, there are over 200 educational programs offered throughout the country by the CFP Board of Standards in which you can enroll. For a complete listing of these programs, call the CFP Board at (800) 487-1497 or visit its web site at *www.cfp-board.org*. One program I work with is the Metropolitan State College of Denver ("Metro"). Metro has the traditional program described above and also an alternative program for students who do not want to sit through an entire one-and-a-half-to-two-year program. It is called *Financial Planning Fast Track (FPFT)* and is offered in Denver three times a year (once in conjunction with each testing cycle), or at various locations of the financial services companies discussed above. FPFT accelerates the process to approximately six months through an intensive course of study. For more information, call (720) 529-1888.

This topic is covered using a cutting-edge, outside-the-box quantification system that can help you measure and manage your practice and determine when you are ready to advance to the next level.

REPEAL OF GLASS-STEAGALL AND THE FORMATION OF TRUE FINANCIAL SERVICES SUPERMARKETS

With the megamerger between Citibank and Travelers that formed the financial services supermarket Citigroup, all future barriers to combining banking, brokerage, and insurance companies have been lifted. The reason for this partnering is to provide one-stop shopping for all customers. Cross-selling can now exist among the different companies of the newly formed entity (i.e., Citibank (banking and mortgages), Travelers (insurance), and Salomon Smith Barney (brokerage)). With one-stop shopping, the client needs only one financial advisor contact to lead the way into all the ancillary companies.

Many planners I know believe in the "financial supermarket" concept, that if they can house an array of financial planning products and services under one roof, the client has no reason to go anywhere else. It makes sense. Banks, brokerage firms, and insurance companies are no longer identified as separate companies selling only their respective products. That is one reason why the old Equitable Insurance Company decided to move away from the negative insurance industry stereotype and change its name to Axa Financial, which denotes all types of financial products and services.

Companies are also pairing up so they can cross-sell their existing clients and develop new distribution channels. Citibank can now cross-sell bank customers with insurance and annuity products, and Travelers can do the same thing with mortgages, personal loans, and other bank products. Just look at AIG's acquisition of SunAmerica Inc. AIG has access to some of the best annuity products and other venues, while it opens a new door for SunAmerica by enabling them to sell to foreign markets, such as Asia, where they have been virtually nonexistent until now. Look at the H&R Block tax service. With their recent acquisition of Olde Brokerage, they now are in a position to cross-sell their tax clients with financial products and, in effect, become a true year-round business. The list of such companies is enormous and will continue to get larger. Not only that, many nonfinancial service companies will get into this arena as well.

This one-stop-shopping concept is what is happening in the advisor community. Many advisors have partnered with CPAs, attorneys, insurance agents, stockbrokers, actuaries, mortgage brokers, and others to form comprehensive shops. It works with the client as follows: The client comes into the office and meets with the financial advisor to begin the interactive goal-setting and data-gathering session. After that, the client returns to the office to meet again with the planner and the remaining team members. Each specialist, who has direct input into the client's plan, talks about his or her appropriate specialty with the client. If additional products and/or services are warranted as a result of the plan's findings, then the client can be channeled to those areas.

Chapter 5, on using Form 1040, provides an integrated approach to how you can combine various elements when working with your clients.

THE NEED TO BECOME PROCESS ORIENTED RATHER THAN TRANSACTION ORIENTED

Many of the large financial services firms that I train for have come to the realization that it is easier to acquire client assets and sell more products by using a process-oriented approach that looks at the client's entire picture, rather than looking at specific issues and then tailoring products to fit those issues. By uncovering all a client's needs, you end up doing a more thorough job for the client, which, if done properly, can result in the client's having greater ties to the financial services company.

The best way to tackle any issue is to follow one line of thinking through a systematic process. Financial planning is no different. In fact, one system can be used to determine the quantitative needs of any client. Anyone in your office should be able to use the client's information to arrive at the same financial conclusions. This will help you provide consistent results for all your clients.

Planners who incorporate financial planning into their business structure realize that financial planning is a process, and not a product. It could very well end up with the sale of a product, but unlike going into a client call with a specific product in mind, we examine the entire spectrum for the client and are then in a better position to evaluate the client's situation as a whole. The key to establishing a successful relationship is to walk the client through the financial planning process.

The financial planning process as practiced by me is denoted by the acronym PIPRIM©:

- **P**reliminary meeting with the client
- **I**nteractive goal-setting and fact-finding session
- **P**utting it all together
- **R**ecommending solutions
- **I**mplementing the plan
- **M**onitoring the plan

Step 1: Preliminary Meeting with the Client

During this time, you and the prospective client explore whether the client's issues are ones that you can handle. You must ask yourself whether you can work closely and successfully with the client. Some of the items of discussion may include:

- The clients' immediate and long-term needs
- All the services you can provide
- Why the client would benefit from these services
- Your financial and investment philosophy
- Estimated time frame to accomplish client goals
- Estimated time frame to complete the plan
- Your method of compensation
- Your role in the process

If the two of you hit it off, schedule your next meeting for sometime during the following two to three weeks. By meeting quickly, you will continue the rhythm you have established from this meeting. Write a letter of understanding (also called an "engagement letter") to ensure that both of you know your complete roles going forward.

Step 2: Interactive Goal-Setting and Fact-Finding Session

In this session—the first paid one with the client—you will ask the questions that will help you design and implement a successful financial plan. The meeting should last for as much time as you need; some planners spend as much as two hours with a client.

Make it as interactive as possible so information is flowing freely from the client. Gather as much information as possible. Have the client prioritize goals for you. This way you will help assure that, at the very least, the most important ones are achieved.

After the interview concludes, set up the next appointment for approximately four weeks later. Before you do any work, send the client a synopsis of the meeting, stating your recollection of the issues and objectives discussed and the conclusions to which you came. Ask the client to sign the synopsis and return it to you.

Step 3: Putting It All Together—Analyzing the Information

Once you have the information you need, you should analyze it to identify your client's strengths and weaknesses. Create a balance sheet and a cash flow statement from all the information given to you so you can analyze the entire picture.

Step 4: Recommending Solutions

Your next step is to develop recommendations on how clients can accomplish their financial goals. These recommendations act as solutions to the client's needs and prioritized objectives. Before you offer these recommendations in a formal and neatly presented plan, discuss them with the client. Often, recommendations need to be modified before the client accepts them. That is because situations may have changed during the process, or the client realizes that some data was not correct. Once you and the client agree, present the recommendations in a clear, concise statement, which will make it easier for the client to implement your plan.

Step 5: Implementing the Plan

It is time to act on these recommendations. Discuss an order and timetable for their implementation. Talk about who will initiate action on each recommendation.

Step 6: Monitoring the Plan

Schedule periodic review sessions with clients to evaluate their progress toward reaching their objectives and to decide whether a given plan continues to meet client needs. At the very least, these meetings should be held annually.

Pay attention to the particular situations of your clients, such as where they are in their lives, as well as to what transpires in the economy, such as tax changes, inflation, interest rate movements, and so forth.

By going through the entire process, you will be in a much better position to correctly diagnose your client's concerns and apply appropriate solutions directly to those needs.

TREND TOWARD FEE-BASED RATHER THAN COMMISSION-BASED PLANNING

We have all witnessed the trend toward fee-based planning and away from commissions. I would say that within five years half of all planners will be compensated through some type of fees.

Fees can come in several forms. You can charge hourly, by the project, or as a percentage of assets under management. You can also have some hybrid of the above. I have an hourly fee rate of $150. For a typical financial plan, I charge approximately $1,200 because I envision it taking me eight hours to complete. My percentage-of-assets fee ranges from 1.50 percent down to .585 basis points, based on the amount managed.

A Top Ten list stating why advisors prefer fee-based business includes:

- *Keeps the client relationship intact.* Trust factors develop and a good dialogue results, thus making your relationship with your clients first-rate. It also encourages annual reviews to monitor the progress in client accounts. Client loyalty may also be an advantage. Possibilities for long-term relationships exist and the number of referrals can be higher because of the dedication between planner and client. Clients also realize that you are not trading products just to generate commissions because you are not getting paid in that capacity.
- *No perceived conflict of interest.* Since your livelihood is not dependent on commissions from product sales, many planners feel that fee-based business is the only way to be ob-

jective for your clients. If your clients realize that fees are your sole source of revenue, they will perceive you as servicing only them.

- *Investment management opportunities.* Since you view the client as first and foremost, you can do what's best for the client without jeopardizing your status as a product provider.
- *More opportunities to evaluate many different types of products.* You can gain access to the latest and highest quality alternatives by gaining knowledge of products yourself; asking client specialists to make suggestions; and using your own specialists.
- *Reduced costs.* Many planners provide full services to the client. Examples include tax return preparation and planning, financial planning, answering questions throughout the year, and other services.
- *Revenues come in the form of a quarterly annuity paid in advance.*
- *Asset management enables the advisor to assist the client lay the foundation for the accomplishment of his or her financial objectives.*
- *Clients may be able to deduct your fees.* Under Section 212, Ruling 73-13, of the Internal Revenue Code, fees for investment advice are tax deductible. Assuming investment advice is an integral part of your practice, these fees may be deductible. This contrasts with commission paid for purchasing investment products, which probably will not be deductible.
- *Less marketing may be required, since your practice is based primarily on referrals.*
- *You may be viewed more professionally,* since clients are used to paying hourly or per-service/job fees for other professionals, such as doctors, lawyers, CPAs, and the like.

To set the record straight, there is no right or wrong way to charge your clients. What does count the most is whether you believe that you are doing the right thing for the client. Clients are not dummies. They understand that you need to be paid in order to make the system work. Therefore, as long as you have developed trust with them and have fully disclosed how you are being compensated, and how much (if product-related), you are doing right by your clients.

Chapter 2 provides a brief overview of the various compensation methods used by planners.

TREND TOWARD SPECIALIZATION, LEVERAGING, AND DEVELOPING ALLIANCES IN OTHER AREAS

With the increasing knowledge base that exists, it is impossible to know all the areas of financial planning. You cannot be all things to all people! Strong planners work with what they know and farm out what they do not. Choose your areas of concentration and become a qualified expert in them. You are better off knowing a lot about a little than a little about a lot. Just look at doctors. Years ago, doctors made house calls and were general practitioners. They knew a little about a lot. Nowadays, they are all specialists. Whenever you have a particular ailment, you go to someone specific in that field. Just think how poor a job they would do if they were responsible for every part of the body. Look at other professions. Law and accounting have specialties. Now, we must also as financial planners.

You may be able to pick a specialization based on your past experience. I came from the insurance industry. Many years ago, I worked for Metlife in its Management Executive Training program. I got to learn a lot about insurance and estate planning while I was there. I have always been partial to insurance. Even though I worked in all the financial planning disciplines with the American Institute of Certified Public Accountants (AICPA), I always had a fondness for insurance. I have taught insurance classes more than any other subject and have come to be known as an insurance specialist with clients. You might have come up through the investment ranks and feel the same way about investments. Another alternative is to designate a specialty area and become an expert in it. Take continuing education classes, find a mentor, and make other connections in that area. It is easier to bill yourself as a specialist than a generalist. There is more money to be made in specialization; just ask any doctor!

I also see the partnering of various specialists under one roof. I know of several firms that have six planners on staff. Each one is responsible for a different part of the client's overall financial well-being. There is usually a CPA for income tax preparation and planning, an attorney for estate planning, an investment specialist (many times a Chartered Financial Analyst (CFA)), an insurance broker (who handles not just life and health, but property and casualty as well), a retirement specialist or actuary, and a general practitioner, who handles the client interview (the first *P* and *I* in PIPRIM). This last person also is responsible for numerical calculations, such as retirement or life insurance needs analysis, college forecasting, and so forth. These arrangements are really advantageous because they eliminate the competitive factor, bringing planners of different interests and abilities together and enabling each one to fine-tune his or her specialty.

I learned long ago that the only way to expand your capabilities is to leverage yourself through various channels and to leverage others. You need to know when to rely on yourself and your specialty, when to reject an opportunity because it does not follow your model, and when to rely on the work of outside specialists to provide proper training and support. You need to learn how you can work with your peers—CPAs, attorneys, and the like—to achieve a stability not seen before.

Aligning yourself with CPAs and attorneys provides important technical expertise. Wholesalers provide much-needed product information, technical expertise, and funds to help market yourself. Chapter 4 covers ways in which you can master your relationships with alliances and affiliates to encounter win-win situations all the time.

Chapter 4 also discusses specific strategies on how to take advantage of becoming an expert in various areas of financial planning so you may advance your practice in this area.

TREND TOWARD TECHNOLOGICAL ADVANCES AND BECOMING MORE RELIANT ON TECHNOLOGY AND LESS ON THE PERSONAL TOUCH

With clients demanding more information and advisors needing to cover all bases, technology is increasingly becoming the most important as well as possibly the most expensive asset of a firm. Networking is critical for the success of any firm, because for a team, all information must be shared. Any person in my office can access any file or any printer from any computer. And by the time it is all in place, you have to update the system or it can become antiquated very quickly. You should hire a "technology consultant" to take care of any hardware and software issues that arise. I have one. His name is Stewart Goldfarb. I would be lost without him. With limited time, you cannot be all things to your business. You need to know what you can delegate and what you should directly work on. Have the technology consultant design the networking system you will be using. Describe to that person what it is you are trying to accomplish and let that individual figure out your system requirements. You need to make sure you get a system that can be upgraded quite easily and quickly for future growth. It is easier to have someone who is a specialist handle all these issues so you can maintain your billable hours.

It is pretty ironic. I always thought technology was supposed to make life easier. Not so! There are more demands on me because of technology than every before. When I travel, I have to be completely reachable via e-mail, cell phone, and fax. In essence, I am taking my whole office on the road every time I travel. And that is why I make it a point to have technology follow me across the country. I can have my telephone calls forwarded to me at all times and clients never know where I am when I am speaking to them. They may think that I am in the office, but chances are I am as far as 3,000 miles away or just hanging out at home.

I also try to buy the most advanced technology possible so that we can grow into it, and that we do not have to continually replace computers and other equipment.

Chapter 2 will discuss the best use of technology to advance your practice by providing you with background and questions to ask that will enable you to make apples-to-apples comparisons for purchasing the most appropriate items technology has to offer.

TREND TOWARD A REVAMPED INDIVIDUAL MARKETING APPROACH: IT IS A DIFFERENT BALLGAME NOW

My undergraduate degree is in marketing management from the City University of New York at Bernard Baruch College. Much of what I learned in preparing for the economic system in the late 1970s is irrelevant in today's economy. With technology changing as rapidly as ever, the rules of the game will continually change as well.

You need to constantly adapt to the changing strategies of the marketplace today. We are no longer a society in which companies produce without regard to consumers' needs. The policy "if you make it, they will buy" really doesn't cut it anymore. Rather, we are a society of very specialized needs. Before we do anything, we need to field test, survey, and conduct focus groups and the like. Many big companies do this regularly; they can spend millions of dollars throughout the test marketing stage and then pull the plug without making the product a reality. The reason why many companies fail is because they do not adapt to our changing society.

This "consumer-first" mentality is actually a pretty good thing. We apply these concepts to our financial planning process. If we do it right, we find out about the client before we make any recommendations. This leads to the heart of the "trust factor." All purchases and relationships are based on emotional factors. Your clients think emotionally before acting, and then try to justify their decisions. Once the appeal is made, your clients will want someone telling them what to do.

Chapter 3 lays the foundation for the changes in marketing. It is set up with radical thinking that can help you see alternatives to issues you encounter on a regular basis. I provide 50 ways to leave your existing marketing.

TREND TOWARD BUILDING FROM WITHIN: IT IS CHEAPER AND MORE EFFECTIVE TO DEVELOP YOUR INFRASTRUCTURE RIGHT THE FIRST TIME

If you look at all the successful professional sports teams, the one thing they have in common is this: they know how to build from within. They develop players through the farm system, bringing managers up from the minors. They have the components in-house and they know where to put them once they mature. Our business is no different. We, too, have to build and promote from within, and hire the right people from outside only after we have exhausted the other approach.

That is the sign of any good organization. We should promote our staff to positions of authority, thus providing ownership of certain responsibilities. If staff members can do the job, it is easier because they already know the culture of the office, they fit in, and they are more eager to undertake an assignment that will help them prosper with the company. Second, it is cheaper because internal staff generally are paid less than employees brought in from the outside. (That is why you have always heard that the only way to rapid advancement and rapid salary raises is to keep taking new jobs with outside employers.) Third, and most important, it shows a staff member that there is life beyond what he or she is currently doing for the organization, and that hard work, discipline, and persistence can lead to a position of responsibility and power.

Chapter 2 lays the foundation for properly structuring your business, with 25 proven methods to use in building your system to the next level.

TREND TOWARD COMMODITIZATION OF SERVICES

Unfortunately, much of what we are doing is fast becoming a commodity. That means that many qualified people can provide the same service or product. In these circumstances, economies of scale will always suffice because, as Costco, Sam's Club, or any big purchaser of items can attest, there is strength in numbers. Much in the way of number crunching can be done with readily accessible free software over the Internet. And how do you compete with free? CPAs and other accountants are learning this the hard way. With tax software available on the Internet for free, and bookkeeping/write-up software available for practically nothing, it is no wonder why these professionals have to look elsewhere to continue their livelihoods.

Our only approach is to truly provide value-added service. Sure, you have heard this before. But what you may be unaware of is that very few people really do anything about it! That is why there are so many mediocre financial planning firms, and why so many big firms like to give away the store, offering a low cost or free financial plan with the purchase of investment or insurance products.

What you need to do to avoid commoditization is to rank your services, focus on those aspects of the business you like, and take it to the highest level. We provide the necessary tools through a scoring mechanism in Chapter 6, a quantification system to evaluate your existing business.

As you will see, this book is designed to take you through your existing practices, inform you of what you are doing well or not, and help you achieve the next plateau. We will make sure you focus on what is working and get rid of what is not. We use a somewhat unorthodox approach, but will get you there nevertheless.

Take a moment to complete the questionnaire below before proceeding through the book.

Self-Assessment: Where Does Your Practice Fit In?

1. We are moving toward fees in our compensation strategy.   Yes   No

2. We are housing various specialties under one roof.   Yes   No

3. We are leveraging our expertise and forming alliances with other professionals.   Yes   No

4. We are up to date on the most recent technology.   Yes   No

5. We are taking the client's needs to heart before we promote our firm.   Yes   No

6. We hire from within, where possible.   Yes   No

7. We use a financial planning process-oriented approach, rather than a transactional approach, when working with clients.   Yes   No

8. We are providing value-added services all the time.   Yes   No

9. We are trying to educate ourselves to the highest degree by attaining the CFP™ designation or other professional certification.   Yes   No

10. We are well-equipped to compete in a rapidly changing environment.   Yes   No

2

The Practical Effect (An Internal Focus): 25 Ideas to Generate a Stable Business

Build it once, build it right, then move on! These are words I live by. They demonstrate that life is too short to waste time on unproductive means and things that are not beneficial. Every planner has ideas about building a practice. Unfortunately, most focus on the short-term results, rather than looking at the big picture. You need to sacrifice in the short term to gain any true and meaningful rewards later on. It is like the client who is concerned only with short-term disability. This should not be an issue. For example, if a 25-year-old has only a short-term disability policy with a benefit period of two years, what happens at age 27 if that person becomes disabled? Short-term needs should be taken care of from emergency fund, and liquid reserves. In everything you do, you should have the long term in mind.

But how do you go about building your empire? There is so much to take into account, many t's to cross and i's to dot, that you do not want to shortchange anything. Remember Dave Thomas, the founder of Wendy's? He said that the reason Wendy's has square hamburgers is that one of the women close to him while he was growing up said that he should not cut corners! Make the investment up front. At this level, it is not about expense—it is about investments and what you can expect to earn from them.

From my experiences and those of the many planners I have encountered, I have assembled the do's and don'ts of building your practice internally. The following are 25 ideas that can help you take your practice to the next level.

1. NO LOSS LEADERS—GRATIS ISN'T SMART OR PRODUCTIVE IN THE LONG TERM

The cardinal rule of business is to make a profit. If you don't, you won't be there long term when your clients really need you. Many insurance and investment companies give clients financial plans for free so that they can sell the client a product. This is a huge mistake, and demonstrates poor judgment on behalf of the company.

If you receive something for free, then chances are it is not worth much to begin with. Every aspect of your business should be a separate profit center (as discussed below in the marketing section). Why assign a staff person to work on something that is generating no money? If your clients or prospects see that all you are concerned about is selling them a product, the trust factor will disappear. Remember, think of your clients as long term (process oriented), not just transaction oriented.

Develop a price list for the different services you provide. You can offer discounts if the client purchases more than one service from you. However, do not hesitate to provide "throw-ins" to close deals. If you work in huge quantities because you represent many clients, and so forth, you can narrow the gap in your profit margins. But do not eliminate them. All big law or accounting firms have billable time in each area of expertise. You should be no different.

2. HOLD THE APPROPRIATE DIRECTORS ACCOUNTABLE

A staff works best when they are held accountable for an action, project, or result. Ownership made this country what it is, and you should provide ownership opportunities to your workers, in the form of responsibility. The more success an individual has, the more ownership opportunities should be awarded. And compensation should be commensurate with the responsibilities you have assigned.

Every person in your organization should have an ownership interest in his or her turf—his or her work area. Someone in the firm should be responsible for overseeing each discipline. All of these people should reap the rewards of success and share in the consequences of failure. Every person needs to be held accountable for his or her own actions. That is the only way you can see whether employees are doing the job they are being paid for and whether you are excelling in a particular area. You should tie raises or bonuses to performance. In addition to salary, staff members should have a second form of compensation tied to the success of what they are doing for the firm. This creates a huge motivation for staff to want to do well.

I have worked in firms where one size fits all and people were interested in giving no more than the minimum to their company, just as long as they were out the door by 5:00 p.m. These "minimalists" do whatever is barely necessary to justify their existence, but raise the bar, and that means more work is required. If everyone shares in the rewards, then everyone is working toward a common goal. This would be an example where the whole is worth more than its individual parts.

Build a Management Team of Your Appropriate Directors

Without a competent management team, your firm will be unable to respond quickly enough to new opportunities, and will miss warning signs of trouble. There are three things in particular to look out for as your business expands:

1. The business may grow faster than your employees' skill levels.
2. Without good job descriptions worked out in advance, and an understanding of adequate salary requirements, your expanding business can very easily hire the wrong people.
3. Expanding companies tend to stick with the management structure they already know, rather than making the necessary changes and adjustments as the organization grows.

3. ALWAYS PLAN WITH THE FUTURE IN MIND

Planning involves a long, drawn-out process of achieving a particular goal. You should plan your firm with that result in mind. Look into the future 1, 3, 5, and even 10 years. The numbers will work best for five or fewer years. It is difficult to reasonably predict them beyond that point. Too much is changing too quickly.

You should have weekly management meetings to discuss the entire work environment. Your agenda should look something like this:

Weekly Management Agenda

1. Department head status report (recap) of the past week's events
2. Plans for the next two weeks
3. Financial implications of short-term transactions occurring within the next month
4. Six-month project report on what the department head's main areas of responsibility will be like
5. Same time next year: Where will the department be one year from now?
6. Three to five year projections, if appropriate

The macro-level concepts can work well 10 years out, even though the numbers may not. While you do not know what will happen then, if you commit to being on the cutting edge and adapting your firm and style to the changing elements in the marketplace, your 10-year long-term plan will be successful.

4. SAY TO YOURSELF: WHAT IF I WERE JUST ENTERING THE BUSINESS? WOULD THIS BE THE WAY I WOULD SET IT UP?

The old cliché "if we only knew then what we know now" holds true here. Obviously, we have a much better perspective having "been there, done that." The only difference is that the economic circumstances in which you started your business may have required different methods for achieving the same ultimate goal. For example, if you started your business in the 1980s, you would have had a different focus than if you did so in the 1990s or 2000s. If you worked on a client financial plan in the late 1970s, when interest rates and inflation were in the double digits, all the long-range forecasts would have been way off if the plan were not modified on a regular basis. Basically, now you need to figure out where you are today, where you need to be, and how to get there.

Think of yourself starting a new subsidiary, product line, or branch office. What would need to be said today and done tomorrow for that to happen? Would you be gearing up for any of these big events on all cylinders? The rules of the game have changed since you started. You always need to be playing by the rules that are out there today.

5. ENCOURAGE EVERYONE IN YOUR OFFICE TO BE CREATIVE. HAVE A CONTEST. REWARD THOSE EMPLOYEES WHO THINK OUTSIDE THE BOX WITH PRIZES

There is no substitute for creativity. Creativity feeds upon itself, with everyone wanting to get in on the action. Without it, businesses wither away and die. Your staff may feel that if you take an approach that emphasizes that this is your business and that therefore their opinions do not count, they will not see the benefit of thinking outside the box, and, as a result, nothing will be accomplished.

You should plaster the company mission statement all over the office. This way all staff members start with the same common and ultimate goal. Encouragement should be provided to enable staff to think along the lines of the mission statement. A record of all creative suggestions should be kept as a scorecard. Staff should know when their ideas are welcomed and accepted, and be rewarded. One company I worked for gave out movie tickets for the best idea of the week. At another company, the executive director gave the "rubber chicken" award on a weekly basis to the one employer thinking outside the box who helped the company the most that week. Everyone likes to be the center of attention, and this process helps to recognize those staff who go beyond the call of duty. Still another company kept track of all new ideas, and the staff member who had the biggest impact in terms of marketing the company during the year received a weekend getaway for two.

Remember, every person in your company is in the marketing department. That is because they are representing you and possess the ability to be rewarded based on how they help the business attract more clients and grow.

6. HIRE THE RIGHT PEOPLE WHO UNDERSTAND THE MARKETPLACE. SCOUT THE COMPETITION. IF THEY KNOW ENOUGH ABOUT YOUR MARKET, THEN LISTEN TO THEM

There is no substitute for getting the right people in place and building an infrastructure that can support all aspects of your business. Think of your company as a baseball team. There are nine starting position players and specialty reserves who are used depending on the circumstances facing the team that day. If every staff member acts as a position player, you will have a much better and more balanced team that can handle any situation that arises. You will have nine starters who directly report to you or someone in the chain of command. You will have role players who can delve into the situation from any angle. Remember, you are only as good as the people you have under you who are executing your game plan. Take advantage of the resources available from the local community, the local society of the Financial Planning Association (FPA), and others who can help you identify potential staff.

In my business, I have a full-time planner to whom I can delegate the responsibility of completing financial plans and tax returns. I have a full-time writer who can keep me up to date with the best financial planning curriculum and make it track with that of the CFP Board. I have an administrative assistant who keeps me in check and anticipates the things I am likely to forget. For an administrative assistant, I want someone who can think one step ahead of me and make sure I am prepared for everything I will encounter. Someone who knows what I will need before an appointment, engagement, or lecture and makes sure nothing slips through the cracks. I try to cover all the angles.

It is very important to be a "people person." Knowing how to speak with them, get them involved, or reward them for a good job done are critical. A little token of appreciation is necessary every now and then, as well as group "hang-out" sessions. Every Friday, I bring New York–style pizza in to the office. When it arrives, we immediately stop all office activities. We go to the conference room and eat and talk about ourselves, our lives, our families, our outside activities, and whatever else comes to mind. It is a time to unwind and unleash our inner thoughts and enable the staff to bond. It goes back to what I said earlier about teamwork and the ability to hire the right people. You can't always hire shortstops. You need a first baseman, catcher, pitcher, and so forth. There are nine position players for a reason. You need to make sure that they balance each other out and provide the most productive team available.

However, I also believe in cutting your losses immediately. If I hire an individual who I later find is not right for the job because of technical incompetence, displaying a nasty attitude toward coworkers, and spending too much time dealing with personal issues and talking with friends, I cut the cord immediately. I do not believe that these situations work themselves out over time. I will provide a second chance to such an individual after I explain the responsibilities he or she agreed to undertake when joining our firm. However, if I have other staff coming to me privately and complaining about the person, and such complaints are similar in nature, I will need to keep my infrastructure happy. Therefore, I will terminate the person immediately.

You should have an understanding of what the competition is doing in order to make sure you are still competitive in your marketplace. It is not imperative that you figure out what they are doing in advance and play defense. But in case the rules of the game change, you will not fall behind if you keep abreast of these changes. For example, if the community is going off in one direction, you probably need to figure out why that is happening and if it makes sense for you to pursue that course of action as well. You still need to do your own thing, but you don't want to end up "behind the 8 ball."

7. HAVE ANYONE IN YOUR OFFICE BE ABLE TO SIGN OFF ON A PROBLEM

Many companies have a policy that all staff represent the company and possess a certain degree of control over situations that arise. Some of these companies grant permission to their staff to resolve any client situation that arises with the goal of turning an unhappy client into a satisfied one. That means whoever answers the call in your office has the ability to "right the situation" within certain limits, without having to gain advance approval. The phone company does this by crediting your account, credit card companies do it by waiving a late fee or other administrative expense, and airline personnel can waive a $100 penalty. You would be surprised how powerful a tool that is. If you have ever complained about something and received something of value in return, chances are that you were a happier camper (at least for that moment). Having this policy means that the big boss does not need to be there 100 percent of the time, and things can still be done to keep the office functional in a crisis, as opposed to putting someone on hold. My experience suggests that when the boss or someone in authority has to get involved in micro-managing, it completely slows the company down. You can implement this policy through a chain of command that provides various staff people with a certain level of authority, as explained below.

8. ESTABLISH A REALISTIC CHAIN OF COMMAND

You need to establish a realistic chain of command so that everyone in the office has a work identity and knows to whom they are responsible to report. This helps free the lines of communication, helps organize the staff's responsibilities, and forms a bond with their supervisors or direct reports. Organizations that have no chain of command always find themselves in crises mode or simply chaos. Remember, your firm cannot work as a unit if there is no systematized reporting process for workers.

You should have an organizational flowchart and show it to clients as well as staff. This way, when a problem arises, the client raising the issue will know who to speak with, which will result in a faster resolution for the client. You do not want to get directly involved in each client's problem; otherwise, your role will be that of a troubleshooter, constantly putting out fires. You need to get involved when the chain of command does not work because of an irate client or a situation that is not typical within the industry. That is a better use of your time, and promotes a more structured operating system.

**Include a Business Manager Near the Top
of Your Chain of Command**

A business manager is someone who can look at the big picture
and determine how the information within the company should
flow. This individual maintains ties to the service or product line
and to each staff member within the firm. His or her major focus
is to make sure competent staff handle appropriate issues, that no
bottlenecks occur, and that response times are extremely rapid.
The business manager has a macro-level perspective and can see
the big picture, but also a micro-level viewpoint in order to manage the daily functions and responsibilities of the office. I pride
myself in knowing that when I am away, the office won't miss a
beat. Things get done, everyone's focused, and life goes on. So
much for my importance!

9. TEST MARKET NEW FIRM AND PRODUCT OPPORTUNITIES WITH YOUR "B" CLIENTS. FORM A CLIENT ADVISORY GROUP

In order to provide the best service for your clients, you need to
continually try and upgrade what your firm is doing. Your clients
will notice and appreciate your firm providing better service. The
best way to test out new ideas is to divide up your clients into A, B,
and C groupings. Your "A" clients are your ideal working partners.
Your "B" clients you enjoy, but they can come with some baggage.
Your "C" clients provide the 80 percent of the firmwide issues and
only 20 percent of the revenues out of the accepted 80/20 rule.
The "C" clients we really are not concerned about. We do not want
to ruin our relationships with our "A" clients. Therefore, our best
test case is to try new ideas and strategies without "B" clients. Establish a focus group for select B-level clients.

　　　Select 12 clients from your B list. The list should represent a
diverse group. Business owners, married couples with young kids,
empty nesters, singles, professionals, the self-employed, single parents, and so forth, should all participate, if possible. Ask these chosen 12 to participate in a "corporate makeover" in which they will
have direct input into transforming your business into a "true

client-oriented firm." This involves a one-year commitment to hold two live meetings and an initial conference call describing how to complete a specific questionnaire. The rationale is that if you can address most or all client concerns and specific recommendations, it will be easier to service your clients going forward and that will result in every client's having a positive experience with the firm.

Tell these clients that in order to get an honest assessment of how your firm does business, you want them to fill out a questionnaire designed to determine whether your firm does what it is supposed to do in its relationships with clients. Emphasize that in order to do what it needs to do and ensure that everyone is satisfied, you have to get this information from the clients who keep you in business.

In exchange for that, you will reduce or eliminate a year's worth of fees, and will host a task force dinner meeting after all the results are in, so that the entire group knows the outcome.

The reason I do not suggest doing this with your "A," or favorite, clients is that you do not want to do anything that will offend these clients or cause them to leave you. They are your pride and joy. You will want to continue to provide smooth sailing with them. Your B clients are not as high on the list, and if push comes to shove, they can probably go either way. Yet you still value their opinions because they have been with the firm for awhile.

The agenda for the client advisory group would look something like this:

1. Hold a conference call with all participants so everyone knows what the purpose of the task force is and understands where it is headed.

2. Describe the questionnaire they have received from you, which is in front of them now. (Do not ask for answers now. Just make sure they understand what is required.)

3. Ask them to send the questionnaire back in two weeks, after which the results will be compiled, summarized, and distributed to everyone at a dinner meeting.

4. Tell them the responses are going to be analyzed and integrated into the business and marketing plans for the company, and that you will share the results with them at another dinner meeting.

5. Hold the final party, which should be primarily fun oriented. After dinner, give a Powerpoint presentation of what the company will look like going forward. Thank the clients for their participation and ask them if you can call on them in the future about any specific issues that may arise.

The Questionnaire

The questionnaire allows your clients to "spill their guts" to you and the firm. It provides an open and honest assessment of where you are today and where you need to be to the planner/client relationship and address those issues that may arise if you grow the firm.

The questionnaire below is the one I use for my firm.

Client Satisfaction Questionnaire

1. If you were asked to describe in two sentences what JR Financial Group does, what would you say?
2. In your opinion, does what the company says it does match the value of what you ultimately receive from the company?
3. What is the first thing you think about when you hear the name JR Financial Group?
4. What do you think the primary responsibility of JR Financial Group is to you?
5. Do you feel JR Financial Group is best positioned to help satisfy your long-term goals and objectives?
6. What do you like best about JR Financial Group?
7. What do you most dislike about JR Financial Group?
8. If JR Financial Group grew by 50 percent next year, do you still think we could provide the quality of service you have become accustomed to?
9. What is the central problem you feel the firm possesses?
10. How does the staff treat you when you call into the office?

(continued)

Client Satisfaction Questionnaire (*continued*)

11. Does staff always respond to you within 24 hours of a call?
12. How has JR Financial Group's response been to you when you have a problem?
13. Do you feel comfortable calling the firm and addressing any issue of yours with Jeff or another planner?
14. What information or communications would you like to receive from JR Financial Group on a regular basis?
15. Have you ever thought about moving your business from JR Financial Group?

Keep the questionnaire short and sweet. Having close-ended questions (that is, requiring only yes or no answers) does not really help measure how your clients feel about your firm.

10. KEEP ALL THE PLAYERS INFORMED

Everyone on your team needs to know what is going on. Since all staff members have an integral role in the development and marketing of your business, you need to tell them about the following:

- Macro-level information on how the company is doing
- Micro-level information on how they are managing their sections of the whole
- Strong areas within the company
- Weak areas within the company
- Anticipated changes

Lou Stanasolovich of Legend Financial Advisors in Pittsburgh has a fascinating approach to keeping his players informed. He uses a concept called "open-book management," or basically making all information available to everyone in the firm. All staff members know what is at stake for the firm, and what needs to happen to become profitable, and how to correct themselves if they go off course. Based on results, profits to be distributed to staff are dependent on the way everyone rises to the occasion.

11. FORM A PLANNER ADVISORY BOARD (PAB)

Many times it is difficult to be objective when evaluating your company or deciding to implement plans to follow. This is because you become too close to the situation and may not be able to be objective in your dealings. Sometimes it helps to bring in other professionals who can give you long-term, big-picture guidance. An advisory board can help you define your business, figure out who you are now and what you want to be when your business grows up, and suggest ways to get there.

Your board can consist of neighborhood professionals or peers situated around the country. The local board might meet once a month for an hour to discuss business issues. Another option is to arrange a breakfast meeting before the workday begins that will not cut into busy schedules. Prepare a meeting agenda. For the first meeting, focus the discussion on the mission of the company. For later meetings, select one central theme and spend the hour discussing that. For example, in January focus on client service. In February, focus on pricing. In March, focus on alternative distribution channels. If critical issues come up, like a supplier going out of business or a new competitor in the area, call for an emergency meeting or fax or e-mail your thoughts to the members and let them respond. The board exists to help you take your practice to the next level. Work with them wisely.

12. KEEP YOUR BOOKS JUST AS
YOU ADVISE YOUR CLIENTS TO

It comes back to the auto mechanic who is famous for driving a jalopy around the neighborhood and does not bother to fix his car. You are in the adviser business. You provide many clients with millions of dollars in advice throughout the year. You need to take some of that medicine yourself. I was like the auto mechanic for a while. During tax season, I would do all my clients' tax returns first and then mine. Now I work on mine first! And I do that for several reasons. One is that I want to figure out all the bugs in the program before I do anyone else's return. I want to know how the program operates and I will test it on myself first. Second, I practice what I preach. Therefore, when I tell clients to do it early so they can move on with their lives, that approach also applies to me.

If you do not keep your books well, then you will not have any idea how to analyze your expenditures to determine whether they make good investments. Many times you have to plant seed money over a period of time and then watch as it grows. It may take days, months, or even years, but if you do it right, you will reap the benefits. You should investigate all variances at least monthly and determine what works and what doesn't, and then determine whether what does not work is worth pursuing. Sometimes yes, sometimes no. The key point to remember is that you need to stay on top of all your actions as you develop your business. Remember, the buck stops with you!

13. WHAT TO CHARGE: THE OLD ADAGE "HOW MUCH DOES THE CLIENT GOT?" DOES NOT CUT IT

When I first got into this business, there was a dominant sales mentality. Salespeople would go after clients based on how much they could afford and back into the products and the numbers. How far *most of us* have come!

You need to develop a compensation package for clients based on your underlying principles and nothing else. Here is mine. I have a hard time turning clients away. Yet, as a businessman, I understand the value of getting paid for my time, because, as you know, the first rule of being in business is to stay in business. If I go out of business, it does my clients no good. Therefore, I have to leverage my time based on the pre-determined hourly wage I need to make my business run. This includes paying my employees, the mortgage, utilities, insurances, taxes, and the like.

For clients who have less than $100,000 of net worth to invest, I charge based on product sales. In other words, I provide them with load-oriented products, if need be. My rationale is that it is not fair to charge them a fee for assets under management if they do not have the net worth to justify it. It would end up costing them too much, and it would not be fair to charge them on an hourly basis.

For clients with assets over $100,000, I charge either on an hourly fee basis, a project basis, or as a percentage of assets under management. I charge 1.58 percent and then it goes down to 58.5 basis points depending on the amount invested. Also, I charge $150 per hour, or on projects such as developing a financial plan or investment plan. I will charge a lump sum based on the number of hours I believe that this will take. Typically, it takes me eight hours to do a financial plan. The eight hours includes spending two hours with a client, according to my PIPRIM© process of integrated goal setting and fact finding, another two hours to go over the recommendations and to answer all questions, and four hours of processing and review time. Therefore, financial planning clients pay me $1,200 for a financial plan. The same process holds true for developing an investment plan. Clients with large amounts of assets can typically afford to pay my fees.

PIPRIM is the financial planning process I use with clients. It focuses on clients first, and developing a system of what to do and when. PIPRIM stands for:

- **P**reliminary meeting with the client
- **I**ntegrated goal setting and fact finding
- **P**utting it all together
- **R**ecommending solutions
- **I**mplementing the plan
- **M**onitoring the plan

14. SELECT THE RIGHT FORM OF BUSINESS ENTITY

There is no one right entity type to use in developing your business, only a preferred method based on what you want to accomplish. Your primary choices are:

- Sole proprietorship
- Partnership
- Limited liability partnership (LLP)
- Limited liability company (LLC)
- S corporation
- C corporation

I use both S corporations and LLCs. JR Financial Group, Inc., is an S corporation. The reason is that as I want to add key members to take active roles within our team and feel a sense of ownership within the company, I can sell them stock as we continue to grow. Financial Planning Institute, LLC, is an LLC because it can be included in a family trust where an S corporation cannot. I do not envision other owners of our education company, so the issuance of stock is not an issue for me in this case. However, both types of entity have the key ingredient, which is limited liability. This protection saves me from being personally liable for debts and other issues the company cannot get out from under.

I avoid sole proprietorships and partnerships because of the unlimited liability each presents. Also, a sole proprietor, who has to file a Schedule C, is more likely to be audited by the IRS and faces exposure since all information appearing on the form is up for discussion.

Either way, I still encourage errors and omission (E&O) insurance because nothing is foolproof. Many partners of large CPA and law firms who are married typically own nothing themselves because of inherent liability concerns within their businesses. They are basically poor on paper. However, if you operate in this manner, you had better be nice to your better half!

15. LOCATION, LOCATION, LOCATION

Where should you locate your office? The answer is, "it depends!" Go back to the basic question "what business are you in?" If you are running a business that caters to middle-class America, you need a convenient office. A shopping center or strip-mall location would work best, because it has convenience written all over it and makes your firm fit into the composition of the neighborhood. Sponsoring little league teams and the like shows you are an integral part of the community. An office building may work, but not as well. It depends on parking in the area.

If I were targeting high-net-worth individuals, an office building would work best because appearance is a big factor when this niche evaluates potential financial planners. I do not think marble floors are a necessity, but you need to show that your firm prides itself on its appearance.

Perhaps you should consider buying a small office building or an office condominium, as I did. I bought a place that I can grow into. Our unit is 1,836 square feet and can accommodate about 10 people comfortably. Our game plan is that as we get larger, we can begin to take over the offices we currently rent out. Therefore, we can grow into our space (again, always looking at the big picture) and not have to move because we have outgrown it. Or if you are in a small office building, consider purchasing it and renting out space to others, possibly covering your mortgage, taxes, insurance, and then some.

Planners always ask me about a home office. I say that is good for a short time while you are getting your ducks in order. However, over the long term, I do not believe it works well. While more clients are coming to accept home offices, they do not show your firm off well, and it is very difficult to motivate yourself to work when it is too convenient not to.

When I had my home office, I became too distracted with nonwork matters. Many times your family may not understand that you are home but you are not. If money is an issue, go out and become part of an executive suite, where you can have access to a receptionist, copier, conference room, and other amenities of an office you may not be able to afford on your own. Others rent space, such as a single office, from a company for as little as $400–$800 per month. As long as you have your name on the door and operate as a legitimate business, you will be fine.

16. TECHNOLOGY HANG-UPS

Choosing the Right Software

If I had a nickel for every software program I paid for and tried, I would be a rich person. Clearly, there is no right software package or approach. You need to customize a software package to fit the needs of your clientele, which, again, is based on your business model. This area of development is usually the hardest for planners. That is because there is so much to know, so much to look for, that no one is ever completely satisfied. The investment is huge up front. In many ways, you are buying something sight unseen! Sure, you will try out a demo, see how a "model" program runs, but you really do not know how it runs until you use it on many clients. And when you are done evaluating, there will be no perfect program that takes care of all the issues you want.

Take a moment to review the following set of software questions with your computer consultant, staff, or others to determine whether you are getting the capabilities you need.

- Does the company have a demo disk so I can try it out in advance, or against my existing software?
- What is the initial cost for the financial planning software?
- Are there different prices if you are a standalone user versus installing it on a network platform?
- Does the financial planning software have an ongoing fee?
- What benefits do I get by paying an annual fee?
- What is involved when this software interfaces with other software?
- Should I buy software that requires other third-party programs for operation, and what should I look out for?
- Is there a separate install "licensing" disk for usage?
- Can I install it on my home computer as well as the office computer for the same cost?
- Do I need to possess specific skills to operate a financial planning software program?
- What are the pros and cons of buying one integrated system instead of buying two or three programs separately that might accomplish the same tasks?
- How much effort should I put into talking with the software vendor's existing users?
- Can I reasonably expect my software vendor to download data from the companies I do business with on a client-by-client basis?
- How much time can I expect to spend evaluating a financial planning software program?
- Can I expect the vendor to do a plan with me for one of my clients?

- What type of trial period is available when purchasing a program?
- Can I copy the software and use it on different PCs and/or at different locations?
- What type of training is available and where?
- What kind of support can I expect?
- How often is the software updated?
- Is a fact-finder included, and can I modify it or override some of the components?
- What is the learning curve for using this particular software?
- If I switch to the new software program from the old one, can the new program import my data directly?
- How strong is the software company? Is it part of a bigger company? What is the likelihood that the software company will go out of business?
- Should I expect the software vendor to be able to answer my questions about my computer operation, besides their software programs?
- What optimal hardware (including disk space) do I need to run your program?
- What other software do I need to run your program?
- Can I run the software on a network and does it have multi-user access?
- What software is included in your program?
- What additional features cost extra?
- Can I change the assumptions to fit the specific needs of my individual clients?
- Does the software offer an audit trail of calculations for the reports?
- Is this system decision making?
- If yes, then where did your company come up with these assumptions?
- What attitudes or goals does the system take into account when making decisions?
- Does it run Monte Carlo simulations?

There is a list of software packages in the Resources section of this book. It includes software that I have used, seen in operation, or know planners who use.

Choosing the Right Hardware

In this area, unless you are an expert and really up to date on all the recent developments, I say punt! I rely totally on my computer consultants to provide me with the details I need for purchase and to ensure my system will not become obsolete immediately after I write the check.

Keep these questions in mind when evaluating hardware:

- Is this system state of the art?
- Can I get by without having a state-of-the-art system?
- Can the hardware do the specific things I need it to now?
- Can my existing software run on this hardware system?
- How often should I upgrade my hardware?
- Is the hardware expandable?
- Can it operate fully in a network environment?

You need to focus your energies on the things that make you money and make you the happiest. Some planners are technically savvy in this area. They like to experiment, construct, take apart, and do everything that goes with analyzing hardware requirements. Unfortunately, most of the ones I know are not. There is no rhyme or reason for it, or good or bad. Most planners prefer to earn their money through things they enjoy and pay for the balance. They can make more money doing the things they are experts in and leaving the things they have little knowledge and experience in to others. I say, for all hardware concerns, punt!

Choosing the Right Phone System (office and cell)

You need to be very careful here. I tried several phone systems before I found the one that worked best for my business. I have been misinformed on the prices and ongoing costs from various companies and have learned from experience who to trust. But I am still not sold on the system I currently have and I am always looking for new ones.

The very first thing to do is to sign on with a long-distance carrier. You need to select one based on the type of business you have.

Mull these questions over when considering a long-distance carrier:

- Do I have many in-state long-distance or out-of-state long-distance calls?
- Can I have multiple phone numbers on the system?
- Can they be personal as well as business?
- Can they be for multiple locations?
- Can they support an 800 number?
- Do I get any type of rebate, points, or discounted fees after a certain amount of usage?
- Do I have to have a certain call volume in advance of signing up (based on past phone history)?
- Does the carrier provide cell phone service?
- Does the carrier provide Internet access, DSL, or some other connection to the web?
- Is there some kind of comprehensive package if I contract for all types of electronic service through this company?

These topics are areas where your advisory board can come in handy. Chances are that they have "been there, done that" with regard to setting up a phone system and purchasing hardware and software.

17. TIME MANAGEMENT ISSUES

Less is more! That is the concept you need to instill in your head and in your firm. You are better off doing fewer things well than many things just okay.

You need to develop a schedule that you can adhere to. Do not put 60 hours of work on it. Chances are that 60 hours will turn into 100 hours. Put down 30 hours and you will see that it grows to 40. Then try to cut it off. Most of the planners I talk with are concerned, and sometimes unhappy, because they have overcommitted themselves, promising with the best intentions only to find out that the work does not get done in a timely manner. And to make matters worse, they will delay indefinitely or even renege on issues that generate little or no revenue to the planner or the firm.

The main way to handle this is to adopt a strict schedule and leverage your time. It means stripping away nonessential activities. You can do this through technology and a more disciplined approach to planning. That means getting your other staff members involved in the process and delegating.

18. DO NOT DO IT ALL YOURSELF: DELEGATE, DELEGATE, DELEGATE!

I do not have to tell you that control issues are always a real sticking point. After all, you have attained your degree of success by calling your own shots and doing your own thing. That is the sign of a true entrepreneur. You have succeeded by being hands on, and this behavioral pattern, the result of years of positive reinforcement, is difficult to change.

Based on my years in the business and my observations of other planners' businesses, I confirm that planners are very reluctant to delegate. Even when they know they are too busy to pay attention to the nitty-gritty details, there is still that impulse not to give up any control. Delegating is difficult because you would rather admit that you made the mistake rather than a staff member, because, after all, the client is hiring you. The other issue is that you feel a loss of control by not being involved on a regular basis. Even a planner who hires an outside planner or office manager to work on the businesses always has a sense of doubt about the manager's abilities. By the same token, if you do hire an outside person to assist you in the development of your business, then for heaven's sake, listen to that individual! I have seen many good strategies go unfulfilled because the planner in charge was to proud to listen to anyone else.

Many planners feel that if outside individuals are so smart and so good, why don't they have their own companies? And the answer is that many of the skills necessary in a good manager are different from those of a good executor. Your drive, determination, genius, and overall persistence are what made the company in the first place. And there is no substitute for that. Only true entrepreneurs have these qualities. However, such qualities are not always necessary in the development of good infrastructure. The manager you hire may not have the ability to be a good entrepreneur. But the combination (remember the position player on the baseball team) may be a very solid package and a strong team. The transfer of authority to the position players is a key ingredient for success.

How to Transfer Authority

The transfer of authority is the substance of delegation. To make it work, you need to provide clear ownership of key tasks within defined parameters. It is critical, as well, to encourage team members to take responsibility for maximizing their productivity, thinking beyond narrowly defined areas.

To begin with, develop two lists. The first list details the key uses of your time during a typical week. This list should realistically reflect the things you need to do. Keep in mind that there will be activities for which your presence will be absolutely critical to your business and which a substitute would not be able to handle, because your clients want to deal with the boss or you are negotiating a big deal only you can handle for the company. These are not the things to delegate. I am talking about things you should be doing that another staff member can do just as well as you can. Based on this list, look at your staff directory and figure out which staff members would best be suited for any of these tasks and write their name(s) down next to the appropriate task. More than one person may work in any area of importance. If some components of a task can be isolated and delegated rather than the entire task, then do that.

The creation of financial plans is an obvious case. Here, you can meet with the client during the interview stage of the PIPRIM process, do a quick write-up of the client's objectives and possible recommendations and then delegate the responsibility to an appropriate staff member to do the input and verify the original facts you have collected to ensure that nothing gets overlooked. This is also the ultimate system of checks and balances. You receive it back after it is all complete, and, like a partner in a Big Five CPA firm, you have the final authority and responsibility to sign off on this client engagement. You then meet with the client and go over the recommendations now that you feel comfortable with the numbers that were necessary to get you to have faith in the plan itself.

If you want to have another staff member as a potential client contact, have that person in the meeting as well. This will free you up from ongoing daily responsibilities with the client. Doctors are famous for operating in this manner. They will have many patient rooms and delegate procedures, like drawing blood, checking height and weight, cleaning teeth for dentists, and other mechanical tasks. The doctors therefore only get involved in the crucial elements of dealing with patients. Apply those same principles to your practice's clients.

The second list categorizes key time-wasting activities, those things that eat up time without providing a value in return. In other words, the activities that consume your time to the point that the week passes by quickly and afterward you realize that you have nothing to show for your efforts. These are activities that cannot be eliminated, but rather are low priority items that someone else can do for you. An example would be answering voicemail messages for team members who are out of the office for more than a half-day. Devise a system in your office to delegate this responsibility to a other team staff members. Have the in-office team member write these messages down for the absent staff member, and, in some cases, return some of the calls or follow up on trivial issues (such as sending out account statements and answering general questions on office procedure). Other critical issues requiring the presence of the absent advisor can be left until he or she returns.

Other tasks to be delegated include sending a follow-up notice after a client meeting and thank you letters for client referrals. You can use a form letter that can be filled in by a secretary, or dictate a summary of the day's events and forward the tape at the end of the day to your secretary to write up and send out. In this case, the task is delegated even though the time required remains the same. Another member of your team is responsible for follow-up and makes the task manageable.

Putting It on Cruise Control

The idea behind delegation is to minimize your involvement in the day-to-day activities of running the firm, in essence, building a system that can be sold because it is not dependent on you. To do this effectively, make sure you follow IDA:

- Identify the key trigger points to make the particular activity happen
- Develop a process to determine what happens and when
- Assign clear responsibility

Managing Delegation

One of the biggest mistakes you can make is to have your assistants give clients the third degree as they call, making it virtually impossible for them to speak with you. Don't run too tight a military ship; otherwise, you will lose more clients than it is worth.

Ensuring Client Contact

One planner I know has his assistant look through the database once a week to see whom the planner has not personally spoken with in 60 days. On Monday morning of the following week, that assistant provides the names of those clients to the planner and it is the planner's responsibility to contact them for whatever reason. This ensures that the planner has made some type of commitment to talking with each client at least once during a 60-day period.

Another planner I know has his assistant send out a firm-wide evaluation questionnaire (essentially a report card) with a stamped envelope after a client has been on board for three months. He repeats the process semiannually to:

- Detect any warning signs of problem areas
- Ensure that the relationship is what the client expected
- Provide any other feedback necessary to continue the relationship in an uninterrupted manner

Promise such clients that you will share all results with them so they understand how the firm currently operates and what they can do to change things that are reported as unsatisfactory.

Another planner has a 10-day autopilot send out a letter or follow-up phone call or e-mail to see whether a client received a statement, package, and so forth, from the firm within the last 10 days. This ensures that no gaps exist between client contact and follow-through.

For all these areas, the assistant or advisor follows up with each client right away as soon as the firm receives information. This constant feedback is a great way to continually refine your practice.

Managing Yourself

I use a tickler filing and reminder system to keep me in check. I have a loose-leaf binder with a tab representing 31 days of a month and then use either yellow sticky pads or write down on a piece of paper whom I need to contact on a given day and for what. It has proved very effective, since I know whom I need to contact at all times.

How to Build a Team

For a team to function well, an understanding of the macro-level picture is needed. Your firm needs to clarify the team's purpose and strategic intent. What are the short- and long-term goals of the firm? Much of this can be found in your business plan. How will the team be measured and evaluated? When the team is done with its task, what will they see and feel? What value will have been created? Only when those specific questions have been answered will the team be able to do its job. Remember, not only do you have to define what the team is going to do for you, you also have to figure out what you have to give back to the team in return.

Information

This information must be complete, direct, concise, and presented in a manner that ensures complete understanding. It helps in building trust with the staff and also allows them to think outside the box. Finally, it enables you to live with the decisions the team makes.

Coaching

Coaching involves personal guidance to enable a staff member to see the way things should be done and to provide him or her with the tools to make decisions without your involvement. This guidance can come in the form of training, both on the job and outside, that allows your staff member to hear other experts on the issues and see how they have been handled. The training can be business related and can be personal growth–related, as well. There is no substitute for personal instruction. Everyone has a learning curve, and the sooner you help your staff members in seeing the issues and the potential for handling them, the sooner you will be able to free up more of your time.

Keeping Score

This involves the creation of a yardstick or benchmark so your staff members can see how they are doing. It quantifies what is going on to show whether staff members are grasping all they can. If the scores are low, you need to go over the issues with the staff members to get them up to par. This constant measurement helps your staff members gauge their performance and take the initiative to readjust their own performance. If scores are continually low, then you probably need to terminate their employment.

19. FAILING TO TAKE RESPONSIBILITY YOURSELF

One of the worst business moves you can ever make is to blame others instead of yourself. This failure is the result of owners, key personnel, and others having egos that are too big to fit in the zip code of their local community. You need to 'fess up to mistakes and misdirections. If I had a nickel for every blunder I made, I could retire now.

You are the captain of your ship, and, as such, you need to go down with it if you goof, or make it better, where possible. I have seen planners who never own up to their mistakes and, as a result, lose credibility with their staff, their peers, and even their loved ones.

One simple rule I live by is that everyone makes mistakes. Period. I will strongly support staff members who reflect on their mistakes and try to do things right the next time. But those who hide behind their mistakes and pawn them off on others I have no tolerance for, and I will probably end up dismissing them.

20. SELECT AN APPROPRIATE BROKER/DEALER

Depending on the type of business you do, you may need to partner with a broker-dealer. There are many around and it is beyond the scope of this book to rank them all. The major magazines *Financial Planning, Investment Advisor,* and *Financial Advisor* all rate these broker-dealers annually. You can probably get this information from their web sites, as well. The only issue here is to make sure this information tracks with your business model and marketing plan. And see what kind of deal they would give you.

Things to consider when interviewing a broker-dealer include:

- Ownership of clients—yours!
- Payout
- Education—training program, online education, live classes
- Annual conference(s)
- Expense reimbursement, for outside classes, continuing education, licenses, professional dues, and so forth
- Back-office support
- Mentoring program to hook you up with other successful advisors in the area or for someone who will accompany you on client cases
- Review specimen contracts in advance
- Names of three current advisors who use the broker-dealer and three who have used the broker-dealer and no longer do
- Only deal with proprietary products, funds, and so forth
- Minimum production requirements, if any

21. SPEND MONEY ON TRAINING YOURSELF AND YOUR STAFF

In order to be successful in this business, you have to constantly learn new things. You have to take advantage of technologies and current issues for your firm's benefit. Do not be afraid to keep learning. Pay to have your people to earn their CFP™ (Certified Financial Planner™), ChFC (Chartered Financial Consultant), RFC (Registered Financial Consultant), CFA (Chartered Financial Analyst), or CFS (Certified Fund Specialist) designations, and take continuing education courses. If your staff is motivated to be all they can be, encourage them. I pay for all my staff's licensing and professional dues, and allow them to go during working hours to society meetings so they can improve themselves both professionally and personally. Pay for advanced licensing, (i.e., Series 24, 4, if applicable).

A happy employee will be a productive employee. I am not of the opinion that if I educate employees, they will leave because they have become more valuable. Some companies I work with are very fearful of that. Remember the old Soviet Union. They had that mindset, too. Now look at them! While there is no way to stop newly educated employees from leaving, I believe that if I am upfront with them about the job, company, working conditions, and so forth, if I am open and honest with them, encouraging them to participate in the process of running the firm and listening to what they have to say, they will be happy to stay and will not want to go anywhere else. While in life there are no guarantees, I treat all employees as owners of their particular sections, their own turf, so their comments are valuable to me and I make that known. I delegate all the responsibilities of their areas to them so that they can participate in the future success and growth of the firm.

Use training to break down the wall! Separate your bad habits from good ones through training you can use to grow the firm. Do not get hung up on doing things only in one way. There is no one right way. Rather, learn from your personal mistakes, firm wide mistakes and those of others, and take the best of what you have learned from each and develop those ideas into firm-wide policy.

22. DO YOUR OWN DUE DILIGENCE ON PRODUCTS, COMPANIES, WORKING RELATIONSHIPS, AND THE LIKE

Don't take anyone's word for granted! Don't rely on others for things you can do yourself. You are obligated to yourself, your firm, and your clients to do your homework in advance. There are many entities you can go to for help, such as rating firms, journals, and other publications, but the ultimate responsibility for checking out things rests with you. I check out all products, funds, training courses, and other things before I form an opinion that could affect others. Also, if I work with alliances, I do the same thing. Remember, your clients are paying you for giving advice. The only way to do that is to double-check the advice that you are giving to clients.

23. WHEN IS IT TIME TO BRING IN A PARTNER?

Sometimes you can take a practice only so far! The old adage "two heads are better than one" holds true here. I know planners who have taken their practices as far as they can and now have a tough decision to make. Do they sell because they cannot go any further on their own for lack of capital, product base, geographical territory, and so forth, or should they bring in another partner to expand the areas in which they are weak or deficient, or should they merge or be bought out by another firm?

The answer is critical because if you miss the boat, you may lose market share, take on too much that you do not have the infrastructure to support, or just get blown away.

I have always held the belief that I would rather receive part of something rather than all of nothing. There is enough money out there for more than one person in a firm to make, as long as it is done right.

When debating on whether to take in a partner, consider the following 10 issues:

1. Does this individual have the expertise needed to grow the firm?
2. Will his or her personality mesh with the existing firm?
3. Is he or she bringing in cash to the firm to help with its expansion or to buy out part of my interest?
4. Is this person technically competent?
5. What are this person's strengths and weaknesses?
6. Is he or she front-line (meaning out in the public eye, a deal maker, or an asset to promote the company) or someone who likes to be behind the scenes?
7. Will this person interfere with the job I am doing? In other words, are we the same type of people handling the same roles for the firm?
8. Is this the only business of this individual? In other words, will he or she be devoting full-time energies to the firm?

9. Does this person have a lot of professional contacts? Are they in the area of financial planning, the community, the banking environment, or with venture capitalists and other investors?

10. Will the perceived value of the company be increased or decreased with the addition of this person?

24. HAVING A SUCCESSION PLAN

The only way you should attempt to grow a business is to see what the value will be on the other end! In other words, are you building something to sell? If the answer is no, then you are doing it all wrong! You need to build your practice with the intention to sell. Whether you do or not is irrelevant. This enables you to grow the business without its being dependent on you, so that if you miss the daily grind or essential activities, it will continue in an uninterrupted fashion.

If the business is intertwined with your family, other significant issues can develop. Typically, problems arise because there is no clear distinction between your role in the family and the role of the business, and addressing these roles could put further strain on the family relationship. In this scenario, you need to identify the underlying reasons for your or a family member's concern, isolate them, and then come up with solutions to address them.

The succession plan can include selling the business outright one day, incorporating an employee stock option plan (ESOP) so your employees can buy you out, or taking in a partner to buy you out gradually and take over the business.

Some of the basic requirements the successor should meet when taking over the business include:

- Competence
- Commitment
- Character
- Leadership skills
- Funds

Notice that these are more objective than subjective in nature. Family issues can only work if all parties benefit. Never hastily make these decisions. It is always best to think them through over a long period so that a win-win situation results for all parties involved.

25. IF YOU DON'T BELIEVE IN YOURSELF, IT WILL NEVER HAPPEN

Of all the concepts I have talked about, this one is the biggest: If you possess the confidence and ability to get the job done, then you will, and if you don't, then you won't! It is like a ball team that strives to win its games. If it does not believe in itself, it will not win. I have a picture in my office of a running back charging with the ball that reads: "Determination, it's not whether you get knocked down, but whether you can get right back up." I always encourage my kids and the basketball teams I coach to use this football analogy. You have to be persistent and determined. Confidence instills a winning attitude. Being around successful people breeds success. That is why when you are playing a sport with better competition, you tend to play better. You have to display the follow-through to make things happen. Remember, you do not have to be a rocket scientist to move mountains and other obstacles that get in your way. Rather, persistence, determination, street smarts, and motivation will guide you to the next level.

Action Checklist: Practical Firm Building Concepts with the following in mind:

- Where our firm stands now
- What our firm can do in this area
- What we would like to see in three years

1. No loss leaders—gratis isn't smart or productive in the long term.
2. Hold the appropriate directors accountable.
3. Always plan with the future in mind.
4. Say to yourself: What If I were just entering the business? Would this be the way I would set it up?
5. Encourage everyone in your office to be creative. Have a contest. Reward those employees who think outside the box with prizes.
6. Hire the right people who understand the marketplace. Scout the competition. If they know enough about your market, then listen to them.
7. Have anyone in your office be able to sign off on a problem.
8. Establish a realistic chain of command.
9. Test market new firm and product opportunities with your "B" clients. Form a client advisory group.
10. Keep all the players informed.
11. Form a planner advisory board (PAB).
12. Keep your books just as you advise your clients to.
13. What to charge: The old adage, "how much does the client got?" does not cut it.
14. Select the right form of business entity.
15. Location, location, location.
16. Technology hang-ups.
17. Time management issues.
18. Do not do it all yourself: Delegate, delegate, delegate!
19. Failing to take responsibility yourself.
20. Select an appropriate broker/dealer.
21. Spend money on training yourself and your staff.
22. Do your own due diligence on products, companies, working relationships, and the like.
23. When is it time to bring in a partner?
24. Having a succession plan.
25. If you don't believe in yourself, it will never happen.

APPENDIX 2-1: FIRMWIDE SELF-ASSESSMENT SURVEY

The purpose of this self-assessment is to determine where your firm is now.

Phase I: Background—Qualifying Questions

(1a) As a Financial Advisor, do you work with clients in providing financial planning services?

_____ Yes   _____ No

(1b) Do you provide investment and asset management services for your clients?

_____ Yes   _____ No

(1c) How long have you offered financial (and/or related) advice to your clients?

_____ 1 to 3 years   _____ 5 to 8 years

_____ 3 to 5 years   _____ over 8 years

(1d) Do you employ paraplanners?

_____ Yes   _____ No

(1e) What is the reporting structure employed within your firm?

_____

_____

_____

(1f) What is the number of nonadministrative/clerical personnel who work in your office/firm?

_____ 1–5   _____ 11–50   _____ 101–500

_____ 6–10   _____ 51–100   _____ 501+

(1g) Please describe your position within your firm:

_____ Owner/Partner/Principal   _____ Employee

_____ Independent contractor   _____ Other:_____

(1h) Are you a Registered Investment Advisor (RIA) with the Securities and Exchange Commission?

_____ Yes   _____ No

(1i) Are you registered with your State Securities Agency?

_____ Yes   _____ No

(1j) How do you charge your clients for services? (*Please check all that apply or write in a response.*)

___ Fee for financial planning (initial, hourly, and/or retainer)

___ Fee based on percentage of assets managed

___ Commission and/or loads on investment products purchased

___ Redemption fees on mutual funds or insurance products

___ Account fees (such as for IRA accounts)

___ Trail fees on mutual funds or insurance products

___ Commissions on insurance products purchased

___ Other:_____

(1k) What approximately are the assets under management that you personally supervise or manage?

___ Less than $500,000

___ $500,000 to $2 million

___ Over $2 million to $5 million

___ Over $5 million to $10 million

___ Over $10 million to $25 million

___ Over $25 million to $50 million

___ Over $50 million to $100 million

___ Over $100 million to $250 million

___ Over $250 million

Your firm's assets under management? $_____
(*Please write in $ amount.*)

(1l) Do you have a dollar ($) minimum client-account size?

_____ No   _____ Yes

If yes, what is that amount?: $_____
(*Please write in amount.*)

Phase II: Marketing

(2a) Do you target or serve a particular market segment or niche? (Doctors, professionals, closely held business owners, senior citizens, civic associations, high-net-worth individuals, etc.) Please describe:

_____

_____

_____

_____

_____

_____

(2b) How do you generate business or prospect for new clients? (Referrals, newsletters, advertising, radio shows, etc.) Please describe:

_____

_____

(2c) Do you belong to any professional organizations or networking groups?

_____ Yes   _____ No

(2d) If yes, which ones do you belong to and why?

_____

_____

Phase III: Financial Planning

(3a) On a scale from 1 to 10, where 1 is financial planning and 10 is asset management, where would you say is the focus of your firm? (*Please circle your response.*)

Financial Planning								*Asset Management*	
1	2	3	4	5	6	7	8	9	10

(3b) From the financial planning services you provide, indicate the percentage of time spent in each area. (*Note:* Total time allotted should equal 100%.)

___ Budgeting	___ Estate planning
___ Cash management	___ General planning
___ Charitable giving strategies	___ Income tax planning
___ Closely held business owner	___ Insurance planning
___ Divorce planning	___ Investment planning
___ Education planning	___ Retirement planning
___ Employee benefit planning	

(3c) Do you sell or recommend insurance products for your clients?

_____ Yes   _____ No

(3c-1) If you answered yes, then please rank the following categories by importance (with 1 being the most important).

___ Financial strength of the insurer

___ Financial performance of the insurer

___ Percent of business in no-load

___ Tracking performance of underlying funds

___ Costs and fees

___ Product availability

___ Product performance

___ Due diligence responsibility

___ Percent of business in product line

___ Average policy size

(3d) Do you prepare income tax returns for your clients?

_____ Yes   _____ No

(3e) To what extent do you perform estate planning services for your clients?

_____

_____

_____

(3f) Are you affiliated with an attorney?

_____ Yes   _____ No

(3g) When performing investment planning services for your clients, what products do you suggest, recommend, or use for your clients?

___ Futures   Other (*please specify*) _____

___ Hedge funds   _____

___ Individual bonds _____

___ Individual stocks

___ Mutual funds

___ Options

___ Real estate

___ Warrants

(3h) Which financial planning software products do you use?

___ FPLAN

___ Financial Planning Toolkit

___ Financial Profiles

___ JP Sawhney Execplan

___ JP Sawhney PlanMan

___ Luman Financial Planning Professional

___ Your own spreadsheets or system

___ Other system (*please identify*) _____

(3i) What investment planning software products do you use?

___ Frontier Analytics

___ Ibbotson Optimizer

___ Morningstar Principia

___ Wilson Optimizer

___ Other (*please specify*) _____

(3j) What trends do you see in compensation within the advisor marketplace over the next five years?

_____

_____

_____

Phase IV: Active Management/Firmwide Recommendations

(4a) Do you use mutual funds as investment vehicles for your clients?

_____ Yes   _____ No

(4b) How do you define your asset classes when you construct your clients' portfolios?

_____

_____

_____

(4c) How do you structure the initial screens on your advisor investment-oriented software to determine when to buy a specific fund?

_____

_____

_____

(4d) What specific events cause you to drop a mutual fund from your portfolios and replace it with another fund?

_____

_____

_____

(4e) Do you prefer funds managed by a single manager or through a team approach and why?

_____

_____

_____

(4f) Do you utilize a strategy of tax-efficient investing?

_____

_____

_____

(4g) What is the general composition of your aggregate portfolio? (*Please check your selections.*)

	Over 70%	70% to 50%	50% to 25%	25% to 10%	Less than 10%
No-load funds					
Load funds					
Individual bonds					
Individual equities					

(4h) Is your use of funds or individual securities increasing? Decreasing? Staying the same?

	Increasing	Decreasing	Staying the same
No-load funds			
Load funds			
Individual bonds			
Individual equities			

(4i) Are you an asset allocator?:   ___Yes   ___No

(4j) On a scale from 1 to 10, where 1 is *not* relevant to your decision-making process and 10 is very relevant, what "key event" might prompt you to add a new fund or replace an existing fund? (*Please circle your response.*)

	Not Relevant Relevant
(a) Discovering need in an asset class?	1 2 3 4 5 6 7 8 9 10
(b) Change in portfolio manager of existing fund?	1 2 3 4 5 6 7 8 9 10
(c) Existing fund in portfolio must be performing poorly for several quarters?	1 2 3 4 5 6 7 8 9 10
(d) Existing fund is closed?	1 2 3 4 5 6 7 8 9 10
(e) "Excessive" fund style drift?	1 2 3 4 5 6 7 8 9 10

(*Please write in any other key events.*)

(f) Other:_____	1 2 3 4 5 6 7 8 9 10
(g) Other:_____	1 2 3 4 5 6 7 8 9 10

(4k) What factors do you consider when selecting a specific fund for your client portfolios? Please "rank order" your selections by placing a: 1 for *critical* factors, 2 for factors that *differentiate* between fund choices, or 3 for *tie-breakers*, when other factors are considered equal.

1. ___ Reputation of portfolio manager
2. ___ Reputation of fund company
3. ___ Name recognition of fund
4. ___ Back-office capabilities of fund company
5. ___ Level of risk
6. ___ Comfort with investment approach
7. ___ Buy and sell strategies
8. ___ Management company philosophy
9. ___ Distribution and growth strategy
10. ___ Portfolio manager availability
11. ___ Historical return
12. ___ Style discipline
13. ___ Marketing support
14. ___ Total expense ratio
15. ___ Brokerage availability
16. ___ Amount and ease of information about fund manager
17. ___ What factors influence whether or not the fund will be closed
18. ___ Frequency of asset mix reporting
19. ___ Relationship with fund company
20. ___ Wholesaler support
21. ___ Revenue-sharing ability
22. ___ No-load/load waived
23. ___ Asset-class of fund
24. ___ Fund asset size
25. ___ Existing shareholder treatment on new offerings
26. ___ Strength of management company
27. ___ Benchmarks
28. ___ Relationships with company personnel

(4l) Do you personally use a service agent provider like Charles Schwab's Institutional Onesource or Fidelity's FundsNetwork to conduct your mutual fund transactions?

____ Yes   ____ No   (*If no, please skip the next question and go to question 4n.*)

(4m) Which one(s) do you utilize and for what percentage of your assets?

Fidelity FundsNetwork:	___%
Charles Schwab's Onesource:	___%
First Trust/DataLYNX:	___%
SEI:	___%
TD Waterhouse	___%
Other No. 1: _____	___%
Other No. 2: _____	___%
Directly with fund company(s)	___%
	100%

(4n) How many times per calendar year do you typically trade in & out of a mutual fund?

___ 2× or fewer   ___ 5× to 8×   ___ More than 13×
___ 3× to 4×   ___ 9× to 12×

(4o) Please rank in order of importance, with No. 1 being the most important, the following characteristics that a fee-only broker dealer should provide to its advisors:

___ Financial strength
___ Service reputation
___ Availability of products and services
___ RIA division
___ Clearing—Self-clearing vs. outside firm
___ Direct contact with customers
___ Direct payment from customer accounts
___ Fee schedule—who pays for what
___ Electronic links
___ Requirements for relationship

Phase V: Firmwide Relationships

(5a) Are you affiliated with a Broker/Dealer?

_____ Yes   _____ No   (*If no, please skip the next question and go to question 5c.*)

(5b) Which of the following best describes your B/D?

___ Independent B/D subsidiary
___ Regional NASD brokerage
___ National NYSE wirehouse
___ Insurance company subsidiary
___ Bank B/D subsidiary
___ National NYSE wirehouse

(5c) Do you hold any securities licenses? Which ones? (*Please check all that apply.*)

___ NASD Series 2	___ NASD Series 63
___ NASD Series 6, 26	___ NASD Series 65
___ NASD Series 7, 24	___ NASD Series 66
___ NASD Series 8	___ ChFC
___ NASD Series 12	___ Life Insurance
___ NASD Series 22, 39	___ Health/Disability
___ NASD Series 27, 54	___ CFP™
___ NASD Series 52, 53	___ CLU

(5d) How often would you like to follow up with portfolio managers?

___ One time per month	___ One time per six months
___ One time per quarter	___ Once a year

(5e) What method(s) would you like to use to follow up with portfolio managers and why?

_____

_____

_____

_____

(5f) What mutual fund company services turn you off?

_____

_____

_____

_____

Phase VI: Choosing a Fund Family/Distributor/Wholesaler

(6a) What are the primary mutual funds or mutual fund families you currently use?

(a) _____   (b) _____
(c) _____   (d) _____
(e) _____   (f) _____

(6b) What other mutual funds have you used, or would you consider using?

(a) _____   (b) _____
(c) _____

(6c) What are your overall impressions of or likes and dislikes about the mutual funds you mentioned in question 6a and/or 6b above?

(Please write in name of company below.)   **Likes**   **Dislikes**

(a) _____

(b) _____

(c) _____

(6d) Please describe how you go about choosing a particular fund or fund family. What is your screening process?

_____

_____

_____

_____

(6e) In general, when determining whether to recommend a particular fund to a client or prospect, is the client's or prospect's familiarity with the name of the fund or fund company:

___ undesirable?   ___ desirable?

___ somewhat undesirable?   ___ doesn't matter

___ somewhat desirable?

(6f) When you are looking for information on mutual funds, what are your major source(s) of information? Please check or write in all those that apply.

___ Teleconferences   ___ External databases:
___ Due-diligence meetings   Morningstar, Value Line, etc.
___ Trade show   ___ Regional/geographic
___ Newsletters   wholesaler
___ Peer referrals   ___ Phone/internal wholesaler
___ Discussions with   ___ Direct mail
Morningstar or   ___ Word of mouth
Standard and Poors   ___ National industry conference
analyst   ___ Local trade assoc. meetings
___ Stories in financial   ___ Broker-dealer
industry magazines and   ___ NTF/Service Agents
newspapers   ___ Internet
___ Advertisements   ___ Other, please describe:
___ Third-party evaluations

APPENDIX 2-2: WORKING WITH MUTUAL FUNDS

Financial advisors typically work with mutual funds. The following questions were derived to help you sort through the rubbish. Please address each of the following questions with approximately three sentences.

1. How important is it for you to have a specific person within the organization to answer all your questions and address your investment concerns?

    _____

    _____

    _____

2. How important is it for the company to have experience in working with fee-only and fee-based advisors?

    _____

    _____

    _____

3. How important is it for you to receive information about your competitors?

    _____

    _____

    _____

4. How important is it for you to receive information about other fund families you currently do not use?

    _____

    _____

    _____

5. How important is it for you to receive information about the state of the investment planning industry in general?

    _____

    _____

    _____

6. How important is it for you to have access to a fund portfolio manager?

_____

_____

_____

7. How often do you have to receive information for it to be considered timely?

_____

_____

_____

8. What do you consider to be timely information? (for example, what does the portfolio look like statistically at certain intervals?, what percentage ranking does it hold within its particular class?, what is the prospect of the fund right now?, or what is the prospect of the fund going forward?)

_____

_____

_____

9. How important is it for you to receive access to company information, pertaining to any of the subject areas discussed above? (For example, do you need information 24 hours a day, at your disposal, such as that available on the Internet?)

_____

_____

_____

10. Do you need any scripted information to address your clients about a mutual fund company's funds? (For example, a sheet comparing one fund versus another within the same class, or legitimizing the expenses of a fund.)

_____

_____

_____

11. How important is it for the company to have a network of branch offices?

_____

_____

_____

12. How important is it for you to receive direct fee payment from client accounts?

_____

_____

_____

13. How important is it for the company's application and forms to be easy to work with?

_____

_____

_____

14. How clear are the company's ongoing requirements for you to be in compliance?

_____

_____

_____

15. How important is it for you to receive continuing education for any professional designation or license you currently hold from a fund company?

_____

_____

_____

16. How important is it for you to network with your peers through annual or regional conferences that a fund company can provide to you?

_____

_____

_____

17. How important is it for a fund company to act as a clearinghouse for selling other companies' funds?

_____

_____

_____

18. How important is it to have the company initiate face-to-face meetings with you?

_____

_____

_____

19. Do you expect any rewards or incentives from the company to offer its mutual funds to your clients?

_____

_____

_____

20. What characteristics should an institutional advisor-oriented fund have when compared to a retail-oriented fund?

_____

_____

_____

21. What additional products or services do you want from the industry?

_____

_____

_____

22. Do you participate in conference calls and fund manager interviews?

_____

_____

_____

23. Would you read white papers and other research documents from your mutual fund company, and, if so, why do you believe that this is important?

_____

_____

_____

24. How do you think investment information should be packaged?

_____

_____

_____

25. How do you feel about mutual fund companies offering advice directly to consumers?

_____

_____

_____

26. What sources do you use to find out about new funds?

_____

_____

_____

APPENDIX 2-3: INVESTING FOR RETIREMENT (IFR) BUSINESS PLAN

Investing for Retirement (IFR), an asset management firm, has developed the following business plan. This is a sample plan designed to give you insight into the issues that need consideration before you open your doors for business.

Executive Summary

Company Description

Investing for Retirement, Inc. (IFR), is a Colorado-based company providing asset management services to individuals. 100 percent of the company's stock is owned by Jeff Rattiner.

Mission Statement

IFR's mission is to provide fee-based financial planning services to individuals with income above $100,000 and a net worth above $500,000.

Products and Services

IFR provides fee-based comprehensive and modular financial planning services for high-net-worth individuals. Hourly fees of $200 are billed to clients. Financial plans generally take 10 hours to complete. IFR is also licensed to receive insurance and securities commissions from sales of recommended products.

Target Markets

IFR targets the greater Denver area. Greater Denver has a population base of over 2.2 million persons of whom 20 percent are in the $100,000 salary range and $500,000 net worth range.

Marketing and Sales Strategy

IFR aims to differentiate itself from other financial planning firms by taking a knowledge-based approach with the ultimate goal of educating its clients so that they may achieve a good comfort level throughout the investment process.

Competitors and Market Distribution

There are approximately 120 other providers of fee-based financial planning services in the Denver metropolitan area.

Competitive Advantages and Distinctions

IFR's chief advantage is its educational approach. By educating the client, IFR helps manage the client's expectations. This helps keep the client on track with us.

Management

President Jeff Rattiner has been a practicing financial planner for over 20 years. He specializes in working with high-net-worth individuals.

Operations

IFR conducts its business at its offices at 6410 S. Quebec Street, Englewood, CO 80111.

Financial Numbers

Annual revenue projections for 2003, should be $300,000. In 2004, we expect revenue to equal $400,000.

Long-Term Goals

IFR's long-term goals are to open offices in Phoenix in 2004 and San Diego in 2005, running the same type of operation in those locations. IFR hopes to bring in two partners to run the additional two offices (at fair market value of gross billings).

Company Description

Company Mission

IFR's mission is to perform fee-based financial planning services for high-net-worth-individuals earning $100,000 who have a net worth in excess of $500,000.

Services

IFR provides comprehensive and modular planning services for a fee. If appropriate, it may also recommend and sell various investment and insurance products. It has ongoing relationships with clients with whom IFR meets at least once annually. It also performs hourly financial planning services where clients can meet with a financial planner and have specific questions answered or researched.

Legal Status

IFR is a Colorado-based company providing fee-based financial planning services to individuals. 100 percent of the company's stock is owned by Jeff Rattiner. IFR is a Subchapter S corporation.

Industry Analysis

IFR is well positioned to take advantage of the significant opportunities presented by the intergenerational transfer of wealth. With the baby boomer generation expected to share in the general wealth, IFR sees the need for expanded investment and retirement planning services. IFR does not see many other fee-based financial planning firms taking this "knowledge approach" toward working with high-net-worth individuals.

Barriers to Entry

With the commoditization of financial planning services and products, which means that many planners are selling the same products and offering the same services without distinguishing themselves from their competition, profit margins may be coming down in the future. Consumers are demanding more free services from their advisors. Advances in technology also make it harder since many financial service organizations offer free calculator software and other helpful tidbits on their web sites.

Current Environment

The current environment supports additional fee-based financial planners entering this marketplace. With 260 million people living in the United States, [and 50 percent of them (or 130 million households to service)] and approximately 100,000 licensed or registered financial planners to service them (excluding the 150,000 additional self-proclaimed planners), there are many consumers who will need IFR's help in bettering their financial lives. Focusing on the middle market (which is where the majority of these people fall) provides an opportunity to work with many clients.

Long-Term Opportunities

Long-term prospects appear excellent for the reasons stated above. More consumers are working with licensed financial planners and understand the importance of planning ahead for their future.

Target Market

IFR targets households in the greater Denver area that fit the following profile:

- Age: 45–65
- Income range: $100,000
- Net worth: $500,000
- Occupation: People close to retirement or self-sufficient
- Location: Metro Denver
- Technically adept

Competition

IFR's primary competitors include fee-based financial planning firms:

- Jones Financial
- Bert & Ernie Financial
- Big Daddy Financial Services
- We-Are-It Financial

IFR does not intend to compete with these firms directly. Rather, IFR intends to provide knowledge-based programs to its clients to select appropriate investments to meet long-term goals and objectives.

Market Share

None of the competitors listed above has significant market share. This is due to the large number of fee-based financial planning firms in the marketplace.

Strength of Competitors

IFR's competitors are strong in the following areas:

- 55 salespersons soliciting accounts

Marketing Plan and Sales Strategy

To educate its client base and explain its services, IFR plans to use the following marketing media:

- Public relations
- Brochures
- Consumer trade shows
- Direct mail
- Advertising through newspapers

Operations

IFR conducts its physical business at its location at 6410 S. Quebec Street, Englewood, CO 80111. However, the heart of IFR's operations lie with its education program and its web-based customer training center. This center makes it easy for clients to access financial data and recommendations over the Internet. Further, it lets clients pose questions in a chatroom and have them answered by qualified financial planners.

Management and Organization

President Jeff Rattiner has been a practicing financial planner for over 20 years. He specializes in working with middle-income families and their concerns. He is a graduate of City University of New York.

Long-Term Development and Exit Plan

IFR will grow steadily over the next 10 years. By 2012, IFR plans to have a 7 percent market share in the Denver area.

Strategy for Achieving Goals

IFR will consider opening additional offices in various locations throughout the United States.

Risks

The greatest risk of expansion is the chance that IFR might become too decentralized in its operation and management of the company.

Financial Numbers

Income Statement

The following is a projection of cash flow for the next three years.

	2003	2004	2005
Income			
Gross revenue	$300,000	$400,000	$500,000
Operating Expenses			
Salaries and wages	$100,000	$140,000	$200,000
Employee benefits	$ 10,000	$ 14,000	$ 20,000
Payroll taxes	$ 15,000	$ 21,000	$ 30,000
Professional services	$ 2,000	$ 2,500	$ 3,000
Rent	$ 12,000	$ 12,600	$ 13,200
Web development	$ 2,000	$ 2,500	$ 3,000
Depreciation and			
amortization	$ 1,500	$ 1,800	$ 2,100
Insurance	$ 2,000	$ 2,200	$ 2,400
Utilities	$ 4,000	$ 4,400	$ 4,800
Postage and supplies	$ 500	$ 630	$ 700
Marketing and advertising	$ 5,000	$ 5,500	$ 6,000
Travel	$ 2,000	$ 2,500	$ 3,000
Entertainment	$ 3,000	$ 3,300	$ 3,600
Bad debts and doubtful			
accounts	$ 2,500	$ 3,500	$ 5,000
Total operating expenses	$164,500	$219,730	$299,700
Net income before taxes	$ 85,500	$130,270	$200,300
Provision for income taxes	$ 17,100	$ 26,054	$ 40,060
Net income after taxes	$118,400	$154,216	$160,240

Balance Sheet

Assets

Current assets

Cash	$ 80,000
Accounts receivable	$ 10,000
Prepaid expenses	$ 5,000
Total current assets	$125,000

Fixed assets

Building	$250,000
Equipment	$ 50,000
Furniture	$ 60,000
Total fixed assets	$360,000
Total Assets	**$455,000**

	2003	2004	2005
Liabilities			
Accounts payable	$ 75,000		
Accrued payroll	$ 15,000		
Taxes payable	$ 5,000		
Short-term notes payable	$ 20,000		
Long-term notes payable	$150,000		
Total liabilities	$265,000		

Net Worth (This is the difference between assets and liabilities, or in other words, your plug number)

Shareholders' equity	$ 30,000		
Retained earnings	$160,000		
Total net worth	$190,000		
Total Liabilities and Net Worth	**$455,000**		

Appendix

The appendix should include detailed information not included in the main contents of the business plan. It should not include new information not previously presented in the plan. Rather, it should reinforce positions and statements you have previously made and provide that additional detail necessary to make the plan complete. For example, if you used certain projections in your plan, the way they were computed should be included here. Detailed information on the shareholders and what they own should also be included here. Also, strategies that were summarized in the plan should go into more detail here, such as what methods were used to draw the conclusions and perhaps why other methods were not included. Since many individuals do not read appendices, the base part of your business plan should be able to stand on its own.

A business plan is an essential ingredient to the success of your business. It really helps you think it through and acts as a catalyst in getting things done, simply because you are able to describe, in detail or in concise form, what your business is, where you want it to go, and how to get there. But probably even more importantly, it helps define what you want in your life both personally and professionally.

3

The Nifty Fifty: 50 Ideas About Marketing

WHAT DOES MARKETING REALLY MEAN?

We have all heard definitions of marketing and have seen examples of marketing plans in action. But have you really thought about what it means to you in the context of your business? Think about it. Are people really "sold" things nowadays, or are they positioned to buy them? In the old days, we use to "sell" insurance because nobody woke up in the morning and said, "Gee, honey, I think I'll buy myself a nice big juicy insurance policy today!" Although, if your spouse kept suggesting it, you might have had other issues! The whole point here is that marketing occurs through a series of brand repetitions whereby the end user (your client) becomes comfortable, familiar, and self-assured that what he or she is buying from you is essential, worthwhile, and most important, necessary.

Marketing, therefore, is making you "the brand" and putting that brand in front of your intended audience. It is figuring out a way to get noticed and become known. It is gaining essential exposure so that you can create clients from prospects, who end up making a conscious decision to find solutions to what has now become a problem, and then figuring out the best way to address it. It is soliciting your brand to conquer your niche marketplace. It is getting prospects to act, to become clients.

Sure, we have all heard the traditional marketing stuff. You know, the four p's: product, price, promotion, and place. It makes great textbook reading and a lot of sense in traditional product-oriented channels. But how do you translate it to the service side?

Here we are talking about using yourself as each of the four p's. Your marketing must sell you always! You are the product. Your product addresses the needs of clients who want you to work with them and guide them to financial independence. The intended clientele you desire will help set your price. To whom do you want to market? Will you provide a premium product to a sophisticated clientele to demand those prices (fees)? How do you promote yourself to reach your intended market? How do you decide what areas to promote yourself in? Who do you promote, yourself or your firm? Which services or products do you promote? Where do you promote yourself? And then where do you distribute that service, in what place? In what manner do you distribute it? These are all key questions that must be answered when laying out your marketing plan.

I know what they say. Only give your readers an easy reference list. Call it the "Top Ten" or make it have some ring to it. I broke the cardinal rule by giving you as many relevant pieces of marketing advice as you will need to reach that next level of your practice and in a number that is not rounded up or down!

1. BRANDING

Let's talk about branding. My brand is Jeff Rattiner. It is my ticket to gaining recognition and acceptance in what I do best—training planners and practicing financial planning. It is the way I want my target markets to recognize and remember me over time. It is the perception I want people to have when they associate me with some type of financial product or service. I want them ultimately to trust and like me, so they feel comfortable when they select me to guide them down a very important road.

The entire process is time-consuming. It cannot be created in a day, week, or even a year. Many times, it takes years to develop yourself and your practice to be recognized the way you want to be. It is developing an image and transforming that image through uniform communication, firmwide conduct, and touching emotional bases. Positioning your firm (as explained later) is the sure-fire way of being what you want to be for your intended audience.

The main reason for developing a brand is to get your intended market niches to recognize you in a particular light, whatever it is. Look at some of the more successful financial service brands. Merrill Lynch reminds you of the bull—being bullish with client accounts, being aggressive in managing client funds, and so forth. Prudential gives the impression of strength; when you deal with Prudential, you purchase a piece of the rock, which symbolizes strength, financial stability, long-term protection, and so forth. What you are doing is branding yourself on a small scale in a manner that makes you known to your market audience.

In an industry like ours, where many of the qualified planners can do similar things through technology and have the ability to access superior research, the only way we will stand out to our clients and prospects is to brand ourselves. So what is your brand? Or, in other words, how will your clients or prospective clients identify you? Will it be friendliness to clients, low costs, quality products, quick service? The best way to begin identifying this branding is to figure out what your firm is, who you are, and what you stand for. See Appendix 2-1, "Firmwide Self Assessment Questionnaire." You may look at these things and like them, or not like them and want to change them. In any case, your goal is to figure out these attributes and develop and market the ones you like to prospects. The stronger your brand identity, the more likely it is that people will think of you and what you can provide them in your areas of expertise. That brand identity gets reinforced through constant repetition, as discussed below.

2. THE NEXT LEVEL

This book is not about entry-level marketing. It is about figuring out who you already are and then taking that to the next level by using marketing channels that work in your chosen field. You should not be using cold-calling or impersonal solicitation avenues at this stage of the game. Those techniques do not provide long-term, proven results. Rather, you should be using some of the outside-the-box strategies discussed in Chapter 2.

Moneys you use to fund your marketing activities should be considered an investment, not an expense. After all, you are planting the seeds for future growth. All marketing dollars should be designed to deliver an immediate (within the next 12 months) return. Advertising dollars that are spent to deliver awareness for a small financial services firm do not deliver the necessary ingredients to keep afloat. We are small potatoes compared to many of the larger firms in the marketplace. We do not have the funds necessary to pay a retainer to a medium outlet to promote the concepts of good general financial planning and not key specifics of what our firm does.

Getting to the next level means leaving our comfort zone. It means getting naked in the world and going for the gusto. It means doing things you thought about but were too scared to actually do. The idea of thinking outside the box holds true here. Taco Bell has just come out with a marketing campaign taking off from this concept. Theirs is "thinking outside the bun." I think it is brilliant and will eventually get customers who do not want hamburgers to come to their stores.

What have you done lately to get to the next level? Perhaps you have been to a seminar and heard a speaker provide you with way to the riches he encountered. Maybe he even sold you a system outside the breakout session room. To begin with, you need to sit down and write down everything you want to accomplish within your business. You have to determine which items are doable and which ones are not. The list you develop can be made from many of the topics that follow.

3. FORMING ALLIANCES

Many planners like to form alliances to provide their clients with the best services and products. Others like to form them because of the payout they are going to receive from the alliance membership. Whatever road you choose, you need to protect your clients' interests above everything else while operating in an ethical manner. All other issues are secondary.

The Reality of Working with CPAs

I know many financial advisors who have strong relationships with CPAs. They get most of their business from the CPAs in what is supposed to be an equal referral exchange. That means that each party is supposed to provide the other with an approximately equal amount of referrals and dollars each year. But in reality it usually is one-sided; according to my best estimate it is more like a 10 to 1 ratio in favor of the advisor. Most of the CPAs I train at the California CPA Education Foundation, the American Institute of CPAs, the Arizona CPA Society, and other organizations are tired of this exchange and want to get into the game themselves. They see their core businesses literally dying, and feel that at present there is a wonderful opportunity to help their clients. To start with, most CPAs have a leg up on everyone else, since they are deemed to be America's most trusted advisors. So more than 1,000 CPAs come to my training classes looking for ways to get into the business. With the number of audits dwindling because of mergers, bankruptcies, and so forth, and the cheap and effective technology available for tax preparation and record keeping, it is no wonder they need to look for greener pastures. While you may hear that CPAs are the way to go, and many books and seminars tell you how to work them in as a referral source, the truth of the matter is that it won't happen. They want a piece of the action, as well. They are not naive about the amount of money that exists in this business. And most of the CPAs I speak with who have made the transition into the business end up making three times what they did as CPAs within three years. It is not a secret anymore. Therefore, you need to figure out how to co-exist with them and legally split fees and commissions where both parties co-own the business. Perhaps you can start a joint venture or partnership where you each are responsible to do some of the business with the CPA. For example, all clients who come into the partnership are split 50-50. You take care of the investment and insurance angles, and possibly the education and specialty niches, like working with small business owners and suddenly single individuals. Have the CPA take care of the income, retirement, and estate tax angles. This way you each get to work in your area of specialty, there is no overlap, and you are both providing a truly beneficial service.

Another way of doing this is to work with the CPA's clients where they remain under the CPA's control. You are brought in as a specialist in financial issues and house yourself in the CPA's office. You meet with the CPA's clients either with the CPA present or not, but all moneys that are made are split in an appropriate proportion (assuming the CPA is licensed). Letters go out under the CPA's letterhead or that of a new entity and refer to you as the financial advisor who is trained to deal with issues for the types of clients the CPA works with. This approach will pay dividends rapidly. According to many of my CPA students, once such an alliance is formed, they can get a 50 percent or higher cross-over (cross-sell) rate, which means that the same tax clients are now buying financial products or having their assets managed by the CPA firm. In my experience, an equal partnership tends to work best over the long term. Remember, there is enough money in this business for everyone, and then some!

In the insurance and brokerage areas, all parties who share in any commissions or fees must be licensed. No exceptions. If the parties are not licensed, they are prohibited from sharing a fee-splitting arrangement with you. No exceptions! However, what you can do to work out the relationship so that each party can profit from an association and physically keep both parties in the same location for client convenience, is to exchange moneys through rent payments, consulting arrangements, or some other charge-back that is a legitimate expense. As long as one firm is renting space from another one and remaining in the same location for ease of dealing with client referrals, that will probably work out well. You should form these alliances with insurance and brokerage specialists who have different strengths from yours and can complement the work you do for existing clients. By forming an alliance, all parties can market their respective strengths without overlapping.

With lawyers, you need to be careful. First, not all states permit lawyers to accept commissions or other fees typically paid in the financial services arena. Therefore, let state law be your guide. One possibility is to employ an attorney in your office to handle all the estate planning issues and be paid customary fees charged for the drafting of wills, trusts, powers of attorney, and other documents. It is a strong asset to have a practicing and competent estate planning attorney in your office.

This brings me to my ideal office: Five players, including the CPA, who handles all the income tax issues; the attorney, who handles all the estate planning issues; the insurance agent, who handles all of the insurance issues; the investment advisor (probably you) to handle all the investment planning aspects; and the generalist, who handles client appointments (prior and subsequent to the development of the financial plan), performs the interactive goal-setting and fact finding session, develops the financial statements (balance sheet and income statement), understands educational planning and various miscellaneous topics, and can be a resource to look up general financial planning issues. By performing specialties, you do not run the risk of overlapping work and everyone can be paid by splitting all fees thrown into the pool (again, assuming all are licensed).

4. CHARTING YOUR COURSE

Your strategy derived from considering the big picture enables you to lay out a path to follow, establishing key guidelines and providing you with the necessary framework for following through. Creativity should be an important factor in working through all the elements. Use the road map as your chosen path that provides a certain amount of leeway to allow you to tailor your plan.

I do not think you want to try all the techniques discussed below. I believe that this would be an expensive path to choose because you really do not know what is going to work. The problem with this approach, having learned from experience, is that you may not be working in the areas you really like. You may end up with a tidal wave of accounts, funds, and other goodies upfront, but they may dwindle over time because you begin to lose interest and focus and decide that that is not what you want to be when you grow up.

Remember, you had time to experiment with all this stuff when you began your practice. Now, you are in the fine-tuning mode. As such, you need to be crystal clear of what that is. Basically, you need to ask yourself what business do you want to be in when you grow up. See the discussion on quantifying your practice in Chapter 6 for more details.

I have a very basic philosophy about marketing and business. If you are talking to someone with no knowledge of the business and cannot describe to that person what you want to do in one to two easy sentences, then you do not have a clear and concise plan of attack to follow. It is that simple. The mission of a marketing plan should be concise enough to be written on a matchbook cover. If you cannot explain it to people, how are you going to be able to carry it out? When I explain the KIS model to people, some call me fresh! Keep It Simple! Don't overanalyze and write a thesis or dissertation to explain your model. Remember, you are not dealing with Ph.D.s. You are dealing with Joe and Mary Public, who have to understand what it is that you do and how you charge for what you do so they can determine whether what you do will work for them!

5. DO NOT SELL OUT ON VOLUME

Do not try to do the most financial plans or sell the most products in the league! Do not ruin the integrity of your brand by heading up a factory of generic financial plans. Rather, personalize each plan to ensure that you are meeting the needs of your clientele. The drive to do more of everything obsesses many planners. They think "more is better." That is just not true. More would be better if you were able to retain a high volume of high-net-worth individuals and hire new staff to service them appropriately. However, the likelihood of that happening is probably small if you are not well connected in your community or your niche market. Therefore, it is better to do a few plans well and thoroughly than offer a processed package that provides a lot of meaningless rubbish and does not enable the client to work within his or her own level of expertise.

Many planners use the creation of financial plans as a loss leader into other areas. I don't agree with that principle. It goes back to the principle of profitability. You need to be able to sustain a profit on each aspect of your business, which means that you have to cover cost and mark-up on all the services that you provide. Do fewer plans at more dollars, rather than more plans at fewer dollars. That will provide you with the cash flow necessary to expand into other areas.

6. DO NOT OBSESS ABOUT THE COMPETITION

I have said it over and over again. There is plenty of money to be made out there without worrying about what the competition is going to do next. Just focus on what you are good at. Streamline the process, systematize it, so that anyone in your office can do it. If you spend your time worrying about what others are going to do, it will divert your energies and talents away from what you know best and have you playing catch up or defense.

Playing defense never allows you to take the lead. You are always running behind and never get to be on top of your game. Your offense dictates how well you are going to score with clients. Many clients prefer planners who are proactive, rather than reactive, or just chasing the pack. There is plenty of business to go around and we all will end up making a fine living year after year.

7. YOUR MARKETING PLAN IS A WORKING DOCUMENT

Just like clients, many planners think that once they draft their marketing document, they do not have to worry about it again. In fact, the opposite is true. A marketing plan is an ongoing, living and breathing piece of work that continually needs to be updated and modified. One of the reasons is that conditions are always changing and you need to stay ahead of the curve. Therefore, you should be highlighting it, rewriting it, and, more importantly, changing it where and when it is no longer working. Remember, you have limited funds to perform marketing functions. Marketing is an investment. You are not going to invest in something that does not meet ongoing criteria. Otherwise, it is a lost cause. Just as you would measure an investment, so should you measure your marketing plan.

Give your marketing plan three to six months to see whether or not it is working. If it looks like the trend is away from your stated objectives, it needs to be reworked to get it back on track. These decisions need to be made by the committee whose responsibility it is to oversee this area. You, your marketing person, and others who may have the ultimate responsibility for the success of the plan need to be the people who evaluate it and sign off on changes when necessary. You can also involve some of your clients in the process to provide good, honest, objective feedback (see Chapter 2, The Practical Effect).

8. KEEP YOUR FOCUS

The biggest reason for planners failing in their practices is that they lose focus. They end up taking business from all over the place, and eventually cannot relate to where their business is coming from. This can be partially resolved with an appropriate business plan that identifies where your concentration will be. When you advance to a higher level, it is imperative that you play the game at that level. Look at professional athletes. They have such focus and intensity and determination that they play at a higher level. That is how you should consider yourself now. You are reading this book because you find yourself at a crossroads. You need to begin thinking "What can I do to play competitively and successfully at the major league level of financial advisors?" Your competition at your operating level helps you remain competitive. You tend to stay focused on what you are doing versus the competition.

How do you determine what that focus is? You need to develop a niche-marketing plan to determine whom it is you wish to target. Become as knowledgeable as you can in that arena and determine distribution angles to get your message across. Your focus should include goals that are high but attainable, requiring some effort on your part.

9. LEARN FROM YOUR MISTAKES

If I had a dollar for every mistake I have ever made, I would be a millionaire!! Do not be afraid to make mistakes. In fact, that is the only way you will succeed. Ray Kroc did not hit it big until age 55. Many others have gone bankrupt only to be bailed out. Even the Donald (Trump) became rich, lost it all, and became rich again. The point is that if you don't take risks and chances, when you have lost before, then you will never have anything to learn from.

I have a theory I tell my children all the time. It is called the "at-bat" theory. The more times you get to bat, the more hits you will have and the more runs you are going to score. You will make many mistakes when you come up to bat. You will strike out swinging, looking, foul-tipping the ball, bunting with two strikes, and so forth. Each time you will walk back to your dugout (office) and figure out what you did wrong. You will look at game films to determine what you need to do to succeed the next time. It is not the batting average that counts. It is the number of times you come to the plate. I would rather be 50 for 1,000 and batting .050 than 3 for 10 and batting .300. I will have learned more this way, made more mistakes, and come out of it all the better.

Every time you make a mistake, you should plaster it on the wall. You know the old saying, "fool me once, shame on you, fool me twice, shame on me." Pick a corner of the office and write the mistakes down on a whiteboard or flipchart and hang it up. It will remind you of all the things you have tried and failed, and what not to do next time around. Everything you encounter will make you and your firm that much stronger the next time around. Believe me, no one has failed more often than I have. But each time it has made me that much stronger.

10. REALIZE THAT IT IS ALL INTERRELATED

Everything you do in life is interrelated. One area affects another and the cycle continues indefinitely. You need to be aware of the consequences of your actions in a particular event because they may adversely affect another. For example, marketing to one group and accelerating the process may affect the second round of marketing to that group. Another experience I have had was that after we sold out our first round of Financial Planning Fast Track™ (FPFT™), I was tempted to do another round for that session in Dallas. However, the Dallas class would have taken away students from my next Denver class. I decided I would not do it until I could completely justify it and each location could stand on its own merits and not draw from the other. Ultimately, we were able to achieve just that.

11. KNOW YOUR COSTS (BEFORE YOU PROCEED)

Any good businessperson knows what the bottom line is, and how much money it takes to succeed. You should work out your pricing structure and your expense allocation to the micro-details and keep a watchful eye on the budget. You can also have your accountant or financial person do a backup check to ensure that nothing gets overlooked. Minimize your expenses. Most entrepreneurs get themselves into big trouble by spending more than they take in. They want to reach the big time sooner rather than later, and spend accordingly. I witnessed a very successful knowledge-based company do that. It expanded to 17 people after one year and then went belly-up after the necessary cash flow was not being generated.

Any business owner knows that the first rule of thumb is to have positive cash flow. That means bringing in more than you spend. Most businesses fail because they do not follow that rule. Once you acquire a base of capital, then you begin spending to get to the next level. This does not mean going to a bank and getting the biggest line of credit you can find to finance your marketing plan. While I am a believer in leveraging in many situations, leveraging for the sake of growing is not always wise. Build the infrastructure slowly and sure-handedly. Once you reach the necessary financial benchmarks, only then is it right for you to expand to the next level.

12. ANALYZE AND MEASURE YOUR RESULTS

It does you no good to design a marketing plan, implement it, and then quit on it. In order to know that the money you are spending is promoting the growth of your business, you need to hold yourself accountable for your marketing results. You should design a preliminary cash-flow plan before the year begins, monitor the progress throughout the year, and then analyze your actual marketing results. Give yourself some leeway, but not too much. All variances should be investigated to determine what you need to correct going forward. You have to accept the fact in advance that changes will be forthcoming and not fret over them. All companies have to constantly refine their marketing budgets. If you see things are not going the way you thought, you need to change the budget throughout the year, rather than wait until the end of the year.

I tell the same thing to my clients. If we end your planning in the middle of my PIPRIM© financial planning process, then the plan is not worth the paper it is written on. We have to make every attempt to constantly distinguish what works from what does not and continually refine the plan to get just the right mix.

13. DERIVE A MARKETING ANALYSIS

Answer the question "Why am I here?" Or, more correctly, "Why is my company here?" Obviously it has to fill some sort of need; otherwise there will be no industry to target, no clients to be had, or any money to make. Market analysis provides the information on needs and wants of clients required to make your firm responsive and marketing oriented. Market analysis also provides information to guide strategic planning, since studying the desires, beliefs, images, attitudes, and satisfaction levels of clients can reveal weaknesses. In addition, marketing analysis supplies information to guide all the finer points of a marketing program, from decisions about fee arrangements to decisions about the best appeals to use in personal communication. It allows the firm to avoid costly marketing mistakes.

Market analysis focuses on individual client behavior issues. Therefore, issues concerning why clients select, contract with, retain, engage, or fire planners should be covered. It should also cover post-decision blues ("Why did I do that?").

Therefore, the marketing analysis should begin with a needs assessment. Sit back from it and determine whether all, some, or none of your clients' needs are being satisfied. List your typical client's needs in priority order and then list your "A" and "B" clients. Analyze and evaluate them. See if a pattern develops. If you notice that you are missing the same needs for each client, you will need to go back and rework them. Then develop a plan of action to target them going forward. Keep score to see if you are making progress. If that works, you may want to incorporate these changes for your other clients.

The marketing analysis should contain the following information:

- Who are you trying to service?
- How are you doing? (Is it working?)
- How do you rate your clients (fully satisfied, somewhat satisfied, not at all satisfied)?
- What can you do to rectify the situation?
- What group are most affected by this?
- Have you rectified the situation?

14. COMPARE PAST AND CURRENT MARKETING INFORMATION TO DETECT PATTERNS

Even though I am not a proponent of market timing on the investment side, there is some merit to developing a system that detects business patterns before you make any significant moves. For example, if advertising, direct mail, or some other promotional event works at a certain time of the year, then you should focus on it only at that time. The best example is advertising for tax preparers. When do you see them advertise? It is only in January and February. Why? Because that is when the returns need to be worked on and that is where the money is.

H&R Block advertises on big shows, like the Super Bowl, during tax season in anticipation of having clients coming in to their offices dazed and confused. Their approach to the client stresses the complexity of the tax law: There are too many tax law changes, so come to us as the experts on the new laws. Now, for example, if that approach did not work in the current year, a reevaluation of this strategy would have to be made and possibly an alternative tried in order to reach the same audience in a different manner.

15. LISTEN, COMPREHEND, QUESTION, THEN INCORPORATE ALL SUGGESTIONS INTO THE MARKETING GAME PLAN

Inquisitive advisors will not just listen to their own instincts. They will incorporate the thoughts of those around them, including clients, coworkers, peers, and the like, in developing an appropriate marketing game plan.

The Art of Listening

Listening involves incorporating the thoughts of those around you. The first rule in listening is to respond to the central point. Always attempt to determine the speaker's main message. It is not uncommon for your client to send a number of messages at one time through words, actions, or inaction. As a listener, you need to be attentive and have the patience to get at the primary message. Your goal in listening is to understand the client's message as soon as you can and to make sure that the main point is clearly understood.

It is important that you respond to emotional messages. As you know, emotions can block rational decision making. Your objective is to have your client respond fully to your recommendations and to carefully separate the emotional tie-in from the end result, where possible. You should listen to indicators of emotion. For example, if your client has concerns about running out of retirement funds at the later stages of life, you need to attack that fear head-on. Point out specifically what has to be done to ensure that money will be around throughout retirement. Put the client at ease. Your listening skills will help you decide when you need to pull out all the stops in addressing the client's concern.

You also need to remember significant details. Use your memory to focus your thoughts on what the client is telling you. Your clients will undoubtedly share important information with you when they feel comfortable opening up to you. Pay strict attention to all the information that the client shares with you, especially the minute details. Seek clarification on vague issues and reiterate what the client says after he or she finishes. This approach ensures that the client will value you and your opinions when the time comes to implement your plan.

Make interjections where possible. For example, if the client is concerned about running out of money for retirement, jump on the bandwagon and explain the value of investing appropriately during retirement to avoid that occurrence. Explain that by spending too much, or not planning adequately, the client runs the risk of defeating the very thing he or she sets out to accomplish.

Maintain an objective and unbiased approach when repeating client information. If the client wants your opinion, then by all means give it. You need to relay that you are open minded and all-inclusive in your decision-making and your recommendations. Listening is a process that makes you responsible, and that, my friends, comes with the territory.

Comprendo!

Do you understand? It is all a matter of following up the client's initial concerns with a synopsis of what was said. By repeating the major points in a variety of ways, your clients will conclude that you are listening to them and that you care because you are taking the time to digest the information. Don't "yes" them to death! Rather, interject with comments specifically about what they are telling you that may make them think, rather than spilling out all the information at once.

Question

Never take things for granted. If you leave it up to the client, chances are the information being communicated and then documented will be incorrect. Better safe than sorry. Question everything up front, early, and often, if need be. By ensuring a proper understanding from the outset, you will be in a better position to rely on your data.

Incorporate All Suggestions

More is better . . . in information gathering and recommendation planning. The old adage "two heads are better than one" applies here. In addition, more heads are even better, because that means many people are thinking about the same issues and chances are that it will incorporate all the client's main issues will be addressed. After all the facts are down, you can streamline and stick with the very best.

16. IT IS ALL A MATTER OF NUMBERS: WIN MORE THAN YOU LOSE

The more, the better. You cannot be a home run hitter if you never get up to the plate! You have to seize every opportunity possible to try your stuff out so that when you do get to the plate, you will have more chances to produce. There is no such thing as a bad idea. Every idea has merit and is worth looking into. Some work and some do not. But you don't know until you try. For example, a bad idea that did not work was the introduction of "New Coke" in the early 1980s. The Coca-Cola Company tried it, failed, regrouped, and still managed to plow forward. Many of the ideas that have worked are out in full force today. You can tell from all the successful new brands and companies of recent years.

When a wire house or insurance company instructs new sales people to "dial for dollars," the premise is that if you do it long enough and remain persistent and dedicated, more leads will be generated and a higher level of sales will follow. That old-school mentality has been in existence for quite some time. I have learned long ago that it is about getting the opportunity to strut your stuff.

17. DO NOT PACKAGE ALL YOUR SERVICES UNDER ONE IDENTITY THAT COULD BECOME CLOUDY

Many planners I know figure out their core service, become successful at it, and then try to capitalize on it assuming they will have the same luck as before. The problem is that they proceed into areas where they do not have the same expertise. Therefore, their new product and/or service is not as strong as their core area. Over time, the firm loses the identity that got it where it is in the first place. For example, assume ABC Planning Corp., which specializes in retirement planning for teachers and basically dominates its local marketplace, decides to try its hand at income tax preparation and mortgage brokering. The company reassigns some of its staff to perform those functions. They cross-sell their existing clientele and market these services to all newcomers. ABC learns later on that the mortgage arrangements they have with banks and real estate brokers are not as competitive as those of other players in the marketplace and that the lack of CPAs on staff proves costly as mistakes galore are made on clients' tax returns. This is an example of a real planner scenario that occurred. The company subsequently determined that they did not have the right tools and procedures in place to continue operating in these areas and decided to go back and focus on their core business, planning.

18. PICK ONE THING OR THEME AND DO IT WELL (MARKETING FOCUS)

Which leads us into the next topic: pick one thing and do it well. I learned long ago that you cannot be all things to all people. Companies that try to do that end up getting burned in the long run. Take the now-bankrupt K-Mart Corporation. After a successful retail run and unlimited growth opportunities in the 1970s, they decided to open specialty stores, like Borders Books and Office Max. Ironically, both of these companies are doing just fine, but K-Mart did not do anything to improve its core.

The question then becomes how do you pick your one best thing? When I started in business, I used the old spaghetti approach. Throw the spaghetti against the wall and see what sticks. The strands that stick is where you ultimately end up focusing your business. In my case, it was business consulting based on all the corporate contacts I had lined up during my tenure at the AICPA, CFP Board, and ICFP. That is the route I took and I was very glad I did that. Then I thought about it and asked myself, "What do I want to be when I grow up?" I decided I wanted to be an information company that emphasized the training and development aspect of financial planning, which, if structured properly, could result in a financial services supermarket that emphasized training and development to advisors and consumers. I hired capable staff to head each of those areas and then did what I do best, negotiate deals with advisors and consumers to provide these types of services.

Now, while it may appear that I do more than one thing, I pride myself on being an educator and training advisors and consumers on the essentials of financial planning. With the FPFT™

training on the advisor side, and the planning services that emphasize an educational approach on the consumer side, I consider my firm a training ground for those clients who want to better themselves by understanding and using the financial planning process to satisfy their own goals and concerns.

While there is no one right way to succeed, you need to have a clear vision. Mine is that through training, my clients can understand more about financial planning and advisors can understand what they need to work with when dealing with their own clients. I use the training approach by developing the interrelated fields of financial planning, tax return preparation, and general advice to build my consumer-oriented practice.

19. KEEP RAISING THE BAR

I am a firm believer in continuing to grow and prosper, taking things to the highest level possible. You should never accept mediocrity or the status quo. I learned long ago while working for the CPA firm Arthur Andersen and Company that things and people do not stay stationary. Its philosophy, like that of any Big Five firm, is an up-or-out mentality: If you do not get promoted to the next level (i.e., junior staff, senior staff, manager, or partner), then you are out as a staff member. I believe the same basic principles apply here as well. Clearly, if you just try to maintain your market share or keep your practice on autopilot, you are doomed to failure simply because you are losing that competitive edge and are not taking advantage of the new situations that come up. Think about it. Ten years ago, how was your practice structured? Clearly, in 1992 we did not have the Internet to trade e-mails or research items. Fifteen years ago, faxes were not commonplace and not everyone had a computer. My, how things have changed. Just think what would happen if you did not keep up with the changes in technology. You need to take advantage of every opportunity presented and capitalize on it by learning more about all the issues and leveraging yourself, where possible. Think about all the new reports, fund information companies, financial planning software and packages, and financial supermarkets out there.

How do you attempt this? It goes back to your business plan and the financial targets you have set for the firm. Initially, you prepared a projection based on estimates you believed you could meet. Now consider the other types of services, product offerings, alliances, and other relationships you can become part of and include those numbers as well. Ideally, you should be looking at growing anywhere from 5 to 20 percent per year, based on your location, type of business, and support staff. Write down the things you wish to accomplish every year. For example,

- Year 1: Introduce comprehensive financial planning to all clients.
- Year 2: Incorporate income tax preparation as a subset of the income tax section of the financial plans you provide for clients.
- Year 3: Form an alliance with a broker-dealer, Registered Investment Advisor (RIA), or someone through whom business can be channeled at more favorable rates than you have.
- Year 4: Take on more independents in locations you currently do not service but that are part of the territory included in your growth plan. Open up new offices run by trained staff members. This "opening up offices" team has as its mission to go to new locations and stay there for 6 to 12 months in order to hire local people to run the office. By having an independent team, you are standardizing the process even more. Remember, it's the system that counts. Your goal is to develop a business model in which your presence is not necessary for the firm to succeed.

If that does not appeal to you, consider a franchising arrangement. Some planners have developed niche markets and sold their system and rights to a territory where their system operates. Sheryl Garrett of Garrett Financial Systems in Overland Park, Kansas, has a program that specializes in working with middle-income America. This system enables other planners to provide uniform services to their clients and cultivate new ones in their local areas.

One of the other issues that comes up here is how you define your service. If you can continually change the definition of what you are doing, the services you are providing, and the requirements to meet your clients' needs going forward, your peers will continually lag behind. Look at the electronics industry. It comes out with new products (although I personally do not see the need) every few months, so the manufacturers do not become stale. I truly do not believe there is any real difference in these new products. But the perception of the public is that something new has been added to the products, so, as they say, the "out with the old, in with the new" rule applies.

People in general have a "comfort zone" where they feel everything is fine, and they would prefer to stay within this circle of safety. That is why many businesses do not survive; they fall into a rut. Take a look at what you have accomplished within your practice thus far. What are the things that make you stand above everyone else? How have you distinguished yourself in the marketplace? You should challenge the very things that made you successful in the first place. Because if you don't do this, your peers will. And with that, they will be defining the future for you and you will be playing the game by someone else's rules.

As you can see, the up-or-out philosophy holds true here as well. By taking the gamble outside the comfort zone or thinking outside the box, you can do what it takes to keep your practice competitive and dynamic.

20. KNOW YOUR MARKET (UNDERSTANDING YOUR PROSPECTS AND CLIENTS)

You cannot begin to gain any ground unless you know who you are dealing with. To know your market you need to become a specialist. For example, my main market for clients in Denver is airline pilots. I work with many from all different airlines. I made it my business to read employee benefit manuals, employee handbooks, union manuals, and other literature. When anyone asks a question, I immediately can provide an answer on the spot, or I know where I can find it in one of my reference materials. I read all written changes concerning airline personnel that I receive, and many of my clients forward such information to me.

You can do this, too. In fact, if you ended up in this profession after another career, chances are that you are very familiar with the things you did and the people you associated with at that time. Face it, who would understand the market better than someone who sweated it out? If applicable, your former career would be a great market for you to focus on, since you are more than halfway there.

The following are some examples of maximizing a former profession's contacts.

- *Doctors.* Between malpractice costs and dealing with insurance companies, a doctor I know was ready to hang it up. At the time, he was making $300,000 a year as a doctor. After 15 years in the profession, he decided to change his focus and started getting into the financial side. He now helps his fellow doctors invest their money, and makes three times his prior income dealing with his former peers.

- *Lawyers.* Two lawyers I know decided to do the same thing. They started out specializing in corporate law, followed by estate planning, and then decided to recommend appropriate investment vehicles to those estate planning clients who needed guidance.

- *CPAs.* Many CPAs I know have taken down their shingles and decided to use their trustworthiness with their clients. Still others I know gave up any type of accounting or tax work and now market financial planning products to their fellow CPAs' clients. Since they do not do any traditional accounting and tax work, fellow CPAs have no problem referring clients to the non-accountant CPAs.

- *Teachers.* I know a former teacher who retired after 25 years (he was only 46 at the time) and decided to give this career a whirl. He hung out in the school cafeteria three times a week talking about investments, the market, and anything else related to finances. Needless to say, he more than quadrupled his income within the first two years of his so-called retirement.

- *Nurses.* I know of several nurses who also have done this. Again, these workers tend to be loyal to their own kind and prefer to have one of their own who truly understands the profession deal with their particular issues.

21. UNDERPROMISE AND OVERDELIVER

What can I say here? Isn't it better when your clients are surprised because they got more than they bargained for? Go back to one of the very first rules I covered. The main reason why planners get sued is because they do not know how to manage their clients' expectations. Think personally now. Haven't you been in situations where you realized that something delivered to you was junk compared to what you had expected it to be? If the expectations had not been there you would have had nothing to be unhappy about. In essence, you would have gotten everything you bargained for. When I am working on a deal or trying to take my practice to the next level, I do not plan on any of it happening until it is a done deal. Before the contract is signed, the t's are crossed and the i's are dotted, my expectations are not raised. As in the movie *Jerry McGuire*, "show me the money!" Do the same here. Set the expectations low and when you overdeliver, you will have happy clients for life.

22. PICK YOUR PIECE OF THE PIE: STAKE OUT YOUR TURF AND GUARD IT

There is so much room out there to roam that it should be easy for you to pick your turf and guard it. My feeling is that there is so much money out there that everyone is entitled to some of it. With over 140 million adult Americans and roughly 40 to 50 million baby boomers, focusing on retirement would clearly work. With an increase in school age kids in some communities, education planning may make sense. The nice thing about all this is that it does not matter what you select if you believe that a market exists for its growth; just pick something and do it well! I always chuckle at planners who say their competition is "thus and so," or we need to find out what this company is doing to help us plan better. That is nonsense! Worry about yourself, be creative, develop and run with an idea, and be the best you can be at it! Remember, you do not need to become greedy. Accepting part of something is always better than receiving all of nothing. All you need to do is figure out how to differentiate your firm from others.

23. DIFFERENTIATE YOUR FIRM
FROM THE COMPETITION

As K-Mart has shown, you cannot imitate another's (Wal-Mart's) game plan and compete against their strength, in this case, pricing. You need to determine what makes your firm truly different from your competitors'. Evaluate your own strength. What do you believe you can do differently from and better than your peers? The best avenues to explore are follow-up and service. If your clients ask you to check something out and then get back to them—do it! Make a 24-hour response time part of your service philosophy. Remember, anyone can provide investment advice, perform financial plans, or crunch tax numbers. Unfortunately, very few of us have the capability to provide the macro-output and follow up on the micro-detail. What has worked for me in past years is seeing what is being done in the marketplace, picking the things that work, and combining them into one overall game plan.

24. WHEN YOU STEAL FROM ONE, IT IS
PLAGIARISM; WHEN YOU STEAL FROM MANY,
IT IS CALLED RESEARCH (KNOW THE INDUSTRY
AND TAKE THE BEST OF THE BEST)

There are many companies that perform superior research. Companies such as Standard & Poor's, Morningstar, CDA Weisenberger, and Value Line are some that focus on mutual funds. Fund companies have a field day providing research to their customers and advisors. There are also many independents who have done research analyzing the financial advisory profession. Take advantage of it.

You can also do your own research. Poll your own clients to see what they want. Most of your clients will fill out questionnaires you design if they know the purpose is to improve the product and service they receive. Develop a standardized questionnaire and modify it when need be. Poll those prospects who never signed on with you to see why. Send out a survey to your target market and see what they are looking for in a financial advisor. Developing your practice according to the consensus of the survey could be a source of new clients.

25. NEVER COMPETE ON PRICE

Pricing is perhaps the most sensitive topic when it comes to dealing with clients. Many people associate price with value, which may or may not be a valid connection. You should not aim to be the lowest or the highest price in the marketplace. Your price should be the one you believe offers a fair profit margin and enhanced value to the client. The funny thing is that most planners do insufficient or no price research.

Think about it. Do you want to be known as the "cheap financial planner"? Price issues will always get you into trouble. Pricing is a poor focus unless you can truly offer the lowest price. And still, that is no guarantee of success. First, someone will always have a lower price than you. Second, people might get the impression that since you are cheap, you are not good at what you do. Third, pricing tends to take the emphasis away from the real focus, which should be your service or product—in essence, it is you.

Consider a "cost-plus approach" to your pricing structure. If you itemize each component, the client knows what he or she is paying for. For example, an itemized bill might show the number of hours worked on a financial or investment management plan, the cost of any products associated with the recommendation, any additional charges built in, or even any materials or supplies charged. Psychologically, the client feels better knowing that the planner did not charge an unjustifiably high price, or, even worse, a "made up" price. Clients will feel good knowing that the pricing structure represents a breakdown of the services provided. Everyone is entitled to a fair profit, and the client will understand and accept that. Clients realize that if you do not protect your profit margins, you will not be able to stay in business and help bring them full circle. In essence, good pricing protects everybody.

I knew a CPA who targeted new homeowners in his area. He sent out a flier with a coupon stating he would do a tax return for all new homeowners for $95, A CPA doing a client's tax return for $95; what a bargain! Well, he did really well. He built up a practice from no clients to 95 in one year. He did it again the second year and added another 130 clients. 225 clients you say? Not exactly. He lost 35 percent of the 95 clients from the first year. Why? Because they all called him up looking for the $95 coupon for the next year's taxes only to be told that the coupon was only an introductory offer for new homeowners. These 35 clients then proceeded to search for the next cheapest CPA at a similar rate. You cannot build a brand-loyal client base solely based on pricing. That is the wrong criterion. You need to emphasize quality, service, and other attributes that are not very common in our marketplace today. While the idea seemed good at the time, and the CPA kept himself busy, you know the old saying: It is cheaper to retain existing clients than to go out in search of new ones. The CPA continues to use this approach. He calls it "planned obsolescence." Just like a Big Five accounting firm or a large brokerage firm, it is a numbers game, and they expect to lose a specified number of clients each year. He figures if he can retain 65 percent of each year's client base, then he will have a substantial CPA tax practice in five years. He did and he sold it; this was also part of the master plan.

Even though "price" is one of the "four p's" of marketing, it is tough to compete on that basis, especially if you are not a big financial supermarket, which can do things in bulk and make purchases or provide services on a cooperative basis much more cheaply than you can. Just look at the less expensive financial plans offered by American Express or Merrill Lynch. Look at the discounts Costco or Sam's Club receives and the pricing structure that results.

If you really want to test the pricing waters, you need to go back to your advisory group. Ask these 12 clients what they would pay for various services you might offer and why.

26. MAKE IT CONDUCIVE FOR THE PROSPECT OR CLIENT TO ACT

When a client comes into my office, everything is up for grabs. We review the key things that are important to him or her, but many times the conversation goes off on a tangent, resulting in uncovering and reviewing a need that has moved to the forefront in the client's lifestyle. For example, be prepared to get into a life insurance discussion and be prepared to have one of your team members run an illustration. Who knows? You make be able to satisfy certain client needs and take care of your own at the same time. When reviewing an investment portfolio, have funds, stocks, bonds, or other investments available to discuss with clients in light of their financial plans, conversations, and so forth. Remember, if you let clients leave without giving them the opportunity to act, you have done a disservice, since they walk out the door with their needs unfulfilled.

27. SERVICE ME

You know the Rolling Stones 1960s song "Gimme Shelter." Maybe if they updated that, it would be called "Gimme Service," or something like that. I have been repeating this *ad nauseum*. Clients are tired of being passed around to persons who are not competent to handle their situation, or, even worse, passed along to voicemail. Just think of all the times you have become annoyed because you felt like you were getting the runaround. One of my fundamental rules, "treat others the way you would want to be treated yourself," certainly applies here.

The best way of going about it is to ask the staff what are the most common reasons that clients call the firm. Prioritize the results and make it known that if a client calls relating to a specific situation, the staff should follow the playbook and provide the service required. This is the one aspect of your business that you can control completely.

28. LET YOUR CLIENTS LEAVE ON A PLEASANT NOTE

Nothing is worse than when the client leaves your office feeling confused, or, even worse, cheated. Many times such a client has a type of "client remorse" after finishing with you. It is sort of like "product remorse," except that what we are really talking about here is an intangible service, rather than a tangible product.

You always have to reassure your clients that their ultimate decision was in agreement with their prioritized objectives, and everything was discussed thoroughly between you and husband and wife clients, or a single parent, or a single person, and run by you for "a vote of confidence or assurance." Make sure clients understand just what it is they are looking into. Provide the pros and cons so they can make that decision with the most information available.

29. IF YOU WANT SOMETHING—ASK FOR IT: GETTING REFERRALS IN YOUR MARKETPLACE

I grew up asking for everything. I did not get much, but I knew how to approach what I wanted. I figured the worst that could be said to me was "no." That is okay too: If you don't ask, you don't get!

You need to position yourself as someone who is using valuable concepts, tools, and strategies that your clients can use to achieve the things they are after. Tell them, "Since my approach has worked for you, Mr. and Mrs. Client, can you put me in a position to grow my business using these concepts for others, people who you really care about and who can benefit from my services?" About 90 percent of the time, my practice has shown me that clients truly want to help. If you ask them for referrals, they will go out of their way to help you get them. Try it! You have nothing to lose!

30. AWARENESS: DO YOU KNOW WHAT YOUR CLIENTS NEED TO ASK AND LOOK FOR?

Part of the cause of client indecisiveness stems from the fact that they are confused and do not know what to look or ask for. One way to handle that is to ensure that clients have a clear understanding of what they are trying to accomplish. I do this using a three-pronged approach to reinforce the basic reason why they are coming to me in the first place.

First, after I visit with clients during our preliminary meeting stage (the first 30-minute freebie), I ask what they are looking for and how they think I can help. If I am comfortable that I can provide this service, and the client is happy to have my assistance, I send an engagement letter. The engagement letter is a summary of what I will do for the client and, in return, what the client will do for me. It is a basic letter of understanding between the client and myself as to 1) what I plan to do, 2) how I plan to do it, 3) what I charge (with an hourly rate and a price cap), 4) what I can expect from the client, 5) the time frame, 6) the level of commitment, 7) future responsibilities on my part (for example, whether there will be an ongoing relationship, or if this is a one-shot deal) and other relevant issues.

Second, we begin an interactive goal-setting and data-gathering session that lasts approximately two hours and covers all the relevant issues of the client from soup to nuts. After our session, I send a one-page fax, e-mail or letter of the minutes of our meeting, summarizing what transpired, what we each set out to achieve, how we plan to get there, and how I am going to proceed. I ask the client to sign it and return it to me for my files. This way we both have a true understanding of the process and what the client will be attaining. I have minimized the number of discrepancies this way to virtually zero.

Third, after I meet with clients to go over a financial plan, investment plan, and so forth, I provide them with a first draft and give them a highlighter and pen and tell them to mark it up for our next discussion. I tell them it is a working document and should be used, not placed on a shelf. I meet with them approximately one week after they have had a chance to digest it, and fish for questions or concerns about what they need to do to proceed and what happens if things cannot be worked out. In between these visits, I send them a follow-up letter alerting them to certain issues and letting them know what to ask and look for. When the clients return, they are basically signing off on what I did, and they are comfortable with the approach we have established and have appropriate expectations. Remember, the main reason planners have trouble is that they do not know how to manage their client expectations. This approach enables us to take the high road and prevent misunderstandings. Such "preventive defense" can help you to avoid lawsuits resulting from miscommunication.

31. GIVE YOUR CLIENTS MORE REASON TO ACT NOW

As a former salesperson, you have learned never to give the client an out. In your new life as advisor, the same premise basically holds true. You may have to emphasize to clients that the longer they wait, the tougher it will be for them to accomplish their goals. Timeliness is one of the most important features in the success of any plan. Having done the first four steps of the financial planning process without performing the implementation and monitoring is, in my view, completely worthless. Therefore, if they decide not to act now or to put the plan on the back burner, then significant consequences will. Ultimately they will have to save more over the shorter time period prior to realizing their goal. That is one of the reasons I tell my clients that they have to pay me at the time of their visit. Act now. If you don't get paid now, it may never happen!

32. PACKAGE YOUR PRODUCTS— IN A RETAINER-BASED ARRANGEMENT

Since I started working on my own, the foundation of my business plan has been to develop retainer-type relationships. I have done that with many of my corporate clients. For instance, I know that I will bring in a certain amount in a particular year. That provides me with sufficient operating capital to expand the business and do the things I need to in order to achieve success. Make it work for your clients. By now, you have listed an inventory of the services you will provide. Package them and make them available to your clients, offering more discounts the more options they take.

Establishing retainer relationships will help you manage your staff's workload. Knowing upfront what has to be done and for whom, you can make appropriate assignments and bring in temporary help when necessary.

33. CONSTANTLY REITERATE YOUR REASONS WHY IT IS WORTHWHILE FOR YOUR CLIENTS TO HAVE YOU AS THEIR FINANCIAL PLANNER

Everyone wants to be reassured about everything! Your clients are no different. They have to understand that your involvement with them is essential to getting things done. No client wants to be taken for granted. A little remembrance at birthdays, anniversaries, school graduations, client appreciation dinners, picnics, and the like work well in telling the clients that you're nothing without them and their trust in and dedication to you.

One way to accomplish this on a steady basis is to use a drip marketing system, sending direct mail to all your clients at least monthly. This lets them know that you are always thinking about them and keeping them current on important and timely information.

34. REDEFINE THE MARKET—FPFT AS AN ALTERNATIVE TO TRADITIONAL CFP™ EDUCATIONAL PROGRAMMING

Sometimes it helps to redefine your marketplace and provide the tools and other services that will make your company appear fresher in the eyes of your clients and prospects. For example, FPFT is a fresh approach for people who want to become CFP™ licensees, offering an alternative to the traditional educational channels. While the goal of becoming a CFP™ licensee is the same under either approach, the method of getting there is different.

Redefining the marketplace in the electronics industry is called "planned obsolescence." Just look at Bill Gates and Microsoft constantly reshuffling its Windows operating system every few years. Microsoft creates an "industry confusion" so consumers and businesses will constantly purchase its products. And Microsoft is no different than any other electronics manufacturers. Just look at all the new model stereos, computers, televisions, and even cars.

The point here is that as a planner, you need to constantly redefine your marketplace, either intentionally by changing your work habits, the way you do things and the services you provide. Also, the marketplace can change as well (i.e., the trend toward fee-based asset management, one-stop shopping at financial service supermarkets, and specialization). Therefore, in any industry, sometimes the bar needs to be raised or changed. The leaders out there control the market by redefining it periodically.

35. KEEP SCORE OF YOUR PROSPECT CONVERSION RATIO

As mentioned above, you cannot stand still in this industry. It is either up or out. Moving up involves taking on new responsibilities and new clients. The only way to determine whether the prospects you encounter are becoming clients is to keep score. You need to know how many of the prospects the firm sees can become permanent clients, and in what ways. By knowing the detail, you can see what brings the firm the greatest chance of success and focus your marketing opportunities in those areas.

Conversion ratios also depend on where the leads are coming from. Referrals and warm leads should generate better closing ratios than cold leads. You can have contests among the staff to see who can close the most leads and bring in the resulting dollars.

36. MARKET IN THE PLACES THAT WILL
LIKELY REAP THE MOST BUSINESS

You have to analyze your marketing plan to see what brings the most success. Jesse James was asked why he robbed banks. His reply was, "Because that's where the money is." You have to remember that you have limited resources to use in marketing. If there were an unlimited supply of dollars, it would make sense to do it all. But, obviously, that is not the case. So you need to be selective and figure out in priority order what makes the most sense with the few dollars available. Keep score over time. Perhaps over a three-year period you can get a sense of the trend that's shaping up. Noticing trends that do not work or are falling out of favor also is an accomplishment here since it helps you focus the remaining dollars on attaining valuable results.

37. DO NOT OVERLOOK THE HOME FIELD
ADVANTAGE—YOUR OWN BACKYARD

This is an important concept. Here, you can specialize your practice based on your home field location. For example, I know a planner who resides in the suburbs of Detroit and specializes in planning for the Big Three's auto executives. Since many of those types of clients live in that area, he has become familiar with their issues and can use this to his advantage. I am another example. I live in Denver near Denver International Airport, where many pilots and other aviation personnel fly through or live. I do significant work with these airline personnel and know their business inside out. I know a CPA planner in Malibu who specializes in working with movie industry personnel, and several planners who reside in Silicon Valley and know more about stock options than I ever will. Two other planners I know have based a career on the knowledge of the oil producers' hot spots in Texas and have been handsomely rewarded. Other planners I know live in little towns where a big employer dominates. In these cases, such planners make it their business to know all about the ups and downs of working for the big firms. Geographically, it makes sense to take advantage of marketing to personnel in your area who represent something substantial.

38. CREATE A SEPARATE PROFIT-AND-LOSS (P&L) STATEMENT FOR EACH FIRMWIDE FUNCTION

This book has emphasized the importance of finding your niche, specializing in appropriate areas, and trying to provide one-stop shopping to clients, where possible. In order to know whether that is working, you need to do a separate profit-and-loss (P&L) statement in each area of the practice to determine whether some can keep going, need to be modified, or should be eliminated altogether. It does not have to be anything fancy. It just has to show where the money is coming from, who is responsible for bringing it in and by what activities, where money is leaving the firm, whether it can be attributed to one group or many, is it leaving by location, and whether any trends exist.

39. DO NOT NECESSARILY CURTAIL YOUR MARKETING EXPENDITURES DURING DOWN MARKETS

Many planners I know have cut back substantially during the down market of the last two years. Worse yet, look at all the brokerage firms, insurance companies, banks, financial supermarkets, and others who have severely cut spending. This is the most appropriate time to spend, since you can develop your firmwide infrastructure and take it to new heights. For example, you can send your staff to training courses so that when the market reverses itself, your firm will be one of the most prepared to tackle new clients. Some firms, for instance, have sent their reps to classes to become CFP™ licensees so that they can incorporate the financial planning process into their clients' lives. Some have passed on opportunities for purchases, and so forth, because they have not had sufficient resources. That is why sometimes a cash position is worthwhile. In this instance, you may be fortunate enough to reap the benefits from someone's misfortune. Not that I like to tell you to take advantage of someone, but the fact remains, it is inevitable. These things do happen, and you should have sufficient cash to ride out all storms. Some big companies spend more for research and development (R&D) during these periods because they know that in order to differentiate themselves, they have to be the first ones out of the gate when the economy turns. And it always does.

40. WHATEVER MARKETING PLAN YOU CHOOSE, MAKE SURE YOU HAVE THE INFRASTRUCTURE AND THE RESOURCES TO SUPPORT IT

I have seen firms attempt 180-degree marketing shifts only to be stopped short because they do not have the required infrastructure to support them. The only way your firm will succeed is to have the necessary infrastructure to take on more and more, rather than scrambling and playing catch-up ball. The only thing worse than a business not having sufficient cash flow is a business not having the infrastructure to support what it is doing.

It is like the question about which came first, the chicken or the egg? You need to build infrastructure and your business simultaneously. That means you need to decide that when your business reaches a certain level, you will begin to add staff. This way, you are measuring the business by the dollars that come into the company and can keep your staffing up to pace with those dollars that are generated because you have that additional staff working there. Don't get too far ahead of yourself and begin hiring staff in anticipation of the next wave of income, just in case it does not come soon enough.

41. IF YOU SAY YOU ARE CHANGING YOUR SERVICE OR PRODUCT, THEN CHANGE IT—DON'T JUST SAY IT

One of the most embarrassing things that can happen is when you say you have done something, only to be told by a client that it did not really happen. Many planners try to change only the name of a service or product while saying they are offering something new for the client. Even the slightest genuine change can be beneficial because it shows the client that you care enough to continually refine your products and services. Change forces you to reexamine your business and rethink your strategy.

If you have ever gone into an electronics store over a period of time, you will notice the models constantly change, usually as quickly as every six months. They call it "planned obsolescence." I call it a pain in the butt, because all those products I look up in *Consumer Reports* are never there. They have already been discontinued.

42. THE COMMODITY EFFECT

The worst thing we can do as a profession is to take for granted the service we are providing and get on our high horse and completely shut out the world around us. With financial planning, crunching numbers is not the specialty. It never has been. There are enough software programs in the marketplace that your clients can get it done for free. And you cannot compete against free! Unfortunately, there are enough so-called financial planners who will also offer this service for free.

Look at the accountants out there. With the TurboTax or another tax program available for free over the Internet, why do clients have to pay a tax preparer to do their returns when there is a cheaper, quicker, and maybe a better way already out there? Services or product offerings inundate our marketplace to begin with. If prospective clients do not recognize or perceive the real value of the service you provide, the result is a commodity.

Clients can always find a cheaper and possibly more reliable source than you. The real value of your service is in the strategizing compartment, where you analyze the data and derive appropriate solutions to address specific client objectives. That is what you want to be doing anyway. That is where the fun and creativity lie. You are never going to make a living crunching numbers.

If your service is a commodity, you are competing on a whole other level. And as mentioned above, you do not want to compete on pricing, because it is a no-win situation.

43. ADVERTISE YOUR FINAL PRODUCT OR SERVICE

There is no substitute for market exposure. Clearly, advertising your product or service can be done with an awareness ad to let your target market know exactly who you are and what you can do for them. You can also advertise by writing a column for a local newspaper. This will let the readers know who you are and what you can accomplish for them.

It is critical when advertising to know your business and come out with a very specific message to describe the services you provide. The effectiveness of the advertising lies in the constant repetition of the message.

Teaming up with product sponsors can be beneficial, since these companies have the funds to help you run an effective advertising campaign. If you have ever been published, perhaps a magazine article of yours can have a sponsor awareness or product ad included in the reprints. After a concerted mailing effort, prospects will see you as an expert in the field because you have been published by a major magazine. If the article benefits the sponsor, he or she may pay for bigger and better things, like a luncheon, dinner, or client participation event.

You can also e-mail newsletters to continue to advertise through your existing clientele and for new prospects. Such newsletters are cheap and efficient. Anything that can get your name out to your target market is advertising. Remember, advertising based on price is not a good thing.

44. CREATE DEMAND THROUGH YOUR OWN MARKETING

Sometimes you need to create your own demand. Awareness ads can help spur that. Showing prospective clients the benefits of retirement planning, college funding, and so forth, can encourage someone to act. If you are living or working in a particular community that has very specific needs, you can create the demand for the satisfaction of these needs. For example, in Silicon Valley, there is a need for stock option planning. Placing ads for this type of planning at the time these techies can and should exercise their options would create a demand in this particular community. In San Diego, there are many military personnel who need help with their finances, especially when they are relinquishing their duties and are coming back to the civilian workforce. Find out what specifics exist in your community and target a campaign directly at them.

There are many television ads run by companies you never heard of displaying brand awareness. Also, there are many financial service companies showing an older person in retirement, a young couple planning for the children, and so forth. These ads are all designed to do one thing, to raise awareness of a problem, create the need for the targets to act on it, and show them how that company can help achieve their goals. This is like the movie *Wag the Dog*, when the president tries to boost his ratings and stages a war to have the country forget its domestic problems, or when J.R. Ewing tries to do a similar thing on Dallas. But do not go to these extremes!

45. DEFINE YOUR MARKET

If you want to size up your prospects, you need to figure out the common characteristics of each particular niche and how to approach it. There are four types of prospects you will run across. We will call them:

1. Adventurers
2. Celebrities
3. Individualists
4. Guardians

   a. The *adventurers* are people who are willing to put it all on one major bet and go for it because they have confidence and know what they are about. Those with the adventurer personality are typically entrepreneurial and strong-willed. They are difficult to advise because they have their own ideas about what they want to do. They are willing to take risks, and are volatile clients from an investment counsel point of view.

   b. The *celebrities* are people who like to be where the action is. They are afraid of being left out. These are people such as doctors and dentists, as well as typical celebrities such as sport figures or entertainment personalities. These clients will keep coming to you with the latest hot topic and asking: "Gee, should I be in this, or should I be in that?" Celebrities are fashion followers. Although they may have their own ideas about other things in life, they really do not have their own ideas about investments.

c. The *individualists* are people who tend to go their own way; they are typical small business owners or professionals, such as lawyers, CPAs, or engineers. These are people who are out trying to make their own decisions, carefully going about things, having a certain degree of confidence about them, but also being careful, methodical, and analytical. Individualists are also strong-willed and competent, but not rash. These are the ideal rational investors that everybody is looking for—the clients with whom you can talk sense. Individualists like to do their own research, are thoughtful people by nature, and tend to avoid volatility. They are often contrarian investors because they sit back in a chair and think about where they want to go and what makes good value sense (individualists are typically value investors). They are good investment counsel clients only if they are too busy to do it themselves.

d. The *guardians* are older people who are beginning to consider retirement. They are careful and a little bit worried about their money. Guardians are people who are cautious and try to preserve their wealth. They are definitely not interested in volatility or excitement. Guardians lack confidence in their ability to forecast the future or to understand where to put money, so they are looking for guidance. They tend to be very careful about selecting their investment advisers, but once they have chosen you, as long as you never surprise them with anything too dramatic or disappointing, they could be loyal to you for 20 to 30 years or more.

46. DEVELOP EFFECTIVE COMMUNICATION TOOLS

If your goal is to get excellent information to the right prospects and reinforce your excellent communication with existing clients, you have to make sure your image is sound. Notice that I did not say "expensive," just sound, classy, and to the point. The whole idea behind this is that your message should be brought out in a clear and concise manner, saying very simply what needs to be said.

The tools you need for this include:

- Appropriate logo displaying uniqueness of your firm
- Letterhead
- Business cards
- Customized envelopes
- Customized presentation kits
- Company description
- Fact sheet indicating the types of services you provide
- Uniform biographies on each of the planners in the firm
- Article reprints
- Testimonials from key clients
- Pricing structure

These tools will help get the right message out to your existing clients and new prospects. If you are missing any of these, now is the time to complete your puzzle.

47. DO NOT BE AFRAID OF THE INSTITUTIONAL SIDE

Many advisors never attempt to go after where the bread is buttered—the institutional clients. These are firms that have deep pockets, with significant cash flow coming in on the asset management side and, even more importantly, great long-term prospects. The downside is that working with them involves a lot of committee meetings and can be a long, drawn-out process. However, if your image is right, your message is clear and concise, and your presence is strong, you may surprise yourself and find you have a shot at this type of client.

Potential prospects include:

- Public charities
- Private foundations
- Municipalities
- Unions
- Qualified retirement plans
- Nonqualified retirement plans
- Public school districts
- Other nonprofits

48. FORM A MARKETING TASK FORCE

Your firm may be confronted with difficult markets and be in difficult times. Demanding clients may complicate the process. To help you reach decisions more quickly and remain focused, a marketing task force should be formed and given three responsibilities:

1. Identifying marketing problems and opportunities facing the organization
2. Assessing whether key people are needed throughout the organization for professional marketing assistance
3. Recommending whether the organization should establish formal marketing positions

The marketing task force should represent a cross-section of your firm's staff with a key stake in the outcome of the marketing operation. You may also want to include an outside marketing consultant or staff involved in proposal writing and public relations.

The task force should gather information from various sources, including clients, referral sources, other staff, and experts, regarding their perceptions of the firm's strengths and weaknesses, as well as any opportunities and threats facing the firm. Once this information is gathered, the task force should develop a written plan of action and present it to the decision making within the firm. Such a report is called a "marketing audit." A sample marketing audit is included at the end of this chapter.

49. IF YOU WANT TO GO BIG TIME, HIRE A PUBLIC RELATIONS FIRM

Public relations (PR) is used to make yourself known as who you want to be. It lends credibility, which is a proven asset in building your business. It can help you become an expert at organizing your own resources and taking confident steps toward your own marketing success. It could be created on your own or by hiring a public relations firm.

Publicity building blocks include:

- Establishing a drip marketing system
- Writing a book on your specialty

- Doing a book tour
- Instructing a college course
- Sending out reprints of your publications
- Building a dynamic Internet web site and presenting yourself on it
- Giving investment and financial planning seminars
- Speaking at trade shows and membership association annual meetings
- Positioning yourself in your target market
- Writing investment or financial planning problem and solution articles
- Aligning with the media
- Developing a publicity marketing plan

I have always handled my own public relations. I knew I always wanted to be a front-line player rather than a back-office supporter. There is nothing good or bad about either approach. Rather, it is just a matter of what you prefer doing and how you want to work in your chosen profession.

That decision was forced upon me when I was working for the AICPA. My boss at the time, John Hudson, asked me to take over a fledging conference called the "AICPA Personal Financial Planning (PFP) Technical Conference." It had just ended for 1989 and some 110 attendees showed up, of which 60 were comped. At the time, I was the editor of the PFP Division newsletter *The Planner*. John called me into his office and asked me to take the other responsibility. He said it was more high profile, and that he was not sure that was where I wanted to be. The conference needed a complete makeover, and I would have to be very visible running it, recruiting speakers and authors to participate in AICPA events, and so forth. I ended up doing it and effectively engaging in high-profile PR.

I began writing the AICPA PFP Technical Manual, which helped establish me as an expert in the field. I was then offered a side job writing the audio newsletter *Totaltape Audio Financial Planning Report* (now called *Bisk Financial*). And because I became widely known and credible as a technical expert, I have since been asked to do many publishing projects for Harcourt Brace (book series and a newsletter), American Management Association,

Bloomberg, Aspen Publishing, Research Institutes of America (RIA), the ICFP, *Financial Planning Magazine*, the *Journal of Accountancy*, John Wiley & Sons, and many others. I have used reprints from my magazine articles and columns to help spread the word that I am an expert in this particular area. I have also done book tours at Barnes and Noble, Borders, Tattered Cover, and many other fine bookstores. At every consumer seminar I do, I can hand out relevant and credible articles. And now with the planning business we have, we can continually send out relevant mailers to prospects based on our firm explaining the dos and don'ts of various financial planning topics.

In addition, I became known on the speaking circuit, beginning with my stint at New York University's Personal Financial Planning program, followed by the College for Financial Planning, Metropolitan State College of Denver, and many for-profit and nonprofit firms nationwide. Currently, I am on the road speaking approximately 120 days a year for different firms. So yes, public relations can work, and work well.

A good book on this topic is *The Guide to Financial Public Relations*, by Larry Chambers (Boca Raton, FL: St. Lucie Press); (805) 640-0888.

50. SPEAK WITH ONE VOICE

One thing I have learned over the years is that consistency means a lot. You need to display the same message to everyone; coming out with uniform communication is important. The look and feel of all correspondence is important to the message for your intended audience. Such consistent identification of the firm should be displayed in all mailings, and external and internal correspondence. Your business revolves around a brand identity that is crucial to the firm and its long-term success.

The marketing angle here is that every staff member needs to know the corporate positions about all topics so that when they are communicated to others the same message comes through loud and clear. When marketing materials on a variety of issues are received by prospective clients, the same look and feel informs them that the firm handles all these issues in the same manner. Whether each staff person agrees individually is irrelevant. Surely, you would like to have everyone thinking along the same lines as you do. But a diversity of opinion is always welcome, because people do not always see the world as you do. Therefore, whoever delivers the message needs to do so with the same zest and convincing argument that you would do. Remember, there is always a firm policy or position, and there can also be individual positions that are independent of the way the firm conducts itself.

My angle is that all correspondence says:

JR Financial Group, the financial information provider.

This educates prospects and clients that we are there not only to manage their money and provide them with products and services, but also to educate them during the process.

Action Checklist: 50 Ways to Change Your Marketing with the following in mind:

- Where our firm stands now
- What our firm can do in this area
- What we would like to see in three years

1. Branding
2. The next level
3. Forming alliances
4. Charting your course
5. Do not sell out on volume
6. Do not obsess about the competition
7. Your marketing plan is a working document
8. Keep your focus
9. Learn from your mistakes
10. Realize that it is all interrelated
11. Know your costs (before you proceed)
12. Analyze and measure your results
13. Derive a marketing analysis
14. Compare past and current marketing information to detect patterns
15. Listen, comprehend, question, then incorporate all suggestions into the marketing game plan
16. It is all a matter of numbers: Win more than you lose
17. Do not package all your services under one identity that could become cloudy
18. Pick one thing or theme and do it well (marketing focus)
19. Keep raising the bar
20. Know your market (understanding your prospects and clients)
21. Underpromise and overdeliver
22. Pick your piece of the pie: Stake out your turf and guard it
23. Differentiate your firm from the competition
24. When you steal from one, it is plagiarism; when you steal from many, it is called research (know the industry and take the best of the best)

25. Never compete on price
26. Make it conducive for the prospect or client to act
27. Service me
28. Let your clients leave on a pleasant note
29. If you want something—ask for it: Getting referrals in your marketplace
30. Awareness: Do you know what your clients need to ask and look for?
31. Give your clients more reason to act now
32. Package your products—in a retainer-based arrangement
33. Constantly reiterate your reasons why it is worthwhile for your clients to have you as their financial planner
34. Redefine the market—FPFT as an alternative to traditional CFP™ educational programming
35. Keep score of your prospect conversion ratio
36. Market in the places that will likely reap the most business
37. Do not overlook the home field advantage—your own backyard
38. Create a separate profit-and-loss (P&L) statement for each firmwide function
39. Do not necessarily curtail your marketing expenditures during down markets
40. Whatever marketing plan you choose, make sure you have the infrastructure and the resources to support it
41. If you say you are changing your service or product, then change it—don't just say it
42. The commodity effect
43. Advertise your final product or service
44. Create demand through your own marketing
45. Define your market
46. Develop effective communication tools
47. Do not be afraid of the institutional side
48. Form a marketing task force
49. If you want to go big time, hire a public relations firm
50. Speak with one voice

Action Product/Service Application Checklist

Self-Assessment for Products and Services Offered by Your Company

- What Product or service?

  _____

  _____

- What are its features?

  _____

  _____

- What are its advantages?

  _____

  _____

- What are its disadvantages?

  _____

  _____

- How is it used?

  _____

  _____

- Who are the providers (fund, insurance, or brokerage companies)?

  _____

  _____

- Miscellaneous information

  _____

  _____

Action Target Market Worksheet

Self-Assessment for Matching Up Target Market with Appropriate Service/Products

Target Market	*Product or Service*	*Benefits to Group*

Action Marketing Progress Report

Self-Assessment for How Your Firm Is Progressing in Marketing Its Services

Product or Service	1st qtr	2nd qtr	3rd qtr	4th qtr	Annual
_____	_____	_____	_____	_____	_____
_____	_____	_____	_____	_____	_____
_____	_____	_____	_____	_____	_____
_____	_____	_____	_____	_____	_____
_____	_____	_____	_____	_____	_____
_____	_____	_____	_____	_____	_____
_____	_____	_____	_____	_____	_____
_____	_____	_____	_____	_____	_____
_____	_____	_____	_____	_____	_____
_____	_____	_____	_____	_____	_____
_____	_____	_____	_____	_____	_____
_____	_____	_____	_____	_____	_____
_____	_____	_____	_____	_____	_____
_____	_____	_____	_____	_____	_____
_____	_____	_____	_____	_____	_____
_____	_____	_____	_____	_____	_____

Action Marketing Wish List

**Self-Assessment of Prioritized Listing of Products
and Services Your Firm Wants to Offer**

1. _____

2. _____

3. _____

4. _____

5. _____

6. _____

7. _____

8. _____

9. _____

10. _____

11. _____

12. _____

13. _____

14. _____

15. _____

16. _____

17. _____

Action Marketing Management Audit

Self-Assessment of Firm's Marketing Activities

Please assess whether each of these areas is being run adequately by the Firm.

Audit Performed By: _____

	Yes	No
I. Sales and Marketing		
A. Pricing		
Is the Firm pricing structure in line with current industry practice?	_____	_____
Is the Firm pricing policy based on your cost structure?	_____	_____
Have you conducted price sensitivity studies?	_____	_____
B. Market Research		
Has the Firm identified niche markets?	_____	_____
Does the Firm segment its markets?		
Has the Firm identified client wants and needs?	_____	_____
Does the Firm know how markets perceive our products or services?	_____	_____
Has the Firm taken advantage of market potential?	_____	_____
Has the Firm analyzed and evaluated the competition?	_____	_____
C. Personal Selling		
Do you know what your sales practices are?	_____	_____
How does personal style influence your sales practices?	_____	_____

D. Customer Service

    Is customer service a Firm priority?   ____   ____

    Does the Firm solicit customer
feedback?   ____   ____

    Is there a rational balance
between the Firm serving its
customers' needs and good
business practice?   ____   ____

E. Advertising and Public Relations   ____   ____

    Does the Firm select media for
measurable results?   ____   ____

    Is the Firm's advertising consistent?   ____   ____

    Does the Firm's advertising budget
make sense in terms of the level
of business and its anticipated
growth?   ____   ____

F. Sales Management

    Are the Firm's staff and outside reps
properly directed in their duties?   ____   ____

    Does the Firm establish individual
sales or asset management goals?   ____   ____

    Does the Firm provide adequate sales
support?   ____   ____

    Are your salespersons trained?   ____   ____

G. Market Planning

    Does the Firm have a marketing
budget?   ____   ____

    Does the Firm have a market plan?   ____   ____

    Has the Firm taken advantage of
market opportunities?   ____   ____

(continued)

	Yes	No
II. Business Operations		
A. Purchasing		
Is there a Firm policy for purchasing?	_____	_____
B. Quality Control		
Are superior products or services being used all the time?	_____	_____
Does the Firm have a "do it right the first time" policy?	_____	_____
C. Business Growth		
Has the Firm grown at least above the rate of inflation?	_____	_____
Has the Firm met your asset growth, sales, and profit goals?	_____	_____
D. Site Location		
Is the Firm located at the right business site?	_____	_____
E. Insurance		
Does the Firm have an annual insurance review?	_____	_____
Are the risks to the Firm business (including yourself) properly covered?	_____	_____
Does the Firm put your errors and omissions (E&O) insurance package out to bid every year?	_____	_____

	Yes	No
III. Financial		
A. Bookkeeping and Accounting		
Are your books adequate?	_____	_____
Are records easy to access?	_____	_____
Can you get information when you need it?	_____	_____
Do you have monthly P&Ls?	_____	_____
Do you have annual financial statements?	_____	_____

B. Budgeting

    Do you use a cash flow budget?   ____ ____

    Do you use deviation analysis
monthly?   ____ ____

C. Cost Control

    Is the budget used as the primary cost
control tool?   ____ ____

D. Raising Money

    Have you been successful in raising
capital when it was needed?   ____ ____

E. Credit and Collection

    Do you use credit to judiciously
increase revenues?   ____ ____

    Do you know your credit and
collection costs?   ____ ____

    Is your current policy successful?   ____ ____

    Do you review credit and collection
policies regularly?   ____ ____

    Do you have a receivables
management policy?   ____ ____

F. Dealing with Banks

    Is your relationship with your lead
banker open and friendly?   ____ ____

    Do you use more than one bank?   ____ ____

G. Cost of Money

    Do you compare the cost of
money (interest, points) with your
profit ratios?   ____ ____

    Are interest rates and loan conditions
appropriate?   ____ ____

(continued)

H. Specific Tools:

Do you know and use:

1) Break-even analysis? _____ _____

2) Cash flow projections and analysis? _____ _____

3) Monthly P&Ls (income statements)? _____ _____

4) Balance sheets? _____ _____

5) Ratio analysis? _____ _____

6) Industry operating ratios? _____ _____

7) Tax planning? _____ _____

IV. Personnel   Yes   No

A. Hiring

Has the right mix of people been hired? _____ _____

Do you hire from a pool of qualified applicants? _____ _____

Do you maintain a file of qualified applicants? _____ _____

B. Training

Are your employees suitably trained for their jobs? _____ _____

C. Motivating People

Do your employees appear to enjoy what they are doing? _____ _____

D. Enforcing Policies

Does there seem to be logic and order to what goes on in the business? _____ _____

Are reviews and evaluations performed on schedule? _____ _____

E. Communicating

Are people informed and brought in
on decisions?   _____   _____

Do you create opportunities for
employees to set their own goals?   _____   _____

V. Administrative Management   **Yes**   **No**

A. Record Keeping

Are records of past transactions and
events easy to find?   _____   _____

Are records retained for at least the
minimum legal time period?   _____   _____

Is access to personnel files limited?   _____   _____

B. Problem Solving

Are there few unresolved problems?   _____   _____

C. Decision Making

Are you decisive?   _____   _____

Is there a decision process (chain
of command)?   _____   _____

D. Government Regulations

Are you aware of local, state, and
federal regulations that affect
your business?   _____   _____

E. Leadership

Do you actually take charge of the
business and its employees?   _____   _____

F. Developing Subordinates

If you were to die or be suddenly
disabled, is there a ready successor?   _____   _____

(continued)

G. Business Law

Do you have a working knowledge of
applicable business law: contracts, agency,
Uniform Commercial Code, etc.?   _____   _____

Do you know how current contracts
and other legal obligations affect
your business?   _____   _____

H. Dealing with Professionals

Do you have and use an accountant,
attorney, or business consultant?   _____   _____

Do you use outside advisors?   _____   _____

4

External Forces: Controlling Your Own Destiny (The Baker's Dozen of Leveraged Activities)

One of the best ways you can build your empire is by leveraging your expertise and the talents of those around you. In other words, building a close-knit circle of confidants whom you can come to rely upon and with whom you can exchange clients as you work toward a common goal. Also, it involves leveraging your talents to generate new client activity. There are many talented people in the world and we need to associate with some of them to provide the best services to our clients. There are also many desperate individuals who need our help and we need to leverage our time and commitment to them. The people you relate to and join forces with ultimately help you control your own destiny. This chapter provides you with insight on how to work with the external forces that are important to the future growth of your practice.

THE VALUE OF NETWORKING

Networking is a two-way process of sharing information with other professionals, clients, and staff that has the effect of generating potential client leads. To make the process work properly, it is essential to keep track of where the leads originate and whether the response is generated from a specific activity undertaken by the firm.

You can begin the process when your firm is conducting research into new market areas. Initially, the contacts would be made with key people in a particular market in order to gather pertinent information. Later, these contacts, plus those made at association meetings and seminars, can bring networking opportunities.

Rather than taking a shotgun approach to developing a network, you will probably find it better to target several appropriate individuals at community organizations or business and trade associations. These are people who can provide invaluable information about prospective clients. And don't forget past employees. Many CPAs I worked with at Arthur Andersen left the firm and went to work directly with the client, providing an inside contact at their new firm for as long as the former Andersen employee was working there. These former employees can also meet with similar employees from other firms and spread your name around.

To work, the process must involve giving as well as taking. You cannot tap people's resources and give nothing back. And the results you want may not be immediate. You need to be patient, get the entire staff involved in various organizations and activities, and make every effort to expand your network of contacts.

The easiest way to increase the number of key contacts is to take an inventory of those you presently have, note how you met them, and then go out and do the same. Supplement this approach with a drawn-out strategic and tactical strategy. Once you develop these relationships, the next step is to nurture them so that they remain clients of your firm. Constantly try to refer business to them, send them material, information, and articles that may affect their businesses, families, and other important matters, invite them to firm functions, phone or e-mail them periodically just to say hello, and keep them on the mailing list. You may find that they do not need you until years down the road. Remember, client retention is the next level of networking. And the best way to develop the entire picture is to affiliate with outside resources.

AFFILIATING WITH OUTSIDE RESOURCES

Don't even think that you can do it all. No one can. I pride myself on being someone who is technically skilled and has marketing savvy, yet I would not pretend that I know it all. There is too much information out there to be current on everything. That is why you need to affiliate with outside resources. Outside resources enable you to leverage yourself in key areas using known experts whose opinions can be relied upon. On the professional side, these include CPAs, attorneys, insurance brokers, investment specialists, money managers, stockbrokers, employee benefit specialists and actuaries, wholesalers, business brokers, and your peers. On the personal side, leveraging means influencing human resource personnel, performing client-generated activities, and providing multigenerational marketing. You will find that leveraging results in a whole that is greater than its individual components.

LEVERAGE ACTIVITY NO. 1: WORKING WITH CPAs

Who Are the CPAs?

CPAs are historians who have the ultimate trust of their clients. In survey after survey, the American public trusts CPAs more than any other financial services professionals. In the world of financial services, CPAs can dominate the profession if they ever get their act together. This would involve recognizing the potential of financial planning and how best to service their clients in this area.

CPAs have been having their own identity crises of late. They have toyed with having a global designation and changing their call letters to present a more updated or "hip" job function, and have been leaving traditional accounting services in droves to focus on related areas that are both more interesting and better paying. CPAs want to become involved in other aspects of their clients' business. They realize that they are providing many services in an informal manner without compensation. They realize that the game is changing and that they must strengthen their ties to their clients if they want to be called upon to serve as financial advisors. They need to finalize a process that can be used to meet their clients' needs and receive appropriate compensation.

Why Do CPAs Want to Invade Our Business?

CPAs are looking to enter our business. This is evidenced by the number of CPAs taking personal financial planning and investment advisory classes. In the classes that I conduct for the California CPA Education Foundation, I have anywhere from 50 to 100 CPAs attending each class to learn how to enter the financial planning business. These are professionals who realize that their livelihood depends on a variety of factors and that the same tools that are making their businesses better are also making them worse. There are three reasons for this. First, it is tough for CPAs to compete with tax software programs that are provided for next to nothing or even free, like TurboTax, to consumers over the Internet. Second, it is becoming increasingly difficult for CPAs to perform traditional write-up services on a monthly basis for clients when for $100 you can buy a program like Quick Books or Quick Pro that does everything a bookkeeper or accountant will do at a fraction of the cost. And third, the number of audits is dwindling due to mergers, acquisitions, and bankruptcies. Many auditing firms perform audits as loss leaders to keep their staff busy year-round.

Networking with CPAs

The best way to network with CPAs is to act like one of them. No, you do not have to be one, but do get involved in many of the activities they become involved with. I knew a planner who headed up a local community group of CPAs called the CPA club. He was responsible for getting speakers in different subject areas to address the group. He would always introduce the speakers after he introduced himself and his role in the organization. This innovative system of networking enabled the planner to meet many of the prominent CPAs in the community and really get to know them—with the result that he is now the financial advisor to many of them. CPAs command respect from just about everyone. They hold strong opinions about many things the client regards as sacred. From all the surveys I have seen on this subject, CPAs are the advisors' most important source of referrals. As a CPA and based on my experience teaching for many CPA societies around the country, one thing is clear to me: The majority of CPAs tell me that their clients are dazed and confused when it comes to investing and planning for their future. And they always ask the CPA for advice about these issues or a referral to someone who can help. If the CPA of such a client does not participate in the industry, then the referral might well be you.

What should you do when you pick up a client from a CPA? One thing is to learn more about the client. Write, call, e-mail, or fax that client's trade association stating that you have a client who belongs and you want to learn more about the issues these types of clients face and possibly become an affiliate or associate member. You will receive their trade journal, newsletters, and other information, thereby becoming an expert in that client's industry. That is how you can specialize in an industry.

Maximizing the CPA Relationship

Remember a common theme mentioned throughout this book: There is plenty of money to make in this business. Therefore, we can all work together and each take a piece of the pie. The question then becomes "What is the best way to leverage work with CPAs so that everyone can benefit?"

Develop an alliance with one CPA or firm. Have an "exclusive" arrangement, whereby you send all your tax, accounting, and audit referrals to them and they, in turn, do likewise for you. You will notice a strong resistance by some CPAs to getting licensed. Some are tired of additional testing and regulations, and some just have no interest. Obviously, you cannot share any revenues with such CPAs.

I recommend having a planner from your office house him- or herself in the CPA's office to provide assistance on demand. This approach, which addresses client concerns while the client is visiting the CPA, works wonders to establish the CPA as a credible source with all the answers. Your planner would work independently of the CPA firm and would be there only to provide additional services to its clients. Make sure you both think along the same lines. They will not be rubber stamping your recommendations. Rather, they will have the same core belief system on financial planning issues that you do. Having CPAs confirm your recommendations gives them greater weight with your clients.

How Do You Set Up a True Partnership Between Your Firm and the CPA Firm?

The best way is to establish a separate entity, a brand new LLC or S corporation distinct from your traditional practice or that of the CPA firm. All principles of the firm should be licensed. All existing clients are owned by whoever brought them into the new entity specifically for financial services purposes. Each firm should own all new clients equally. An exit strategy should also be developed in case one of the partners wishes to bail out. The main issues of who gets the joint clients and at what price should be addressed. Remember, you are always trying to build a business you will eventually be able to sell!

What Happens When There Is a Split Within the CPA Firm Over Whether to Pursue Investment Management Services and Financial Planning? How Do You Resolve That?

What happens when the CPA firm has a split over who should get licensed to run the new entity? Have the CPA firm form a separate entity with the licensed partner as the only principle in the new entity. All other CPAs should stay with the old firm. Tally up the revenues from each. At the end of the year, make adjustments one way or the other based on an allocation of rent, utilities, and other fixed costs. Keep that line of fixed costs consistent for the entire year and adjust up or down at the end of the year. If you allow it to fluctuate, outsiders may think there is a revenue-sharing arrangement going on. When you share the space, it makes sense to allocate costs based on a single denominator, such as square footage. A working relationship sharing space and the costs associated with it is good business practice.

LEVERAGE ACTIVITY NO. 2: WORKING WITH ATTORNEYS

Many attorneys are joining the financial planning ranks. Attorneys are regulated by their state bar. Therefore, some may be entitled to revenue-sharing arrangements while others are not. Even so, all attorneys should be licensed in order to share commissions and other NASD-type revenue or insurance commissions. Some states have instituted a multi-disciplinary designation that enables attorneys to participate in these types of arrangements.

Since most states prohibit the sharing of commissions with attorneys, you should work in a different manner. Have the attorney become affiliated with your organization. In other words, provide that person or firm with all the leads resulting from clients' needing estate-planning work. Do not expect to share the revenue. Remember, if everyone operates at maximum efficiency, there is enough work and money to go around. The nice thing about associating with one attorney is that he or she will become comfortable with your style of personal financial planning and will develop strategies to complement your approach with your clients.

This exclusive arrangement should provide you with all of the attorney's clients who need financial planning help. Even though no money is changing hands, a professional affiliation has been developed that will make each of you comfortable knowing that the other is basically "on call."

LEVERAGE ACTIVITY NO. 3: WORKING WITH INSURANCE BROKERS

If you don't want to sell products, you need to align yourself with a knowledgeable insurance broker, someone who is up on all the latest developments and truly understands the differences among products and companies. Never go with just one company. Rather, make sure that you can receive quotes from many companies so that you are not dependent on any one company and you are not classified as a captive agent.

Ideally, the broker should represent at least two dozen companies and various product lines. Spend some time with the broker. Classify your clients into different categories and form a "suggested product" list so that when someone comes in who meets the appropriate criteria, you will have narrowed down the field to several products and companies so you can provide the best solutions to client needs.

Remember, you can only receive compensation if you are licensed. Under current law, if you do business in all 50 states, you need to be licensed in each one. In some states such as California, you must be licensed just to provide insurance consulting advice.

LEVERAGE ACTIVITY NO. 4: WORKING WITH INVESTMENT SPECIALISTS, MONEY MANAGERS, AND STOCKBROKERS

It is one thing to say you provide investment advice. It is another to actually scout around and select various investment strategies, calculate risk/return relationships, and determine what is best for the client now and in the future. Hire an investment specialist to take on this huge responsibility for complete back-office investment development. If you do not perform these functions, you need to align yourself with someone who does. Investment specialists should be objective, not tied to any particular company, and able to provide a framework for the advice given. In other words, you do not want someone who shoots from the hip or receives kickbacks, rebates, or some other type of compensation for his investment recommendations. You need someone who subscribes to the same line of thinking that you do. For example, if you believe in modern portfolio theory, the efficient market hypothesis, and the like, your investment specialist should as well.

Remember, it all goes back to process. The investment specialist should have a well-thought-out process in which an investment policy statement is used to measure the risks the client is willing to take and the parameters affecting investment decisions. Each client should be evaluated in terms of risk tolerance, time horizon, liquidity, and marketability issues, income tax consequences, and diversification. Objective criteria for hiring, maintaining, and firing managers should be stated as well as the types of investments most suitable depending on a particular client's risk tolerance level. Measurement techniques should be described and documented when used.

A money manager can ease your burden by creating a diversified portfolio for the client. In essence, you are shifting the responsibility for selecting and managing the money to the money manager; your responsibilities then shift to those of managing the money manager. Looking at the clients' investment policy statement will help to assess whether the client is on track.

If you do not want to work with a specialist and prefer to work with a broker, make sure the broker is not tied to any one company or proprietary fund. The last thing you need is a company with a fund for all purposes. You need objectivity, creativity, and knowledge to assist your clients in hammering out their particular investment criteria.

LEVERAGE ACTIVITY NO. 5: WORKING WITH EMPLOYEE-BENEFIT SPECIALISTS AND ACTUARIES

If you get involved with qualified or nonqualified plan design, you should seek the services of employee-benefit specialists and actuaries. These professionals will help you select the plan most appropriate for your client and ensure that you are following the rules of ERISA, TAMRA, or any other federal act. You don't want to do this yourself. First, the responsibilities and liabilities are enormous. Second, it takes you away from your true game plan of working with all aspects of the client's finances. This type of work involves understanding a specialty so you can be the expert called in to assess these situations.

These rules can be more technical than those of income tax and accounting. Again, you may not want to split revenues with these individuals, but rather try a solid, exclusive referral relationship so that you may call in the expert when needed.

LEVERAGE ACTIVITY NO. 6: WORKING WITH BUSINESS BROKERS

Business brokers are information providers, because they carry a great source of wealth—they know who the people with the money are! They know who is liquid and who has the resources to invest. They are opinion leaders and command the respect of their clients. By staying close to these individuals, you can gain insight on who is selling out and why. But you should also push the envelope and help them out. Why not assist them in this market by being a resource, and provide them information when necessary?

Remember, business brokers always need help finding sellers and buyers and bringing them together. If they get a sudden influx of cash to these individuals, you can be in a position to guide them through the transition and set them up financially for life!

LEVERAGE ACTIVITY NO. 7: WORKING WITH HUMAN RESOURCES PERSONNEL

A great way to get in the door is to establish key working relationships with human resources personnel. Your goal is to educate the workers at a given company and the only way to do that is to get through the human resources door. Offer them product-neutral seminars from a purely educational standpoint; no solicitation or sales should result from the program. In fact, do not give out your business card to anyone. What I do is have my contact information on an outline or handout. If they like what I say and want to get in touch with me, I know they will. Sometimes, they even ask Human Resources for the phone number of the person who ran the seminar.

Once you get in the door, keep the passageways clear. I did many quarterly seminars for the workforce of Douglas County, Colorado, through the Human Resources director. I got into this by answering an ad for a career day in Douglas County and manned a booth on the financial services industry. I hit it off with the executive director for Human Resources and the next thing I knew, I was providing them with objective information on a variety of financial planning issues. We would set up "brown bag lunches" once a quarter for an hour on a different topic each time. Sessions would be designed for 40 minutes, with 20 minutes at the end for questions. There would be anywhere from 10 to 40 people per seminar, depending on the topic. I never sold a product or suggested that anyone see me for any type of planning. Yet they found me! I still service many of them with tax preparation and financial planning, even though I have not had the time to go back there in over three years.

You can also look through your extended network of connections for those who have some ties to larger corporations in your geographic area. Use your connection to get your foot in the door, even if it just means alerting the person in charge that you will be sending a letter to introduce yourself and describe how you can help the corporation's employees plan for their financial future.

LEVERAGE ACTIVITY NO. 8: WORKING WITH WHOLESALERS

Wholesalers are an underutilized group of very successful individuals who know their marketplace extremely well, but do not operate at their full capacity because they are bogged down with minute details. They can assist you in sizing up the market for a particular group and describe the best way to approach it. They can provide a fresh assortment of sales and/or marketing ideas because they know how certain marketplaces react to their companies and their products.

You may want to take it a step further and create a "wholesaler advisory board." This is a group of wholesalers who are knowledgeable enough to put in their two cents to help you expand your practice. Their rationale is that if you grow your practice, you will grow theirs! Many wholesalers have spent considerable time in the business working for a particular company in a technical area and are just dying to share their thoughts and ideas with those who will listen to them. If you offer to keep the doors open to their companies and/or products, they will be ready, willing, and able participants.

LEVERAGE ACTIVITY NO. 9: LEVERAGING YOUR SYSTEM AND EXPERTISE WITH THOSE PROFESSIONALS AROUND YOU AND YOUR STAFF

How do you maximize your effectiveness in working with other professionals? You need to figure out what you have to offer them.

You can do this by taking a self-assessment questionnaire describing the areas in which you are deemed to be an expert. Or you can fall into circles where your peers recognize you for a particular specialty. In many of the Financial Planning Association (FPA) chapters, the membership directory lists your areas of specialty. You goal is to work out provider-oriented relationships that make you the person to go to for certain types of financial planning.

One of the most often overlooked resources is staff. Your staff can bring a lot to the table. They keep the business running. Why not leverage them to the fullest? Keep them aware of what the business is doing and what are clients are doing. Reward them for bringing in new business. Give them a percentage of the business, a finders fee, or a referral fee upfront and for the life of the client as long as the staff member remains with the firm.

LEVERAGE ACTIVITY NO. 10: LEVERAGING YOUR PEERS—GRADUATING YOUR CLIENTS TO THE SERVICES OF YOUR PEERS

The leverage angle here is to free up your time so you can prospect for new and more worthwhile clients. By trimming as much as the bottom 80 percent of your clientele, you will be in a much better position to continue to work on your existing "A" clients (as explained in Chapter 6) and cut out those who cause you problems, are no fun anymore, or just have no more money!

One way is to "cut the cord" if you have reached a dead end with a client. If you cut your losses early and often, you will generate the type of business you want. Life is too short to take on problem clients. The old saying that 80 percent of a business is generated from 20 percent of the clients and 80 percent of the problems are generated from 20 percent of the clients holds true. Constantly review your client database and remove those who fall at or near the bottom on an annual basis. In essence, you will have graduated them! Tell them they have successfully completed your planning program and that you cannot add any additional value to the relationship for the fees they are paying. Provide a referral list of possible planners who are looking to accept new clients as your exit strategy for graduating your clients.

LEVERAGE ACTIVITY NO. 11: LEVERAGING YOUR PEERS FOR YOUR OWN BENEFIT

Once you have been in business for a while, you may want to get your peers involved. You are probably asking, how can they help me? The answer is that they can help you and you can help them. Develop an advisory board of other financial planners who are in the same business as you so you can bounce ideas back and forth and share thoughts. This can be established through organizations like the Financial Planning Association, where members come into contact with other members from all over the country.

You can network with these peers through weekly, biweekly, or monthly half-hour phone calls and discuss each advisor's practice, where it has been, and where it needs to be. Limit the group size to five to six advisors so that each advisor can contribute and receive information back. Form several groups for the same purpose with different members in each. E-mail an agenda to everyone. Have a different advisor be responsible for setting the agenda and arranging for the conference call each time. If you hit a lull in your performance and relationships, the peers can act as a support group encouraging you every step of the way. If any of the members of the group embarrass you professionally or miss calls regularly, remove them from the group and replace them with other willing participants. Competition will be nonexistent because you do not compete in the same marketplace.

You would be surprised how willing these advisors would be to share their experiences with you. Having worked for two membership organizations and a professional regulatory board, I can honestly say that the amount of information being shared within our profession is second to none.

LEVERAGE ACTIVITY NO. 12: LEVERAGE YOURSELF THROUGH CLIENT-GENERATED ACTIVITIES AND THROUGH CROSS-SELLING CLIENTS WITH EACH OTHER

The best way to leverage yourself with your clients is to have a client appreciation event. Many planners use client appreciation dinners, luncheons, picnics, and other events where they can address the clients in an informal and fun manner. This could be your biggest source of referrals. As your "admission price," have the client bring along a friend you do not know yet. Don't make it optional; make it a mandatory requirement. Think about it. If every client brought one friend, relative, or acquaintance, you could potentially double the size of your client base.

Cross-selling enables us to strengthen our relationships with our clients. Part of your client development program should be a review of your firm's client database, specifically to determine how clients benefit from each other. You can also include staff and encourage them to do business with clients. Hold small dinners for 5 to 10 clients of similar businesses, interests, and so forth. This will encourage your existing clientele to (1) know that they all work with the same successful planner, and (2) foster a network of activity among clients who can benefit each other. Showing clients that you are interested in helping them expand their businesses is one of the most effective ways of retaining clients for life!

LEVERAGE ACTIVITY NO. 13: LEVERAGE YOURSELF THROUGH MULTI-GENERATIONAL MARKETING

Every time I deal with estate planning issues and address retirement concerns, I make sure I speak to everyone at the same time. Three generations, if possible. The grandparents, the parents, and the grandchildren all are required to meet with me to discuss issues that will affect each one of them. This enables me to do a few things. First, by meeting with everyone together, issues can be discussed more freely and everyone is hearing the same story and hopefully can agree on all resolutions. Second, if the grandparents do not get it right, it directly affects the parents, and the grandchildren more. So every party has a vested interest in what is being said and how matters are being resolved. Third, and probably most important, I will get to know the other generations and thus have clients for life.

The parents and grandchildren will not feel intimidated by me. They will have known me for a while, having spent considerable time planning with me. When the grandparents die, the parents and especially the grandchildren are less likely to move their money or accounts from me. It is also possible that your clients may have an obligation to take care of other family members and you may have to find the funds to do so. Remember, the percentage of family assets you control and the length of time you control those assets are directly proportional to the number of family members you talk to regularly. In one sense, your best prospects are the ones whose last names are the same!

As you can see, leveraging provides the opportunity to extend yourself and your firm into other areas, establishing many contacts in the process and providing the best solutions from many participants to significant client issues.

5

Financial Planning Opportunities Using Form 1040

We have an easy tool for assessing our clients' current financial position and their likelihood of success in achieving their objectives, it is available to us whenever we need to see it, and it is updated every year! I am talking about the form you file every tax season, Internal Revenue Code (IRC) Form 1040. Reviewing this form is an excellent way for you to partially assess a client's overall financial situation.

As a seasoned financial planner, you can look at the financial planning angles of the tax form (not the income tax angle—leave that to the CPAs). This approach enables you to evaluate the client's financial concerns and uncover key areas that have been neglected. In essence, Form 1040 can be used as a road map of vital financial data and planners can review it after a busy tax season. Assets, expenses, cash flow, and other important financial data can be identified that otherwise may go overlooked. Analyzing a client's tax return can help you unlock the doors to a wide range of potentially vital financial planning issues and opportunities. Remember that considerable analysis should be performed before any recommendations are made and that review of the Form 1040 is only one aspect of such analysis.

INCOME TAX PLANNING IN A FINANCIAL PLANNING ENVIRONMENT

Much of the planning advice you dispense to the client will have income tax planning implications. Income tax planning is using any allowable strategy to reduce, affect the timing of, or shift either current or future income tax liabilities. Ideally, income tax planning is driven by overall financial planning goals, and is not an end in itself. While many planners often perform consultations or engagements that are entirely tax oriented, tax planning as part of a financial planning engagement *assumes* integration with other aspects of the financial planning process. In addition, a tax projection is normally necessary to determine cash flow available to fund goals regardless of any perceived need to apply tax planning strategy. Your quantitative skills and knowledge of your client's tax situation places you in an excellent position to perform this service. Revising the tax projection based on various recommended tax and nontax alternatives is also a natural role for you.

For many families, income taxes represent one of the largest expenditures each year, and planning that expenditure often deserves special attention. This special attention, however, should not isolate tax planning from other financial planning issues. Through the tax planning process, information may be discovered that affects other areas of the client's financial circumstances or goals. Those interrelationships should not be ignored. Even with income tax planning, some level of taxation is usually necessary to maximize the client's after-tax financial growth. For example, if some of your findings point toward recommending an investment strategy, it should be evaluated on the basis of after-tax risk-adjusted yield, not on its tax minimization characteristics. Transactions should never be entered into for their tax effect alone, but transactions should not be concluded without a full understanding of their income tax consequences.

In a financial planning environment, it is necessary to consider tax planning in relation to financial planning goals, thus broadening the role of the planner who chooses to perform financial planning engagements. There is a need to refer constantly to the financial planning goals throughout the tax planning process.

IMPORTANCE OF UNDERSTANDING THE FORM 1040 TAX RETURN

Since Form 1040 must be filed every year with the IRS, it is an important form for your clients to understand. Much of the client's financial activity is recorded on Form 1040, which makes it useful for identifying planning opportunities. When going through the form, a series of questions should be raised with the client that might reveal issues to be addressed in a financial planning engagement. A master checklist is enclosed at the end of this chapter, which has been designed for you to use in practice.

After thoroughly reviewing the data on Form 1040, you should schedule an initial conference with the client to assign priorities to specific financial planning goals. Reviewing should consist of line-by-line detail to ensure that all aspects of your client's financial concerns are being addressed.

Analyzing Form 1040 depends on the basic premise for solving all financial planning problems: the summation of all financial information in a cash flow statement. The cash flow statement summarizes all inflows and outflows over a period of time and can help the client locate resources needed to fund objectives that you have identified during your review of Form 1040. Clients must accept the cash flow concept in order for them to attain realistic goals.

Form 1040 and hence, the client's after-tax cash flow can be affected by life changes. These changes include:

- marriage
- divorce
- moving to another location
- sudden increase or decrease in wealth
- change in investment philosophy
- economic reality questions
- death of spouse and other family members

Marriage indicates that another person will share in the wealth. This could mean that the client must now divide a smaller piece of the pie or additional funds may be necessary to ensure the same standard of living each person enjoyed prior to the marriage. Marriage can also mean that the client's resources are pooled with those of the new spouse and could be lost upon divorce. Furthermore, additional persons might enter the picture, such as children or elderly parents, which could require an even greater amount of resources.

Divorce can dampen or ruin a person financially, especially if one spouse had the majority of assets and income. Financial issues arise, such as what to do with the sale of the personal residence or the vacation house. Other personal assets must be split. If only one spouse has a pension plan, how is it divided? If applicable, a person contemplating divorce should reestablish credit if the other spouse had all the credit in his or her own name.

Moving to another location can result in a significant increase or decrease in expenses. Moving from California to Colorado might free up significant assets, especially if the client downsizes his or her personal residence. Moving to a more affordable location could provide additional moneys for the client to invest toward their financial goals.

Inheritances or ongoing gifts can allow a client to fund certain goals. Certainly, the client might not have to struggle knowing that he or she will receive significant funds. But that course of action may be unreliable, especially if the donor does not gift the money in the timely manner expected. Decreases in wealth could result from a failed business venture or difficult times in the stock market. The result may be that additional funds, above and beyond what was initially thought adequate, will now be required to fund client goals.

A sudden change in investment philosophy may be warranted if the client still seems a long way from accomplishing a particular goal. Clients tend to be "loss adverse," meaning that they desire not to lose any principal. If that is the case, the client must be made aware of the difficulty that could arise in attaining specific goals. The other side of the coin is also true. Being too aggressive in the marketplace may not provide the safety and security the client really desires and may ultimately become too risky in achieving client goals.

Economic reality questions may hit home once the client begins approaching the desired retirement age. Maybe that age has to be pushed back. Maybe certain expenses have to be readjusted to allow for proper funding later on. Clients tend to assume a different picture from the one they really have. It is this constant reality check by the planner on the client that makes the planner truly earn his or her fee.

These are all tough situations that certainly warrant attention. However, there will be many other focal points that hit home while you are doing your analysis. Each one should be followed through from beginning to end to ensure that a rational solution will be suggested.

One final point concerning the income taxes clients pay. Income taxes may be the largest expenditure the client has. But they should not be the focal point of this analysis. While it would be beneficial to reduce the tax the client has to pay today, that approach helps only in the short term and may not help the client achieve his or her goals in the future. Planning opportunities should be defined now to ensure that long-range planning enters the client's financial picture. After all, client goals and objectives are designed to be long term and require an appropriate game plan for many years into the future.

QUALIFYING THE CLIENT FOR
FINANCIAL PLANNING SERVICES

The most appropriate time to qualify a client for financial planning services is during the initial interview when the client is getting his or her tax return prepared. The client should complete a general financial planning checklist while waiting to see you. The checklist should take no more than five minutes to complete and can be administered by you or your staff, or completed while the client waits for you in your waiting room.

The questionnaire should address the areas of concern to clients. It should just touch upon whether the clients have thought about these concerns and should provide you with an indication of where their needs lie. All clients should complete these forms, whether you see them or not. You need this information before you can even begin a basic conversation about investments or planning. It should provide you with sufficient background to schedule an appointment for after the tax season. Remember, if you do not develop an efficient follow-up system, missed opportunities will result.

You should be able to accomplish the following with the pre-interview questionnaire:

- Determine client financial planning or investment potential.
- Find out whether rerouting of unprofitable clients is necessary.
- Provide a uniform procedure for office employees in addressing these concerns when clients walk into your office.
- Raise important issues for your clients to begin thinking about for an upcoming appointment with you after the tax season. These issues should be reinforced with clients when they pick up their tax returns. Briefly discuss some of the implications and concerns you have regarding their financial planning needs and that you will be giving them more attention once the tax season ends.

A post-interview questionnaire consisting of a risk tolerance evaluation and a follow-up to the initial questionnaire should be completed prior to sitting down with the client for the actual financial planning session.

WORKING IN CONJUNCTION WITH A CPA OR OTHER TAX PROFESSIONAL

You may need to work in conjunction with other advisors, especially if you are not the one who prepares the Form 1040. If you do not prepare the tax return, you need to be careful not to criticize the tax preparer's work, especially if the client's referral comes from the tax preparer. You will have no shortage of professionals should you need help in developing and implementing the plan, but at the outset, it will take all of your diplomatic skills to communicate the value of this combined venture to the client.

KEY ASPECTS OF TAX
RETURN PREPARATION

If you prepare the client's tax return, you need to focus on key issues. First, review the past three years' tax returns for the client. There is no need to go back beyond that date because the IRS does not accept amended returns after three years. Check to see if there is any type of trend by the client. If so, it might be easier to spot potential pitfalls and planning techniques. If not, then you need to identify to the client potential problems that may result from inconsistent income and expenses used to fund future goals.

When analyzing the client's Form 1040, consideration should also be given to the particular state(s) in which the client files tax returns. Some state laws follow precisely the federal government's lead while others do not. In order to help you become more familiar with Form 1040, the following discussion identifies the individual components of a tax return.

The Individual Components of Form 1040

Most people have never noticed that Form 1040 is divided into sections (see Exhibit 5-1). The individual components are:

- Name and address label section
- Filing status
- List of exemptions
- Gross income
- Adjustments
- Adjusted gross income
- Deductions
- Exemption amounts
- Taxable income
- Total taxes
- Credits
- Other taxes
- Payments
- Refund or amount due

Exhibit 5-1   Form 1040

Form **1040**	Department of the Treasury—Internal Revenue Service **U.S. Individual Income Tax Return**	2001	(99)	IRS Use Only—Do not write or staple in this space.

For the year Jan. 1–Dec. 31, 2001, or other tax year beginning , 2001, ending , 20   OMB No. 1545-0074

Label
(See instructions on page 19.)
Use the IRS label.
Otherwise, please print or type.

L A B E L   H E R E

Your first name and initial | Last name | Your social security number

If a joint return, spouse's first name and initial | Last name | Spouse's social security number

Home address (number and street). If you have a P.O. box, see page 19. | Apt. no.

City, town or post office, state, and ZIP code. If you have a foreign address, see page 19.

▲ **Important!** ▲
You **must** enter your SSN(s) above.

Presidential Election Campaign
(See page 19.)

Note. Checking "Yes" will not change your tax or reduce your refund.
Do you, or your spouse if filing a joint return, want $3 to go to this fund? . . . ▶

You Spouse
☐ Yes ☐ No ☐ Yes ☐ No

Filing Status

Check only one box.

1 ☐ Single
2 ☐ Married filing joint return (even if only one had income)
3 ☐ Married filing separate return. Enter spouse's social security no. above and full name here. ▶ _____
4 ☐ Head of household (with qualifying person). (See page 19.) If the qualifying person is a child but not your dependent, enter this child's name here. ▶ _____
5 ☐ Qualifying widow(er) with dependent child (year spouse died ▶). (See page 19.)

Exemptions

If more than six dependents, see page 20.

6a ☐ **Yourself.** If your parent (or someone else) can claim you as a dependent on his or her tax return, **do not** check box 6a . . . .
b ☐ **Spouse** . . . .
c **Dependents:**

(1) First name Last name	(2) Dependent's social security number	(3) Dependent's relationship to you	(4) ✓ if qualifying child for child tax credit (see page 20)
			☐
			☐
			☐
			☐
			☐
			☐

No. of boxes checked on 6a and 6b ___
No. of your children on 6c who:
• lived with you ___
• did not live with you due to divorce or separation (see page 20) ___
Dependents on 6c not entered above ___
Add numbers entered on lines above ▶ ☐

d Total number of exemptions claimed . . . .

Income

Attach Forms W-2 and W-2G here. Also attach Form(s) 1099-R if tax was withheld.

If you did not get a W-2, see page 21.

Enclose, but do not attach, any payment. Also, please use Form 1040-V.

7 Wages, salaries, tips, etc. Attach Form(s) W-2 . . . . | 7 |
8a Taxable interest. Attach Schedule B if required . . . . | 8a |
b Tax-exempt interest. **Do not** include on line 8a . . . | 8b |
9 Ordinary dividends. Attach Schedule B if required . . . . | 9 |
10 Taxable refunds, credits, or offsets of state and local income taxes (see page 22) . . | 10 |
11 Alimony received . . . . | 11 |
12 Business income or (loss). Attach Schedule C or C-EZ . . . . . . | 12 |
13 Capital gain or (loss). Attach Schedule D if required. If not required, check here ▶ ☐ | 13 |
14 Other gains or (losses). Attach Form 4797 . . . . | 14 |
15a Total IRA distributions . | 15a | b Taxable amount (see page 23) | 15b |
16a Total pensions and annuities | 16a | b Taxable amount (see page 23) | 16b |
17 Rental real estate, royalties, partnerships, S corporations, trusts, etc. Attach Schedule E | 17 |
18 Farm income or (loss). Attach Schedule F . . . . | 18 |
19 Unemployment compensation . . . . | 19 |
20a Social security benefits . | 20a | b Taxable amount (see page 25) | 20b |
21 Other income. List type and amount (see page 27) _____ | 21 |
22 Add the amounts in the far right column for lines 7 through 21. This is your **total income** ▶ | 22 |

Adjusted Gross Income

23 IRA deduction (see page 27) . . . . | 23 |
24 Student loan interest deduction (see page 28) . . . . | 24 |
25 Archer MSA deduction. Attach Form 8853 . . . . | 25 |
26 Moving expenses. Attach Form 3903 . . . . . . | 26 |
27 One-half of self-employment tax. Attach Schedule SE . | 27 |
28 Self-employed health insurance deduction (see page 30) | 28 |
29 Self-employed SEP, SIMPLE, and qualified plans . . | 29 |
30 Penalty on early withdrawal of savings . . . . . | 30 |
31a Alimony paid b Recipient's SSN ▶ _____ | 31a |
32 Add lines 23 through 31a . . . . | 32 |
33 Subtract line 32 from line 22. This is your **adjusted gross income** . . . . . . ▶ | 33 |

For Disclosure, Privacy Act, and Paperwork Reduction Act Notice, see page 72.   Cat. No. 11320B   Form **1040** (2001)

Exhibit 5-1 (*continued*)

Form 1040 (2001)   Page **2**

Tax and Credits	**34**	Amount from line 33 (adjusted gross income)	**34**

Standard Deduction for—
- People who checked any box on line 35a or 35b or who can be claimed as a dependent, see page 31.
- All others:

Single, $4,550

Head of household, $6,650

Married filing jointly or Qualifying widow(er), $7,600

Married filing separately, $3,800

35a Check if: ☐ **You** were 65 or older, ☐ Blind; ☐ **Spouse** was 65 or older, ☐ Blind.
Add the number of boxes checked above and enter the total here . . . . ▶ **35a**

b If you are married filing separately and your spouse itemizes deductions, or
you were a dual-status alien, see page 31 and check here . . . . . . ▶ **35b** ☐

36 **Itemized deductions** (from Schedule A) **or your standard deduction** (see left margin) . . | **36**

37 Subtract line 36 from line 34 . . . . | **37**

38 If line 34 is $99,725 or less, multiply $2,900 by the total number of exemptions claimed on line 6d. If line 34 is over $99,725, see the worksheet on page 32 . . . . | **38**

39 **Taxable income.** Subtract line 38 from line 37. If line 38 is more than line 37, enter -0- . | **39**

40 **Tax** (see page 33). Check if any tax is from **a** ☐ Form(s) 8814 **b** ☐ Form 4972 . . . | **40**

41 **Alternative minimum tax** (see page 34). Attach Form 6251 . . . . | **41**

42 Add lines 40 and 41 . . . . ▶ | **42**

43 Foreign tax credit. Attach Form 1116 if required . . . . | **43** |

44 Credit for child and dependent care expenses. Attach Form 2441 | **44** |

45 Credit for the elderly or the disabled. Attach Schedule R . . | **45** |

46 Education credits. Attach Form 8863 . . . . . . | **46** |

47 Rate reduction credit. See the worksheet on page 36 . . . . | **47** |

48 Child tax credit (see page 37) . . . . | **48** |

49 Adoption credit. Attach Form 8839 . . . . | **49** |

50 Other credits from: **a** ☐ Form 3800 **b** ☐ Form 8396
c ☐ Form 8801 **d** ☐ Form (specify)_____ | **50** |

51 Add lines 43 through 50. These are your **total credits** . . . . | **51**

52 Subtract line 51 from line 42. If line 51 is more than line 42, enter -0- . . . . . ▶ | **52**

Other Taxes

53 Self-employment tax. Attach Schedule SE . . . . | **53**

54 Social security and Medicare tax on tip income not reported to employer. Attach Form 4137 . . | **54**

55 Tax on qualified plans, including IRAs, and other tax-favored accounts. Attach Form 5329 if required . . | **55**

56 Advance earned income credit payments from Form(s) W-2 . . . . | **56**

57 Household employment taxes. Attach Schedule H . . . . | **57**

58 Add lines 52 through 57. This is your **total tax** . . . . ▶ | **58**

Payments

If you have a qualifying child, attach Schedule EIC.

59 Federal income tax withheld from Forms W-2 and 1099 . . | **59** |

60 2001 estimated tax payments and amount applied from 2000 return . | **60** |

61a **Earned income credit (EIC)** . . . . | **61a** |

b Nontaxable earned income . . | **61b** |

62 Excess social security and RRTA tax withheld (see page 51) . . | **62** |

63 Additional child tax credit. Attach Form 8812 . . . . . | **63** |

64 Amount paid with request for extension to file (see page 51) | **64** |

65 Other payments. Check if from **a** ☐ Form 2439 **b** ☐ Form 4136 | **65** |

66 Add lines 59, 60, 61a, and 62 through 65. These are your **total payments** . . . . . ▶ | **66**

Refund

Direct deposit? See page 51 and fill in 68b, 68c, and 68d.

67 If line 66 is more than line 58, subtract line 58 from line 66. This is the amount you **overpaid** | **67**

68a Amount of line 67 you want **refunded to you** . . . . ▶ | **68a**

b Routing number | | ▶ **c** Type: ☐ Checking ☐ Savings

d Account number | |

69 Amount of line 67 you want **applied to your 2002 estimated tax** ▶ | **69** |

Amount You Owe

70 **Amount you owe.** Subtract line 66 from line 58. For details on how to pay, see page 52 ▶ | **70**

71 Estimated tax penalty. Also include on line 70 . . . . . | **71** |

Third Party Designee

Do you want to allow another person to discuss this return with the IRS (see page 53)? ☐ **Yes.** Complete the following. ☐ **No**

Designee's name ▶ | Phone no. ▶ ( ) | Personal identification number (PIN) ▶ | | | | |

Sign Here

Joint return? See page 19.
Keep a copy for your records.

Under penalties of perjury, I declare that I have examined this return and accompanying schedules and statements, and to the best of my knowledge and belief, they are true, correct, and complete. Declaration of preparer (other than taxpayer) is based on all information of which preparer has any knowledge.

Your signature | Date | Your occupation | Daytime phone number ( )

Spouse's signature. If a joint return, **both** must sign. | Date | Spouse's occupation |

Paid Preparer's Use Only

Preparer's signature ▶ | Date | Check if self-employed ☐ | Preparer's SSN or PTIN

Firm's name (or yours if self-employed), address, and ZIP code ▶ | | EIN | |
| | Phone no. ( ) |

Form **1040** (2001)

1. **Gross Income.** Lines 7 through 21 require you to list wages, interest, and dividend income, net income from businesses and farming, net capital gain or loss, rental and royalty income, farm income, alimony, and miscellaneous income, such as lottery winnings. All items of recognized income, even though reported first on a supplemental schedule, wind up here.

2. **Adjustments to Income and AGI.** Lines 23 through 31a allow you to deduct IRAs, self-employed pension plan, and health insurance deductions, alimony, and (complete). Adjustments have some significance because adjusted gross income is used in several calculations to determine deductibility of other things such as medical expenses, miscellaneous itemized deductions, and overall itemized deductions. Therefore, decreasing your adjusted gross income (AGI) could lead to an increase in deductions.

3. **Deductions.** Line 36 provides you with a certain minimum deduction, whether you have any or not. That is, everyone gets a standard amount he or she can deduct from AGI, no matter what his or her actual deductions total.

   If you can get your *itemized deductions* to total more than your standard deduction, then you will want to use Schedule A and take the larger amount. Itemized deductions are listed on Schedule A as *certain types* of medical and dental expenses, taxes, interest, charitable gifts, casualty and theft losses, moving expenses, and miscellaneous. Each of these items is subject to many rules describing what parts of which expenses under what circumstances, subject to certain limitations, will be deductible.

   Deductions should be distinguished from credits, which will be described later. Deductions are subtracted from adjusted gross income to arrive at a number that has no description, so we will call it "AGI less deductions."

4. **Exemptions.** Line 38 entitles all taxpayers to claim exemptions for all dependents (based on certain criteria). Exemptions, generally speaking, are those folks includ-

ing yourself for whom you provide more than half of the support.

5. **Taxable Income.** Line 39 is taxable income and is derived by subtracting itemized or standard deductions and exemptions from gross income, which finally gives us the amount of income subject to income tax. Using the appropriate set of tables, generally based on filing status, we can arrive at our income tax based on this taxable income with rates applied.

6. **Income Tax.** Line 40 represents tax you may be responsible for in addition to income tax.

7. **Credits.** Lines 43 through 50 are credits. These amounts, if any, are items that come directly off your income *taxes*, not off income that is going to be taxed. That is quite a difference. With a deduction, if you are in the 30 percent tax bracket, each dollar of deduction or exemption is worth 30 cents. In other words, the government is subsidizing you 30 cents and therefore your true net cost is 70 cents. A credit is worth 100 percent or a dollar-for-dollar offset against tax liability. Of course, it may have already had a few percentages applied to it before it ever gets to the 1040. Subtracting credits from your total taxes gives you tax after credits.

8. **Other Taxes and Total Tax.** Lines 53 through 57 list all the taxes you may be responsible for in addition to the income taxes you just calculated. The IRS collects various other taxes in addition to income taxes. These include taxes for Social Security and self-employment, taxes on distributions from qualified retirement plans, recapture of investment credit, and the alternative minimum tax (AMT). Adding Income Taxes After Credits to Other Taxes you arrive at Total Taxes.

9. **Total Payments.** Lines 59 through 65 are a payment section in which taxpayers would have withheld income tax or receive a credit from a variety of options.

INCOME TAX PLANNING AND THE PERSONAL FINANCIAL PLANNING PROCESS

The CFP Board defines the personal financial planning process in six steps:

1. Establishing client-planner relationships
2. Gathering client data and determining goals and expectations
3. Analyzing and evaluating the client's financial status
4. Developing and presenting the plan
5. Implementing
6. Monitoring and updating the client's plan

Establishing Client-Planner Relationships

As you know, this is the point at which you decide whether to establish a relationship with the client. During this 30-minute free consultation, you determine whether you and the client can work together. If so, the next step is to begin the process.

Gathering Client Data and Determining Goals and Expectations

1. **Gathering Client Data.** You must generally develop a core information base for tax planning purposes. This usually starts with copies of the last two or three years' income tax returns (along with any IRS or state audit reports). Additional information is available from the several data-gathering documents used in the financial planning engagement.

2. **Establishing Goals and Objectives.** In a financial planning environment, income tax planning has two primary objectives:

1. Determining the effect of income tax expenditures on cash flow
2. Establishing tax planning strategies to help satisfy the client's overall financial planning goals

An initial projection of income tax liabilities is usually necessary to determine the client's after-tax cash flow available to fund goals. A revision of the projection is often necessary after tax planning strategies and other financial planning strategies have been selected. This will help determine their impact on cash flow and present a final cash flow plan to the client. In many cases, analysis of the tax impact of certain transactions is an important part of the projection process. The income tax projections should cover a time frame necessary to meet engagement objectives, which may vary from one to five or more years.

Analyzing and Evaluating the Client's Financial Status

Tax planning strategies include those designed to reduce, affect the timing of, or shift current or future income tax liabilities. Consider the advisability of strategies in light of the client's overall financial goals and not just in terms of the immediate tax consequences.

Tax reduction results when a strategy produces tax-free income or recharacterizes nondeductible expenditures as deductible. The driving factor in tax-free income planning should be the risk-adjusted after-tax yield, not the tax exemption itself. Tax reduction also results when income is taxed at a lower rate than would have otherwise occurred without planning (for example, timing the recognition of a gain to take advantage of a low capital gain rate). Examples of tax reduction strategies include:

- Converting taxable to nontaxable income by shifting investments from corporate bonds to municipal bonds
- Establishing a home equity loan to convert personal interest to fully deductible interest

Management of timing of income tax liabilities involves tax deferral or acceleration. Tax deferral results when a strategy postpones income to a future year or accelerates a deduction to the current year. The considerations in timing strategy include the time value of money, the period involved, the current and expected future tax brackets, the expected inflation rate, and the client's current and future anticipated cash flow needs. Examples of timing strategies include:

- Contributing to 401(k) plans and IRAs
- Using annuities and certain types of U.S. savings bonds
- Timing the recognition of appreciation in investment assets
- Shifting portfolio income generators into passive income generators
- Determining the right year to make discretionary charitable donations
- Converting income investments to growth investments

Income shifting involves shifting income to individuals or entities in lower tax brackets to lower the overall tax paid on the income. Most income shifting requires some degree of loss of control over the income and related assets generating the income. Therefore, before shifting income special consideration should be paid to the impact of the shifting on nontax financial planning goals. If the client could possibly be subject to estate and gift taxes, these should be reviewed while considering shifting techniques.

It is important to determine the client's attitude toward the risk of audit, adjustments by taxing authorities, the cost and trouble of tax controversies, and interest and penalty payments on potential tax deficiencies. Clients with a lower risk tolerance will generally be less inclined to agree to aggressive tax planning strategies because of the higher risk exposure.

Another consideration is the joint and several liability for the taxes reported on joint income tax returns, which liability can be avoided only under the "innocent spouse" rules in limited cases. You should consider involving both spouses in tax risk discussions to avoid future misunderstandings when it is known a joint return will be filed.

The benefit of a tax planning strategy should be compared with its cost. In addition to fees and direct implementation costs, consideration should also be given to indirect burdens, such as the client's time and effort required and the complexity the strategy adds to the client's financial affairs.

When planning, select an appropriate rate and tax law assumptions on the basis of the planning issue at hand. Current rates are usually the most appropriate to use for current year projections. Pending legislation can be analyzed and used as a basis for estimating rates for relatively short-term periods. Long-term projections may require the use of historical rate averages or expected tax trends. Because this process involves determining what rates they are using in similar circumstances. You disclose the rate assumptions in the report to the client and indicate that they are subject to change. When rate or tax rule assumptions change, the planner suggests a revision of appropriate portions of the financial plan as part of an ongoing engagement.

Developing and Presenting the Plan

After carefully analyzing and evaluating the client's financial situation with information obtained from Form 1040, the client is in a position to address these needs and concerns through the planner's recommendation of one or more types of products or services.

Implementing

As with all financial planning, you may be asked to assist with implementing selected tax planning strategies. Examples include a tax review of proposed legal documents and reminders to clients about tax-related steps to take.

Monitoring and Updating the Client's Plan

Monitoring the client's plan is an important part of the financial planning process and usually includes recognizing and advising the client of changes that have occurred that affect the plan. You are in a good position to recognize the effect of tax law changes on a client's financial plan.

It is important to establish an understanding with clients about the responsibility to determine and inform them of the impact of tax law changes on their financial plans. Generally, you should keep any monitoring and updating services as a separate engagement.

SECTION 7216 OF THE INTERNAL REVENUE CODE

Before you offer financial advice on your client's tax return, you need to become familiar with IRC Section 7216. This essentially says that "any person who is engaged in the business of preparing or providing services in connection with the preparation of (tax returns)" is required to obtain the taxpayer's written consent before the return or any information gathered to complete the return is used to solicit additional services.

According to Section 7216, the signed consent must include:

- the name of the tax return preparer
- the name of the taxpayer
- the purpose for which the consent is being furnished
- the date on which the consent is signed
- a statement that the tax return information may not be disclosed or used by the tax return preparer for any purpose (not otherwise permitted) other than that stated in the consent
- a statement by the taxpayer, or his agent or fiduciary, that he or she consents to the disclosure or use of such information for the purpose previously described

The problem can be solved through the use of a tightly worded engagement letter containing the required disclosure authorization, preferably reviewed by an attorney experienced in these matters.

DETERMINATION OF FINANCIAL PLANNING NEEDS FROM FORM 1040 BY CATEGORY

The following categories highlight some of the financial planning information that can be obtained from the client's Form 1040.

Name and Address Label Section

The address will give a clue as to the taxpayer's lifestyle attitudes and overall wealth, which may indicate something entirely different from the numbers shown on the 1040. This could trigger questions as to the need for or adequacy of personal liability and homeowner's insurance coverage. It could also reveal whether the client has moved (if the address is different from that on the return last year), and, if so, whether the move was to an out-of-state address. If your client's address is different from the prior year's, a number of follow-up questions should be asked. For example, did the client sell the previous residence? Is it now an investment property? Did the client buy a new home or is he or she renting? Was the client entitled to a $250,000 if single, or $500,000 if married, permanent gain exclusion?

The address can also provide the planner with a clue as to the wealth of the individual and the possible need for estate planning. If you have a client living in an exclusive area with poverty-level wages, you know that there may be an inheritance involved. A change in address may also tell you that a change in estate planning may be needed if the client moved from a community property state to a non–community property state, for example.

If the taxpayer moved from another state, does the estate plan need to be modified? Does a new executor need to be appointed? This also may trigger questions about multistate probate. Is there a difference between common law versus community property law? Did the client update his or her will? Is the property properly titled?

Filing Status

Along with the mailing label information, this tells you whether the client may have children who are not shown as dependents. Changes in marital status may affect estate planning or insurance needs. The client's filing status helps the planner detect whether the individual is acting alone or with someone else in achieving financial goals. For example, has the taxpayer been married or divorced during the year? If so, have the beneficiaries been changed to reflect the update in status, or has the estate plan or will been modified to reflect this change?

Has your client purchased disability insurance, especially if he or she is single? If not, who can the client rely on to pay his or her expenses?

Exemptions/List of Dependents

The listing of dependents provides the planner with names and ages of those individuals the client is responsible for and establishes a basis for estate planning, insurance planning, and educational planning. Exemptions can also identify income-shifting opportunities, employing children in business if there is a Schedule C, E, or F, education funding, life insurance, and disability insurance.

With respect to estate planning, are elders, parents, or other relatives listed as dependents? Is future long-term care a concern? If so, has the client inquired about long-term-care insurance? Has the client spoken with an attorney with respect to living trusts, durable powers of attorney, or springing trusts? Does the client have children from a previous marriage?

With respect to insurance planning, you need to determine whether there is adequate life insurance held on both spouses. Has the client named one or more beneficiaries, other than him- or herself, in order to keep the life insurance proceeds out of the client's estate? Have the beneficiaries under the current policy been updated to reflect new children born into the family? Do any of the working dependents have disability or health insurance? Does the automobile policy list all drivers over the state's driving age?

With respect to educational planning, was a new child born during the year? If so, should a college funding program be established for this or any other child? Has the client considered a Section 529 plan, Coverdell education IRA, zero coupon bonds, growth stocks, or other appropriate investment(s)? If a college funding program needs to be established, perhaps the parents may need to reposition their assets by putting funds into growth mutual funds, or other assets whereby the funds would become available when the child is ready to enter college. Or, if funds previously have been transferred to children, does the client understand the consequences of making gifts in trust versus making outright gifts and the impact of the kiddie tax rules? If children are currently in college, will there be a future reduction in expenditures?

If both parents work, have arrangements been made for day care? If so, is the client utilizing a child-care credit (Form 2441)? The parents need to obtain the employer identification number from the child-care facility and maintain adequate records (canceled checks) to obtain the credit. Is there a dependent care program through work?

Other questions may include:

- Are any children employed in a family business? If so, could it be set up as a family partnership or some other type of income-shifting arrangement?
- Do the children file separate tax returns?
- Will the amount of dependency deductions be below the appropriate thresholds (otherwise the deduction may be limited)?

Wages and Self-Employment Income (Forms W-2 and 1099)

Wages can tell you if the client is living within his or her means and whether these living expenses are supported by that income stream. You can learn much about retirement and employee benefits, help determine insurance needs, raise estate planning issues or help define a client's spending patterns through income earned. You can also determine if the appropriate box is checked as to whether the client has group life insurance or is a participant in a qualified retirement plan.

With respect to retirement, when are wages scheduled to stop? Does the client have a pension plan, 401(k), SEP, SIMPLE, or 403(b) as indicated on Form W-2? If so, is the client vested in the company plan? Is the client taking advantage of 401(k) plans and/or pension plans by contributing the maximum allowable amount? If not, does the client appear to be on track toward funding his retirement? W-2s will tell you if the client contributes to a retirement plan, participates in one but does not contribute, has over $50,000 of life insurance at work, or is a key employee who may be eligible for a deferred compensation arrangement. Is a Roth IRA appropriate for the client?

Does the level of wages indicate that the client will qualify for the maximum Social Security benefits upon retirement? If the client needs funds, has he contemplated borrowing against the plan, if permissible?

With respect to employee benefits, perhaps based on the amount of wages or length of service with the company, is the client a key employee? If so, can the client participate in a non-qualified deferred compensation plan, such as a split-dollar, executive bonus, or key employee plan? Is the client participating in a Section 125 Cafeteria plan, if available?

With respect to insurance needs, is current life insurance appropriate? Is the disability insurance amount adequate for wages earned? Is there a protection for this income stream in the form of disability and life insurance? Disability insurance usually covers 60 percent of income. If the client terminated his job during the year and has not found a suitable replacement, did the client participate in COBRA, thereby extending his medical insurance coverage from 18 to 36 months?

With respect to estate planning, does the amount of income suggest that the client will have a sizable estate?

With respect to income, does the level of income appear sufficient to take into account expenses and/or saving? If not, has the client established a budget? Are there any cash flow problems? What are the sources of other income?

With respect to Social Security, could the client benefit from a long-term investment strategy that emphasizes growth rather than short-term income causing Social Security benefits to be taxable? Besides the actual benefit amount, are the client's retirement objectives being met? If Social Security benefits are taxable, would annuities reduce income low enough to avoid it?

Adjustments—"Above the Line Deductions"—IRAs, Keoghs, SEPs, SIMPLEs, and Alimony

In determining what if anything the client should contribute, you need to determine what the client's personal cash flow requirements are. If the client has been contributing to a retirement account, are existing retirement assets properly invested to achieve all objectives? If not, does the client anticipate receiving retirement plan distributions in the current year? Will the client receive between the minimum and maximum distribution from his plan or will it be subject to excessive distributions?

Do both spouses qualify for IRA deductions? If not, does a nondeductible IRA still make sense for the client's retirement plan? If so, is the client disciplined enough to begin making IRA contributions either early in the year or on a monthly basis?

If the client is divorced, determine what amount would be classified as alimony or child support. If child support is an issue, does the client need to establish an education fund for his or her children? Would it be advisable to establish a Section 529 plan, Coverdell (education) IRA, or a 2503(b) or 2503(c) trust? Does the client have an IRA or need one? Is there an SEP, Keogh, or other plan for self-employment income? If paying alimony, when does it end and where will the funds go when payments end?

Adjusted Gross Income

Any opportunities to reduce this number can help in itemizing deductions, and so forth.

Itemized Deductions (Schedule A)

Itemized deductions on Schedule A can tell a lot about the client's personal circumstances. There are many opportunities for the planner to identify key financial planning needs by analyzing itemized deductions, especially since they are taken by most taxpayers we see.

If the client does not own a home and cannot itemize deductions, does it pay for the client to purchase a home, especially since interest rates are near their lowest level in 20 years and home prices have stabilized or even gone down in many areas of the country? If the client does own a home, is there any need to tap into home equity? Do decisions on other forms and schedules ease deductions limited by a percent of AGI calculations to be lost? Moreover, do such AGI increasing decisions (> $100,000 indexed) result in a loss of itemized deductions (maximum loss of 20 percent)? If there is a second home, could the taxpayer benefit from converting that to a rental? Were gambling losses taken to the extent of winnings (not subject to 2% AGI floor)?

Because of the need for the client to exceed the threshold amounts for medical (7.5% of AGI) and miscellaneous (2% of

AGI) expenses and stay below the overall base in order to avoid losing part of the full deductible amount, will the bunching of expenses in alternate years better help the client to exceed AGI thresholds in alternate years? Does it pay for the client to use "married filing separately" status due to an extraordinary amount of expenses incurred by one spouse?

Medical. Is the client's medical insurance adequate? For deductibility purposes, the client's expenses must exceed 7.5 percent of AGI or 10 percent of AGI for AMT purposes. If the client is self-employed, does part of his medical premium expense show up above the line (before AGI) and the remainder as an itemized deduction? With qualifying medical expenses, the client may be able to take an early distribution from a retirement plan without incurring the 10 percent penalty. If not, does the client have an emergency fund that can be used to pay uncovered medical expenses? If the client has a significant amount in medical deductions, has the client reexamined the type of coverage he or she currently has?

Interest. Does the level of interest and debt service represent an acceptable percentage of income? Should the client consider paying off nondeductible/consumer-oriented debt or perhaps consolidating it through a home equity loan? Does it pay to refinance a mortgage now to lower interest rate debt? If so, has a new cash flow analysis been prepared to reflect this change? Does the client have insurance to pay off the mortgage in the event of disability or death? What is investment interest for? If the client has a new residence, were points correctly deducted? Is investment interest being foregone due to a lack of investment income?

Taxes. Should the client prepay state and local income taxes and property taxes depending on the AMT consequences? Or should the client defer deductions because of any future increase in tax rates? Are amounts being withheld appropriate, are they too low, creating underwithholding penalty problems, or are they too high, resulting in foregone investment apportionments?

Charitable Contributions. Has the client thought about making gifts of appreciated property rather than selling the property, recognizing capital gain, and then donating the proceeds? Is the client in a position to take advantage of more sophisticated charitable giving strategies, such as charitable lead or charitable remainder trusts? Would the client benefit from setting up a charitable trust? In all these situations, the client must have a charitable intent.

Other questions you should ask include:

- Is the client properly gifting family assets to reduce income or estate taxes?
- If the client has a second home, can it be converted into rental property?
- Are casualty losses covered by insurance that has not been received by the client?

Overall Increase in Income

If the client's income rose substantially, did the client receive an inheritance? If so, how has the money been invested and did the client change the estate plan, possibly by setting up one or more trusts? You may need to employ asset reallocation strategies to reduce overall tax liability. The client may also need to increase withholdings to avoid an underpayment penalty.

Overpayment of Taxes

If the client overpaid taxes, should amounts paid in withholding or estimated payments be reduced? If the client is one who likes to receive a big refund check at the end of the year as a type of forced savings, how will the refund be invested? Perhaps, if education funding was not previously part of the financial plan, the client can use this refund to begin an education funding program. If not, why has the client given an interest-free loan to the IRS? The client should change his or her exemptions to properly plan for the following year.

Supporting Schedules

Interest and Dividend Income (Schedule B)

Interest and dividend income are listed on Schedule B and separated into taxable and nontaxable. The types of investments indicated by interest and dividend income can provide insight into the client's risk-tolerance level. For example, is the client so risk adverse that all his or her money is in CDs? If this is the situation, the client needs to be informed of purchasing power risk and interest rate risk that could erode the principal over the long term. If the client has been keeping all his or her eggs in one basket, a proper diversification strategy may be necessary. The planner can look to see what specific investments generate the dividends. Unnecessary taxable income may indicate a need to rearrange the client's investment portfolio. Repositioning investments to tax-exempt or tax deferred, or restructuring toward long-term growth with minimal emphasis on annual income, may be more appropriate.

Reviewing portfolio income and Schedule B (discussed below) may help the planner determine the client's investment philosophy in light of the client's (1) stage within the life cycle and (2) capacity for financial risk. Once the risk-tolerance level and time horizon are identified, will the client's investments be suitable for current and future needs?

If the amount of portfolio income appears high in relation to total income, putting the client in a high marginal tax bracket, should taxable income be converted into tax-exempt or tax-deferred income, such as municipal bonds? Because income tax rates have increased over the last few years for certain individuals, it may be more appropriate in the future to steer the client toward tax-exempt investments, especially in high-tax states such as California or New York.

Other questions you should ask include:

- Does the client have an investment policy statement?
- Does investment income suggest a liquid fund has been established for emergencies (emergency fund)?
- Will nontaxable interest income trigger the alternative minimum tax (AMT) or cause Social Security benefits to be taxable?
- Does the client have too much or not enough money in cash (savings accounts)?
- If the client is not satisfied with his rate of return, should the client search for a new broker?
- Are the client's assets divided up in such a way as to minimize estate taxes?

- Is there a net annual decrease each year in portfolio income? If so, does that represent an overall negative cash flow as a result of dipping into savings?
- Is the client diversified?
- Are the investments in line with individual goals?
- Are the investments primarily low yield? Are they too risky? Are they illiquid? Too liquid?
- Is there an opportunity for tax deferral on earnings (annuities) or tax exemptions?
- Are high dividend rates being earned? Have you pulled a Morningstar, Standard & Poor's, Value Line, CD Weisenberger or other analysis to verify?

Capital Gain/Loss (Schedule D)

Schedule D also provides valuable insight into the risk tolerance of the client. The client's investment philosophy comes into play in determining if his or her investments are properly diversified to reflect current attitudes and objectives. If the number of capital gain and loss transactions indicates excessive trading, the client may need to rethink the investment plan.

Questions you should ask include:

- Again, does the client have an investment policy statement?
- Could the client generate capital losses to offset capital gains or ordinary income?
- Or has the client considered the timing of investments sold and purchased for possible tax savings?
- Does the client's estate plan reflect current investments? If so, are they sufficiently liquid and properly titled?
- With regard to Form 4797, are there opportunities to offset unused capital losses with more capital gains? Is the client consistently trading and incurring losses?
- What type of IRA or other retirement plan distributions were taken and why? Where are the funds now?
- Would charitable gifting and the interplay with volumes cause a loss, reduction, or postponement of tax benefit derived from either source?

Business Income (Schedule C)

The planner should help the client determine whether the choice of business entity is still appropriate. Options include a sole proprietorship, partnership, S corporation, C corporation, limited liability company, or limited liability partnership. If the client has working-age children, are they receiving wages or should income splitting be employed through family partnerships? Does the client have a retirement plan in place, such as a Keogh or SEP? Is the client properly insured with errors and omission or malpractice, and property and casualty insurance? Business insurance coverage will show up as a Schedule C business expense. If no insurance coverage deduction is taken on Schedule C, what is the taxpayer relying upon for such protection? Will the client's homeowner or apartment dweller's policy cover business assets when an office-in-the-home (Form 8829) deduction is taken? Is personal liability umbrella coverage appropriate for the given situation and circumstances? For example, if a business owner meets a client at home, how frequently does that occur? Is a vehicle used in a business going under 50 percent business use and will there be any subsequent depreciation recapture? Could disposition of Section 1231 assets create ordinary loss or capital gain? Does the client have a succession plan or buy-sell agreement in place?

Rental and Royalty Income (Schedule E)

In addition to property and casualty insurance, does the client have an umbrella policy or general business liability policy on the property? If so, has the client shopped the building insurance policy or do these expenses appear reasonable? If not, maybe the client can add them on to his personal policy as a liability rider. Has the return on the investment been sufficient? How has the value on these investments fared during inflationary and recessionary periods? Does the client have miscellaneous income, such as director's fees, that may qualify for HR-10 or SEP contributions? Has the client considered setting up an S corporation or partnership for receiving this income? If there is S corporation income, are there ownership or income-shifting opportunities available? Would the aggregation of multiple significant participation undertakings leading to material participation status change the characterization of the activity from passive to nonpassive? Would PLGs (passive loss generators) be appropriate to offset suspendable (taxable) passive activity losses (income)? Are at-risk limitations being considered before application of passive activity loss rules (Section 469)? Will decisions made on other forms or schedules increase AGI levels, thereby disallowing active participation losses? Is multiple-state property ownership appropriately covered in the estate plan? Are investments reported on this Schedule (such as in, partnerships and S corporations) liquid and suitable for the taxpayer? Would a Sec. 1031 exchange be a course of action to pursue?

Passive Income/Loss

Questions that you should ask include:

- Does the client's current estate plan provide for ownership of property in two or more states?
- Could the client benefit by investing in passive income generators (PIGs)?
- Has the client considered the liquidity and suitability of passive investments?

The following questions should be asked in reference to Schedules C, E, and F:

- Are buy-sell agreements in place? Business insurance coverage should show up on these forms.
- Is there any business interruption insurance or disability?
- Are children working for the client?
- Is a retirement plan in place?
- Would PIGs be appropriate to offset suspendable (taxable) passive activity losses (income)?
- Are subchapter S or partnership income losses reported on Schedule E suitable for this taxpayer?

Employee Business Expenses (Form 2106)

Are there any employee business expenses that can be picked up by the employer in order to avoid the 2-percent-of-AGI threshold?

INCOME TAX CONSIDERATIONS OF FINANCIAL PLANNING RECOMMENDATIONS BY CATEGORY

You should have an in-depth knowledge of your client's existing or recommended sources of income and deductions (as well as the type of assets held or purchased) to effectively manage cash flow and tax liabilities. Therefore, it is important to devise economically sound strategies that not only conform to the desires of the client, but also increase cash flow surplus by converting dollars otherwise payable in taxes to funds available for investment. To accomplish this goal, planners and their clients should have a working knowledge of the applicable federal and state income tax laws that relate to the determination of taxable income. Because so much of financial planning revolves around the management of existing assets and investment in assets for the purpose of preserving or increasing wealth, planners should specifically focus on tax consequences related to the acquisition and disposition of assets. Asset allocation decisions thus may be partly motivated by a client's need to reduce or defer taxes or to convert taxable to tax-exempt income.

Because the effectiveness of tax planning in a financial planning environment depends on other financial planning goals, this section develops tax planning concepts in relation to the other facets of the financial planning process. These facets include:

- Cash flow planning
- Risk management planning
- Investment planning
- Education planning
- Retirement planning
- Estate planning

Cash Flow Planning

As stated at the beginning of this chapter, determination of and ability to generate cash flow are the underlying premise in planning for the client's future. Cash flow is reduced by federal and state income taxes, which represent one of the largest outlays that clients make during the year. Because of the magnitude of this expenditure, it deserves special attention during the planning process. However, any reduction in income taxes should be coordinated with other parts of the financial planning process.

You should assist the client in timing income and expenses. In these situations, you should consider calculating the tax effect of accelerating income or deferring deductions. Whenever there are limitations on deductions and the client has the option of timing when the expense is paid, the planner advises the client to time the payments so that they are made in the most beneficial year. Some examples of these deductions are:

- Medical expenses
- Investment interest expenses
- Charitable deductions
- Passive activity losses
- Miscellaneous itemized deductions
- Retirement plan contributions

There are also situations when there is taxable income, but there is little or no cash flow to pay the resulting income tax. For example, a client could also have investments in mutual funds, choosing to reinvest all dividends or capital gains. You would advise the client that funds to pay the taxes either must come from other sources or from redeeming some mutual fund shares. If the client does the latter, the gain or loss generated is considered in the planning process. Finally, a client may have an investment that generates taxable income but no cash flow. Some examples of this situation are:

- A tax-shelter partnership that uses its cash flow to repay debt in years when depreciation and interest deductions do not offset the taxable income that created the cash flow. This taxable income is often referred to as "phantom" income.
- A short sale against the box (selling stock short that is already owned) to lock in a gain. In year one, stock already owned is sold short, the sale to close early in year two; the

cash is received when the short sale is entered and the income realized is recognized when the short sale closes in year two; the tax is paid in year three.

Generally planners advise their clients that windfalls could have tax consequences. Once the client invests the windfall, there may be additional taxes to pay because of the taxable income that the investment generates, or the receipt of the windfall itself, such as winning the lottery. Regardless of whether the windfall results from a planned transaction, such as the termination of a trust, or from an unplanned event, such as the death of a relative who has left an inheritance to the client, the windfall affects taxes and planning.

Windfalls include:

- Termination of a trust in which the client has a contingent income or remainder interest and all the contingencies have been eliminated
- Receipt of gifts from a friend or relative
- Receipt of life insurance proceeds
- Winning the lottery or other contest
- Employment-related bonus

Risk Management Planning

Risk management involves identifying client risks; making informed decisions to retain, reduce, transfer, or avoid each significant risk; and implementing those decisions. While transfer is one option, it is clearly not the only option. The decision to retain, reduce, transfer, or avoid risk usually involves an immediate decision to transfer potentially large losses that are quite severe and occur infrequently with relatively small transfer costs (for example, residential dwelling casualty) to insurance companies and to retain small loss risks by providing for them from current income or an emergency fund. All other risks require more complete analysis to determine the appropriate course of action.

When a risk is retained, clients should create an emergency fund (for example, a three-to-six-months' living expense reserve in case of loss of income) to cover the immediate needs arising on a loss occurrence. Therefore, unless immediate availability is unaffected, the fund should not be invested in a manner that reduces tax on the income or provides some other tax benefit. Clients who choose to use marketable investments (that is, stocks and bonds) with a low income tax basis as an emergency fund should be aware of the income tax cost of liquidating them to meet the emergency need.

Life insurance planning in the context of income tax planning deserves special attention. Generally, premium payments are not deductible and proceeds are not includable in taxable income. Some of the more common life insurance income tax issues follow:

- The death benefits payable under a life insurance policy are, generally, free from federal income taxation. A life insurance policy that is transferred from one policy owner to another may be subject to the transfer-for-value rule. Under this rule, the death proceeds of a policy transferred for a valuable consideration are taxed as income to the extent that the death proceeds are greater than the purchase price plus premiums paid by the transferee. Thus, if an existing life insurance policy or an interest in an existing policy is transferred for any type of valuable consideration, all or a significant portion of the death benefit proceeds may lose income-tax-free status. Policies can be transferred safely to the insured, a partner of the insured, a partnership in which the insured is a partner, or a corporation in which the insured is a shareholder or officer, without subjecting the proceeds to income tax, even if the transfer is for a valuable consideration. The planner can review the income-tax-free status of a transfer before implementation.

- If the premiums on a life insurance contract issued after June 21, 1988, are paid in the early part of the policy life, the modified endowment contract (MEC) rules could apply to treat loans and other policy distributions first as income and then return of investment and subject them to a 10 percent excise tax. Generally, you should obtain a representation from the insurance company that a policy to be issued is not classified as a modified endowment policy before finalizing life insurance planning. Also, when considering policy exchanges, some planners discuss with their clients the advisability of having them continue to hold pre–June 21, 1988, contracts to avoid the MEC taint.

- Exchanges of life, annuity, and endowment policies are generally nontaxable under IRC Sec. 1035. If any exchange would otherwise be taxable, policy loans may be something to consider to avoid income recognition. But the possible limitation on the interest deductions should be considered in evaluating the advisability of the loan option. Gain on any exchange is limited to the policy value in excess of the owner's basis in the policy so the planner should determine if the gain is significant before recommending anything special to avoid it.

The following briefly identifies several of the other income tax strategies related to risk management:

- Providing excludable health and accident benefits for an employer-client through a cafeteria plan (IRC Sec. 125)
- Allowing the tax-deferred buildup within nonterm life insurance policies to reduce insurance outlays or otherwise provide funds to solve a risk management problem
- Using tax-free dividend options to reduce insurance or other risk management costs
- Repaying policy loans with deductible interest-bearing debt or taxable-income-producing asset liquidations to reduce after-tax cost of maintaining a policy
- Timing the payment of major medical premiums to maximize their deduction by avoiding the 7.5 percent limitation
- When possible, allocating homeowners and automobile policy charges to business use and deducting them as business expenses
- Using a current or deferred annuity as a life insurance settlement option
- Using the living-proceeds provisions of some insurance policies to provide tax-free funds for catastrophic illness expenses (the tax treatment of these provisions is still unsettled)

Investment Planning

The tax treatment of investment vehicles affects all clients. The clients, however, may find the treatment inconsistent and confusing. Your knowledge of the taxation of investments is invaluable whether you assist the client's investment adviser in determining the tax effects of various investments or give specific investment advice. Thus, your role in the investment arena varies from practice to practice.

The purpose of good investment planning is to maximize the return on investment. Income taxes are a major expense that can affect that return. Some of the general considerations follow:

Most clients have investments with unrealized capital gains or losses. Often planners encourage year-end selling to offset other realized gains or losses. While this approach could minimize taxes or decrease capital loss carryover, it may *not* maximize return on investment. Some clients are compelled to use their unrealized gains and losses at the first available opportunity. Economics, not taxes, should be the controlling factor. The realization of unrealized gains should be a factor to consider when changing money managers or considering a continuous repositioning strategy.

A client may have current or suspended passive activity losses related to a particular investment and several opportunities to sell the investment. To sell the investment primarily to use the suspended losses may *not* be in the client's best interest. The focus should be on the return on investment. If the return on the sale meets the client's predetermined criteria, the client may consider selling the investment.

Rates of return should be tax and risk adjusted. By computing after-tax yields, you take the first step in putting investments on a comparable basis. The next step is to determine investment risk—the likelihood that the investment's actual return will deviate from its expected return. Determining this factor is very difficult and subjective. However, an after-tax, risk-adjusted rate of return puts investment on a comparable basis.

Some other considerations in this area are:

- Determining the character of gains and losses—for example, ordinary versus capital and short term versus long term
- Converting portfolio income into passive income

- Evaluating municipal private activity bonds in light of their AMT preference status to be certain the advantages outweigh their inherent AMT risk

Several income tax issues are particularly important to mutual fund investors. One issue involves the tax treatment of capital gain distributions. It is possible for a client to purchase a fund share on one day and receive a taxable capital gain distribution shortly thereafter. However, the client may not have received any economic benefit from the distribution because the share value would be decreased by the amount of cash received. A good rule for mutual fund investors is to contact the fund before purchasing shares and inquire whether such distributions are pending.

Poor record keeping for reinvested dividends can cause double taxation. Because dividends received represent taxable income to the shareholder, their reinvestment is an adjustment to basis that the client should consider on the subsequent redemption of shares.

Education Planning

Education planning involves identifying the client's goals for education of children or others, quantifying the cost of achieving those goals, and selecting the appropriate funding methods to provide for the costs of achieving those goals. Although most income tax planning comes to play in the quantification and selection phases of education financing, it is critical that the planner not let income tax savings result in a decision inconsistent with a client's goals established in the initial goal identification stage. For example, most income tax savings strategies involve some degree of loss of control over the resources devoted to them. If the client has significant reservations about the possible diversion of the resources to an unintended use, the planner may want to clearly point out whether there is loss of control in any tax strategy suggested for education funding.

Initial education goal quantification usually involves estimating future education costs and computing the lump-sum amount or periodic payment to deposit to achieve the desired funding level at a conservative rate of return. While income tax ramifications are not usually considered in any degree of detail at this stage, the planner can decide to use either a pre-tax or after-tax rate of return in the initial projection. The rate of return and tax assumption used should be disclosed by the planner in any presentation to the client to avoid misunderstanding and to prevent an unwarranted conclusion by the client that education fund accumulations are tax exempt.

One often overlooked factor is the pressure that funding education on a pay-as-you-go basis might have on the requirement for pre-tax earnings at an age when the client might otherwise like to reduce career time and stress commitments. Recognizing this possibility at the outset is important because it generally will be too late to do much about it if the client waits until the time to pay. If pay-as-you-go funding requires a previously nonworking spouse to go to work, the client may be shocked to see the amount of pre-tax earnings necessary to fund the education costs currently net of the Social Security and income tax costs imposed on the earnings of the spouses.

Education funding methods include using the family's income and assets at the time of the need, financial aid from outsiders, and advance funding with income-producing or appreciating assets. Usually a combination of these methods is used.

Clients planning to use the pay-as-you-go method should include the tax cost of income production or asset conversion to fund the education goal when projecting the resources required. If education expenses are expected to be very high (for example, a large family with an Ivy League education tradition), it may be advisable to plan to recognize the child's taxable income (not required for life-style maintenance) either before or after the educational costs need to be paid to keep the marginal tax rate lower than would otherwise be the case. Deferred compensation plans with the client's employer and other options may be available to assist in this regard. Clients should be made aware that it is not possible to deduct interest on education loans. If borrowing is contemplated, advance planning to free up home equity for a qualifying residential loan may be advisable. Deducting interest may not necessarily result in a lower after-tax funds cost than other forms of education financing.

Obtaining financial aid, while difficult for middle-income families, may be the only way those families can afford to give a talented family member the chance to attend an educational institution that will fully develop that talent. Starting two years before any financial aid application will be filed, a client should carefully consider passing up a college-bound child's dependency exemption. If parents are not getting a tax benefit from the dependency exemption because of their income level, serious consideration should be given to allocating support costs so that their child can claim the exemption and appear self-supporting on a financial aid application at some time in the future. Clients who could benefit from a dependency exemption but decide not to claim that exemption should back that up by using the child's own resources to provide over 50 percent of the support of the child. Finally, the tax advantage of accumulating assets in the child's name should be weighed against the fact that such assets are weighed more heavily than the parents' assets in the financial aid application.

Advance funding of education costs with appreciating or income-producing assets involves many tax considerations. Some of the more common tax considerations follow.

- Contributions to a Section 529 plan. Assets grow tax deferred and can be withdrawn tax free if used to pay for the child's education expenses. This is clearly the best way to go.
- Coverdell Education Savings Accounts (ESAs) offer similar benefits, except that the amounts are capped.
- Tax savings occur in a long-term accumulation plan when income is shifted to a lower-bracket child. However, under the kiddie tax, children under age 14 are generally taxed on unearned income at their parents' top tax rate; therefore, a way to defer income past that age is generally needed to make the tax advantage work. Certain types of income-producing investments (for example, U.S. Series EE savings bonds) can be structured to avoid the kiddie tax. Also, appreciating assets with little or no current income (for example, growth stocks that pay little or no dividends) can be used to accomplish a similar result, although with greater investment risk. Trusts can also be used to accumulate income and avoid the kiddie tax, but

narrowed trust income tax brackets reduce their attractiveness as accumulation vehicles.

- Moderate-income taxpayers may be able to benefit by acquiring U.S. savings bonds to cash in tax free to pay education expenses under IRC Sec. 135. However, the impact of limitations (income ceiling, age of owner, exclusion cap at education, expenses less financial aid received) makes this an impractical solution for most financial planning clients.

- Salaries paid by parent-controlled businesses to children have the tax advantage that they avoid the kiddie tax and, unlike unearned income, can be partially or fully absorbed by the child's own standard deduction. Unincorporated businesses do not have to pay Social Security tax for children of the owner who are under age 18, but incorporated businesses do not enjoy the same exemption. Many parents find it difficult to control their children's disposition of salary income but, if that is possible, there are distinct tax advantages to using this technique. Children must perform services that have a value reasonably related to their earnings or IRS disallowance is likely upon audit.

- Various forms of Section 529 plans, certificates of deposit (CDs) tied to college cost inflation rates, and state-offered zero-coupon municipal bonds are available for prefunding education costs.

- Life insurance products provide tax-deferred accumulation, so they could be considered as another choice for building an education fund. However, mortality costs reduce fund accumulations and there may be more restrictions on withdrawals than with other accumulation vehicles.

Retirement Planning

The retirement planning process begins with identifying and quantifying the client's goals and objectives and then determining whether the client has sufficient to cover those future expenses. Generally, estimated retirement expenses will exceed estimated retirement income. Because of this shortfall, or retirement income gap, clients need to plan for funding a vehicle for accumulating assets. It is important to identify the type of retirement funding vehicle available to the client. The following are some of the more common recommendations:

- 401(k) plans
- 403(b) annuities
- IRAs
- Keogh plans
- SEPs (simplified employee pensions)
- SIMPLEs
- Qualified defined benefit plans
- Qualified defined contribution plans
- IRAs (individual retirement accounts)
- Nonqualified plans

Distributions from retirement plans that accumulate income and capital gain on a tax-deferred basis are generally taxable when the distributions begin. Keep in mind how sensitive the various funding alternatives are to different income tax rate assumptions. In periods of low tax rates, clients may find that it is advantageous to fund the retirement income gap with a mixture of taxable and tax-advantaged investment vehicles. If tax rates rise, using the tax-advantaged vehicles is generally more advantageous.

Rollovers and transfers are techniques available for managing, on a continuing basis, the tax-deferral characteristics of IRAs and qualified plans. There are two basic types of rollovers: an IRA to an IRA and a qualified plan (or a tax-sheltered 403(b) annuity) to an IRA. In an IRA-to-IRA rollover, the funds must be deposited in the new IRA within 60 days. Each IRA can be rolled once every 12 months. Some qualified plan distributions can also be rolled over to an IRA instead of being taxed when received. A distribution made because the employee died, left the employer, or became permanently disabled qualifies. To qualify, the distribution has to be a lump-sum distribution and cannot include any employee after-tax contributions. However, earnings on those contributions can be included. Distributions from an employer's plan can also be rolled over to an IRA and used as a holding account. The funds can later be rolled over to a new employer's plan. The IRA account used as a holding account should not contain any assets other than the original employer's plan assets or the right to rollover to a new employer's plan is forfeited.

Estate Planning

The estate planning process begins by having the client determine who should receive what property and by using legitimate strategies to reduce the estate tax burden. Since you will have a handle regarding the approximate amount of assets the client has (by backing into total investable assets found through the reporting of interest, dividends, and capital gain and loss transactions), you can determine what types of trusts or other documents may be necessary.

INFORMATION NOT FOUND ON FORM 1040

You can estimate house values by looking at addresses, estimate home mortgage and other liability balances by looking at interest paid, and estimate values for stocks and interest income instruments by looking at dividend and interest income on Schedule B.

However, there is certain information that you will not be able to obtain through analysis of the Form 1040. This information includes:

- Whether there are any annuities
- The cash value of life insurance
- Gifts or inheritances received or made recently unless they have been reinvested for dividends or income
- Life insurance proceeds unless reinvested
- Personal injury awards unless reinvested and dependent on their taxability
- Personal property coverage, unless a Form 4684 for casualty and theft loss is attached and the deduction taken on the appropriate schedule
- Preparation software lumped calculations/deductions (e.g., no Form 4562 attached but rather a line item only)

- Previous contributions to IRAs, which may or may not be identified depending upon the need to file Form 8606 for nondeductible IRA contributions

You will probably be able to obtain much of this information during the client interview.

SUMMARY

By determining where a client stands today, relative to finances and assets, and by looking at what will predictably happen to the client over the planning horizon, you are able to assist the client in managing assets and energies toward the fulfillment of goals and objectives.

Using tax returns in determining financial planning needs will help you create a stronger relationship with your client and will provide you with the opportunity to become involved in all aspects of your client's financial affairs. If you are uncomfortable discussing one or more of these issues, consider referring the client to a specialist, such as an estate planner or attorney, an insurance professional, an investment counselor, a retirement planner, or some other individual specializing in a particular financial planning area. Using the client's Form 1040 will help you become the complete financial advisor!

Determining Financial Planning Needs
by Analyzing Form 1040

A Checklist for Financial Planners

Review of IRS Form 1040 is an excellent way for planners to
partially assess a client's overall financial situation. Form 1040 can
be used as a road map or tool to help uncover vital financial data,
and it can be reviewed by planners after the busy tax season. The
following checklist has been designed to help you examine a
Form 1040 income tax return and focus on those areas where the
client may need some assistance.

1. Have you complied in writing with each of the following
   requirements of Section 7216 of the Internal Revenue Code
   prior to determining any financial planning needs of the
   client?

   (a) the name of the tax return preparer   ___ Yes   ___ No

   (b) the name of the taxpayer   ___ Yes   ___ No

   (c) the purpose for which the consent
       is being furnished   ___ Yes   ___ No

   (d) the date on which the consent is
       signed   ___ Yes   ___ No

   (e) a statement that the tax return
       information may not be disclosed
       or used by the tax return preparer
       for any purpose (not otherwise
       permitted) other than that stated
       in the consent   ___ Yes   ___ No

   (f) a statement by the taxpayer, or his or
       her agent or fiduciary, that he or she
       consents to the disclosure or use of
       such information for the purpose
       previously described in (c)   ___ Yes   ___ No

(continued)

I. Filing Status

1. Has the client been married during the past year? ___ Yes ___ No

   - If yes, have the beneficiaries been changed in his or her will? ___ Yes ___ No

   - If yes, have the beneficiaries been changed in his or her life insurance policies? ___ Yes ___ No

2. Was the client divorced during the past year? ___ Yes ___ No

   - If yes, have the beneficiaries been changed in his or her will? ___ Yes ___ No

   - If yes, have the beneficiaries been changed in his or her life insurance policies? ___ Yes ___ No

3. If the client is a single parent, does he or she own a disability insurance policy? ___ Yes ___ No

II. Home Address

1. Does the location of the client's home indicate anything about the following:

   (a) Client's lifestyle and personality? ___ Yes ___ No

   (b) Effect of local taxes? ___ Yes ___ No

   (c) Change in value of the client's home? ___ Yes ___ No

   (d) Potential hazards such as:

      (i) Earthquake? ___ Yes ___ No

      (ii) Floods? ___ Yes ___ No

      (iii) Fires? ___ Yes ___ No

      (iv) Storms or other weather perils? ___ Yes ___ No

   (e) Risk management   ___ Yes   ___ No

      (i) Does insurance coverage appear adequate for where the client lives?   ___ Yes   ___ No

     (ii) Has the client considered additional coverage for hazards not covered by normal policies?   ___ Yes   ___ No

2. Does the client have equity in the home?   ___ Yes   ___ No

3. If (2) is yes, how much is it? $_____

4. Do prior years' returns show any interstate moves?   ___ Yes   ___ No

5. If (4) is yes, has the client considered the following:

   (a) How title is held? _____

   (b) Have wills or trust instruments been reviewed to reflect the change in jurisdiction?   ___ Yes   ___ No

6. How long does the client intend to reside in the current residence? _____

7. Is the client's life state (expanding family, retirement) going to cause a change in residence?   ___ Yes   ___ No

III. Exemptions/List of Dependents

Filing status and exemptions:

1. Does the filing status indicate any nontax considerations? (Head of household or married filing separately may indicate family situations that could affect planning.)

2. What are the ages of:

   (a) Taxpayer? ____

   (b) Spouse? ____

   (c) Dependent children? ____

   (d) Dependent parents? ____

(continued)

3. (a) Do prior years' returns indicate any
        changes in:

    (i) Dependents? ___ Yes ___ No

    (ii) Filing status? ___ Yes ___ No

  (b) If (a) (i) or (ii) is yes, have the
       effects of the change on planning
       been considered? ___ Yes ___ No

4. Does the client claim all children for
   whom support payments are made? ___ Yes ___ No

5. (a) Do any dependent children have
        earned income? ___ Yes ___ No

  (b) Has the impact of a dependent
       child's earned income been
       considered? ___ Yes ___ No

6. (a) Do any dependent children have
        investment or other income? ___ Yes ___ No

  (b) Has the impact of a dependent
       child's investment or other income
       been considered? ___ Yes ___ No

7. (a) Does the client have financial goals
        (such as college) for dependent
        children? ___ Yes ___ No

  (b) If yes, how have these goals been funded?

8. If the client has dependent parents:

  (a) What is the financial commitment per annum? $_____

  (b) How is it being met?

  (c) What are the long-term care considerations and
       related costs?

Estate planning:

1. Are elders, parents, or other relatives
   listed as dependents? ___ Yes ___ No

2. Is future long-term care a concern?   ___ Yes   ___ No

   • If yes, has the client inquired about
     long-term care insurance?   ___ Yes   ___ No

3. Has the client discussed living trusts,
   durable powers of attorney, or springing
   trusts with an attorney?   ___ Yes   ___ No

Insurance planning:

1. Is adequate life insurance held on
   both spouses?   ___ Yes   ___ No

2. Has the client named one or more
   beneficiaries, other than himself or
   herself, in order to keep the life
   insurance proceeds out of his or
   her estate?   ___ Yes   ___ No

3. Have the beneficiaries under his or her
   current policy been updated to reflect
   new children born into the family?   ___ Yes   ___ No

4. Do any of the client's working
   dependents have disability or health
   insurance?   ___ Yes   ___ No

5. Does the automobile policy list all
   drivers over the state's driving age?   ___ Yes   ___ No

Financial planning with children: education, child care, and tax returns

1. Was a new child born during the year?   ___ Yes   ___ No

   • If yes, has a college funding program
     been established for this or any
     other child?   ___ Yes   ___ No

2. If a college funding program needs to
   be established, has the client thought
   about repositioning his or her assets by
   putting funds into growth mutual funds
   or other assets whereby the funds would
   become available when the child is ready
   to enter college?   ___ Yes   ___ No

(continued)

3. If the client has previously transferred
   funds to children, does the client
   understand the consequences of making
   gifts in trust versus making outright gifts
   and the impact of the kiddie tax rules?   ___ Yes   ___ No

   - If yes, is the client using a child-care
     credit (Form 2441)?   ___ Yes   ___ No

   - If yes, has the client obtained the
     child-care facility's employer
     identification number and maintained
     adequate records (e.g., cancelled
     checks) to receive the credit?   ___ Yes   ___ No

4. If the client has in-house childcare, is he
   or she filing Form 941 for payroll taxes?   ___ Yes   ___ No

5. Are any children employed in a family
   business?   ___ Yes   ___ No

   - If yes, could the business be set up as a
     family partnership or some other type
     of income-shifting arrangement?   ___ Yes   ___ No

6. Do the children file separate tax returns?   ___ Yes   ___ No

7. Will the amount of dependency deductions
   be below the appropriate thresholds (other-
   wise the deduction may be limited)?   ___ Yes   ___ No

IV. Wages

Retirement: ___ Within one year   ___ Beyond one year

1. When are wages scheduled to stop? _____

2. Does the client have a pension plan,
   401(k), SEP, or 403(b) as indicated on
   Form W-2?   ___ Yes   ___ No

   - If so, is the client vested in the
     company plan?   ___ Yes   ___ No

3. Is the client taking advantage of 401(k) plans
   and /or retirement plans by contributing
   the maximum allowable amount?   ___ Yes   ___ No

- If not, does the client appear to be on track toward funding retirement? ___ Yes ___ No

4. Does the level of wages indicate that the client will qualify for the maximum amount of Social Security benefits upon retirement? ___ Yes ___ No

5. If the client needs funds, has he or she contemplated borrowing against the plan, if permissible? ___ Yes ___ No

Employee benefits:

1. Perhaps based on the amount of wages or length of service with the company, is the client a key employee? ___ Yes ___ No

   - If so, can the client participate in a nonqualified deferred compensation plan, such as a split-dollar, executive bonus, or key person plan? ___ Yes ___ No

2. Is the taxpayer participating in a Section 125 cafeteria plan, if available? ___ Yes ___ No

Insurance needs:

1. Is current life insurance appropriate? ___ Yes ___ No

2. Is the disability insurance amount adequate for wages earned? ___ Yes ___ No

3. If the client terminated his or her job during the year and has not found a suitable replacement, did the client participate in COBRA, thereby extending medical insurance coverage anywhere from 18–36 months? ___ Yes ___ No

Estate planning:

1. Does the amount of income suggest that the client will have a sizable estate? ___ Yes ___ No

(continued)

Income:

1. Does the level of income appear sufficient to take into account expenses and/or saving?   ___ Yes   ___ No

2. Is he or she running into any cash flow problems?   ___ Yes   ___ No

3. Does the level of income appear sufficient to provide necessities for family members plus a suitable amount of savings?   ___ Yes   ___ No

4. Have career goals been set for the:

    (a) Client?   ___ Yes   ___ No

    (b) Spouse?   ___ Yes   ___ No

5. If 4 (a) or (b) is yes, are they on target for:

    (a) Client?   ___ Yes   ___ No

    (b) Spouse?   ___ Yes   ___ No

6. Is there satisfaction with the earnings level for the:

    (a) Client?   ___ Yes   ___ No

    (b) Spouse?   ___ Yes   ___ No

7. Does the amount of earnings compare favorably with the norms of the occupations for:

    (a) Client?   ___ Yes   ___ No

    (b) Spouse?   ___ Yes   ___ No

8. Is family income dependent on one wage earner?   ___ Yes   ___ No

9. Does the client have any plans if the earnings of the major wage earner are disrupted by death, disability, or illness?   ___ Yes   ___ No

10. Does the major wage earner's occupation require special risk management considerations such as special liability or disability coverage?   ___ Yes   ___ No

11. In reviewing prior years' returns, did
    earned income fluctuate?   ___ Yes   ___ No

12. Does income come in ratably during
    the year?   ___ Yes   ___ No

13. Does the client's employer provide a:

    (a) Medical plan?   ___ Yes   ___ No

    (b) Dental plan?   ___ Yes   ___ No

    (c) Term insurance?   ___ Yes   ___ No

    (d) Retirement plans, such as a defined
         benefit or 401(k)?   ___ Yes   ___ No

14. If the benefits identified above do not
    provide adequate coverage, have
    appropriate steps been taken?   ___ Yes   ___ No

    Does the employer have any unique charac-
    teristics or *corporate culture* that could help
    you understand the client better? (A *high
    flying* start-up company versus an established
    company may indicate something about
    the client's risk tolerance level.)   ___ Yes   ___ No

V. Investment Aspects

Sources of investment income:

1. Does investment income indicate the
   client has successfully managed a financial
   program?   ___ Yes   ___ No

2. Does the client understand the nature of
   the investment vehicles currently in
   the portfolio?   ___ Yes   ___ No

3. (a) Do prior years' returns show
        investment income fluctuations?   ___ Yes   ___ No

   (b) If (a) is yes, is there a pattern?   ___ Yes   ___ No

   (c) Have any conclusions been drawn?   ___ Yes   ___ No

(continued)

4. Does the source of investment income indicate that the client has a grantor-type trust? ___ Yes ___ No

5. Do current or prior years' returns indicate taking of aggressive tax positions? ___ Yes ___ No

6. Is the client's tax return posture consistent with other evidence of the client's risk posture? ___ Yes ___ No

7. Has the client indicated his or her investment philosophy in considering the client's age and capacity for financial risk? ___ Yes ___ No

8. Once the risk tolerance level and time horizon are identified, will the client's investments be suitable for current and future needs? ___ Yes ___ No

9. If the amount of portfolio income appears high in relation to total income, which would put the client in a high marginal tax bracket, should the client convert taxable income to tax-exempt or tax-deferred income, such as municipal bonds? ___ Yes ___ No

10. Does investment income suggest that a liquid fund has been established for emergencies? ___ Yes ___ No

11. Will nontaxable interest income trigger the alternative minimum tax (AMT) or cause Social Security benefits to be taxable? ___ Yes ___ No

12. Does the client have too much or not enough money in cash (savings accounts)? ___ Yes ___ No

13. If the client is not satisfied with his or her rate of return, should the client search for a new broker? ___ Yes ___ No

14. Are the client's assets divided up in such
a way as to minimize estate taxes? ___ Yes ___ No

15. Is there a net annual decrease each year
in portfolio income? ___ Yes ___ No

   • If yes, does that represent an overall
     negative cash flow through a dip
     into savings? ___ Yes ___ No

VI. Capital Gain/Loss (Schedule D)

1. Does the number of capital gain and loss
transactions indicate excessive trading? ___ Yes ___ No

2. Could the client generate capital losses
to offset capital gains or ordinary
income? ___ Yes ___ No

   • Has the client considered the timing of
     investments sold and purchased for
     possible tax savings? ___ Yes ___ No

3. Does the client's estate plan reflect
current investments? ___ Yes ___ No

   • If yes, are they sufficiently liquid and
     properly titled? ___ Yes ___ No

3. Have proceeds from major capital
transactions been reinvested
appropriately? ___ Yes ___ No

4. Does the nature of pass-through items
tell anything about the client's
investment strategy? ___ Yes ___ No

VII. Interest and Dividend Income (Schedule B)

1. Is the client so risk adverse as to have
all his or her money in CDs? ___ Yes ___ No

   • If yes, has the client been informed of
     purchasing power risk and interest rate
     risk that will erode away the principal
     over the long term? ___ Yes ___ No

(continued)

2. If the client has been keeping "all of his or her eggs in one basket," has a proper diversification strategy been considered?   ___ Yes   ___ No

3. Has the client diverted himself or herself from earning unnecessary taxable income? ___ Yes   ___ No

Schedule B—interest and dividend income:

1. Does the client have a foreign bank account or trust?   ___ Yes   ___ No

2. If (1) is yes, have the special rules such as access, currency fluctuation risk, and other restrictions been considered?   ___ Yes   ___ No

VIII. Business Income (Schedule C)

1. Is the choice of business entity for the client still appropriate (sole proprietorship, partnership, S corporation, C corporation, limited liability company, or limited liability partnership)?   ___ Yes   ___ No

2. If the client has working-age children, are they receiving wages or should income-splitting be employed through family partnerships?   ___ Yes   ___ No

3. Does the client have a retirement plan in place, such as a Keogh, SEP, or SIMPLE?   ___ Yes   ___ No

4. Is the client properly insured with errors and omission or malpractice insurance, and property and casualty insurance?   ___ Yes   ___ No

5. Does the client have a succession plan or buy-sell agreement in place?   ___ Yes   ___ No

IX. Rental and Royalty Income (Schedule E)

1. In addition to property and casualty insurance, does the client have an umbrella policy or general business liability policy on the property?   ___ Yes   ___ No

- If yes, has the client shopped the building insurance policy or do these expenses appear reasonable? ___ Yes ___ No

- If not, should the client add it on to his or or her personal policy as a liability rider? ___ Yes ___ No

2. Has the return on the investment been sufficient? ___ Yes ___ No

3. Has the value on these investments fared well during inflationary and recessionary periods? ___ Yes ___ No

4. Does the client have miscellaneous income, such as directors fees, that may qualify for Keogh or SEP contributions? ___ Yes ___ No

5. Has the client considered setting up an S corporation or partnership for receiving this income? ___ Yes ___ No

6. If the client has a second home, can it be converted into rental property? ___ Yes ___ No

Schedule E—supplemental income:

1. Does the gross and net operating income on rentals appear appropriate for locations and debt service? ___ Yes ___ No

2. Does the location indicate anything about the quality of the properties? ___ Yes ___ No

3. If the client has invested in partnerships:

   (a) Are there partnership losses? ___ Yes ___ No

   (b) Are any of the partnership investments limited? ___ Yes ___ No

X. Passive Income/Loss

1. Does the client's current estate plan provide for ownership of property in two or more states? ___ Yes ___ No

(continued)

2. Could the client benefit by investing
   in passive income generators (PIGs)?   ___ Yes   ___ No

3. Has the client considered the liquidity
   and suitability of his or her
   passive investments?   ___ Yes   ___ No

XI. Social Security Benefits

1. If the client receives Social Security benefits,
   could the client benefit from a long-term
   investment strategy that emphasizes growth
   rather than short-term income causing
   Social Security benefits to be taxable?   ___ Yes   ___ No

2. Has the client then elected coverage
   under Part B of Medicare?   ___ Yes   ___ No

3. Beside the actual benefit amount, are the
   client's qualitative retirement objectives
   being met?   ___ Yes   ___ No.

4. Will the client's wage level qualify for the
   maximum Social Security retirement
   benefit?   ___ Yes   ___ No

**XII. Above-the-Line Deductions—IRAs, Keoghs, SEPs,
     and Alimony**

1. If the client has been contributing, are existing
   retirement assets properly invested to
   achieve his or her objectives?   ___ Yes   ___ No.

   • If not, does the client anticipate receiving
     retirement plan distributions in the
     current year?   ___ Yes   ___ No

2. Will the client receive a distribution
   between the minimum and maximum
   from his or her plan?   ___ Yes   ___ No

3. Do both spouses qualify for traditional
   IRA deductions?   ___ Yes   ___ No

   • If not, does a nondeductible Roth IRA
     still make sense for the client's
     retirement plan?   ___ Yes   ___ No

- If yes, is the client disciplined enough to begin making IRA contributions either early in the year or on a monthly basis? ___ Yes ___ No

4. If the client is divorced, does he or she pay alimony or child support? ___ Yes ___ No

5. If child support is an issue, does the client need to establish an education fund for his or her children? ___ Yes ___ No

6. Would it be advisable to establish a 2503(b) or 2503(c) trust? ___ Yes ___ No

7. If the client is paying alimony, has the time frame been factored into the client's plans? ___ Yes ___ No

8. If the client is receiving alimony, has the effect of its cessation been considered? ___ Yes ___ No

9. If the client can foresee paying alimony, has the potential for the commencement of payments been considered? ___ Yes ___ No

10. If the client is currently paying alimony, have plans for the additional funds that will be generated when the alimony payments terminate been made? ___ Yes ___ No

11. Does the current relationship of alimony payments the client is making to income seem appropriate or otherwise make sense? (If the client's income has declined relative to the payments, a court order to reduce payments could be considered.) ___ Yes ___ No

IRA Distributions, pensions, Social Security benefits, Etc.:

1. Have the sources of the client's retirement income been analyzed? ___ Yes ___ No

2. Are distributions of retirement funds being managed effectively? ___ Yes ___ No

(continued)

3. Does the level of the client's retirement income appear sufficient to meet goals such as travel and hobbies? ___ Yes ___ No

4. If the client is entitled to receive Social Security benefits but is not receiving them, does deferral make sense? ___ Yes ___ No

IRA, Keogh, SEP, etc., contributions:

1. Is the client covered by a retirement plan with maximum contributions and deferrals? ___ Yes ___ No

2. Are the investment vehicles used for the client's retirement funds appropriate considering the client's goals, age, risk tolerance level, and so forth? ___ Yes ___ No

3. Considering age, accumulated investments, and levels of debt, does the client appear to be on track toward funding retirement income? ___ Yes ___ No

XIII. Itemized Deductions (Schedule A)

1. If the client does not own a home and perhaps cannot itemize deductions, does it pay for the client to purchase a home, especially since interest rates are at a relatively low level and home prices have stabilized or even gone down in many areas of the country? ___ Yes ___ No

2. Because of the need for the client to exceed the threshold amounts for medical (7.5 percent of AGI) and miscellaneous (2 percent of AGI) and to stay below the overall annual threshold base, would taking these deductions in alternate years better help the client to exceed AGI thresholds in those years? ___ Yes ___ No

3. Does it pay for the client to file "married filing separately" based on an

extraordinary amount of expenses
incurred by one spouse? ___ Yes ___ No

Medical:

1. Is the client's medical insurance adequate? ___ Yes ___ No

2. If the client is self-employed, does 70
   percent of his or her medical premium
   expenses show up above the line (before
   AGI) and the remaining 30 percent as an
   itemized deduction? ___ Yes ___ No

3. If the client has qualifying medical expenses,
   did he or she take an early distribution
   from his or her retirement plan without
   incurring the 10 percent
   penalty? ___ Yes ___ No

   • If not, does the client have an
     emergency fund that can be used
     to pay uncovered medical expenses? ___ Yes ___ No

Schedule A—itemized deductions:

Medical and dental

1. Does the client have extraordinary medical
   expenses? ___ Yes ___ No

2. Do medical expenses indicate:

   (a) Inadequate health insurance? ___ Yes ___ No

   (b) Special needs? ___ Yes ___ No

   (c) Health problems? ___ Yes ___ No

   (d) Insurability problems? ___ Yes ___ No

Interest

1. What types of interest expense does the
   client have? ____

2. Does the client's interest expense indicate
   the debt structure? ___ Yes ___ No

3. Does the client appear to be
   adequately managing debt? ___ Yes ___ No

(continued)

Gifts to charity

1. What types of charities does the client support? _____

2. Is the magnitude of the client's giving
   large enough to consider the use of a
   private foundation?   ___ Yes   ___ No

Interest

1. Does the level of interest and debt service
   represent an acceptable percentage
   of income?   ___ Yes   ___ No

2. Should the client consider paying off
   consumer-oriented debt or perhaps
   consolidating it through a home
   equity loan?   ___ Yes   ___ No

3. Does it pay to refinance a mortgage now
   to lower interest rate debt?   ___ Yes   ___ No

   • If yes, has a new cash flow analysis
     been prepared to reflect this change?   ___ Yes   ___ No

4. Does the client have insurance to pay
   off the mortgage in the event of
   disability or death?   ___ Yes   ___ No

Taxes

1. Should the client prepay state and
   local income taxes and property taxes
   depending on the AMT consequences?   ___ Yes   ___ No

Charitable contributions

1. Has the client thought about making gifts
   of appreciated property rather than
   selling the property and recognizing the
   capital gain and then donating the
   proceeds?   ___ Yes   ___ No

2. Is the client in a position to take
    advantage of more sophisticated charitable
    giving strategies, such as charitable lead
    or charitable remainder trusts?   ___ Yes   ___ No

3. Is the client properly gifting family assets
    to reduce income or estate taxes?   ___ Yes   ___ No

Casualty and theft losses

1. Do losses, if any, indicate anything about
    how the client manages risk?   ___ Yes   ___ No

2. Has the client replaced any lost or
    destroyed assets?   ___ Yes   ___ No

3. If the client has not replaced destroyed
    assets, has consideration been given to
    any alternatives?   ___ Yes   ___ No

4. Has the client replaced any lost or
    destroyed asset?   ___ Yes   ___ No

5. If the client has not replaced destroyed
    assets, has consideration been given
    to any alternatives?   ___ Yes   ___ No

6. Has the client adequately planned for
    managing the risk of similar future losses? ___ Yes ___ No

Miscellaneous itemized deductions

1. Do any consulting or accounting fee
    details indicate anything about the
    client's tolerance of fees?   ___ Yes   ___ No

2. Does the client pay trustee fees?   ___ Yes   ___ No

Employee business expenses (Form 2106):

1. Are there any employee business expenses
    that can be picked up by the employer in
    order to avoid the 2% of AGI threshold? ___ Yes   ___ No

(continued)

Overall increase in income

1. If the client's income rose substantially,
   did the client receive an inheritance?   ___ Yes   ___ No

   • If yes, how has the money been invested
     and did the client change his or her
     estate plan, possibly be setting up a
     trust or trusts?   ___ Yes   ___ No

2. Should the client employ asset
   reallocation strategies to reduce the
   client's overall tax liability?   ___ Yes   ___ No

Overpayment of taxes

1. If the client overpaid taxes, should he or
   she reduce amounts paid in withholding
   or estimated payments?   ___ Yes   ___ No

2. If the client likes to receive a big refund check at the end of
   the year as a type of forced savings, how is the client going to
   invest the refund? _____

   _____

   _____

   _____

6

Quantifying Your Practice

There is no one way to conduct a financial planning practice. Clearly, each advisor has a preferred method for conducting his or her practice. After interviewing more than 50 practitioners, I found that no two do exactly the same thing. All practitioners have a preferred method that works for them based on the trials and tribulations of performing financial planning services and growing their practices to the level at which they now operate. What practitioners have told me is that the way business is conducted is based on the types of services they provide for their clientele. Over the years, they figured out what works for them and what does not, and then they capitalize on what does and streamline it to a higher level. That is my goal. I have taken bits and pieces of what practitioners have told me and quantified it to help you measure success. I have designed a process to help you examine your business.

Isn't it ironic? We talk about using the financial planning "process" in assisting our clients with the development of their life goals. We process the information to show that no one thing can help our clients achieve their goals. They buy into this system to ensure that a slow and steady growth over time will help lead them to the path of success. The only true way to build wealth is in slow and steady increments. The same can be, and should be, said of us. We need to follow that advice and begin using a process to develop our goals for running a business. Quantifying that process helped me derive the SAME© system for success:

- **S**tarting point
- **A**nalysis

- **M**ap
- **E**valuation

Therefore, your mission is to figure out what types of services to provide regularly for your clients. Decide what you like to do and "process" those items into a workable starting point to expand your practice. Work through the various practice alternatives and derive a system of your own. This chapter walks you through the concepts employed by other leading practitioners, takes the best of the best, and works them into developing your own process. When you begin to refine your existing practice, use the SAME approach to value your practice from a business standpoint.

STARTING POINT

Every business examination has a starting point. The starting point is the macro-review of your business. Essentially, this step requires you to figure out where you are in your practice today. That requires incorporating measurement tools to objectively assess the situation. Investigating your business on the basis of random observations without thinking them through can be disastrous.

Begin by going to an off-premises location. If the business is you, then you still need to get away from the property in order to help you evaluate more clearly. If there are other partners involved, all should be in attendance. Take as long as you need. What you want to determine is this: Where you are today, which we will call "Point A," and where you ultimately desire to end up, which we will call "Point B." Develop an authentic road map to connect those points, so you can have a specific game plan for accomplishing those results.

The starting point consists of the following tasks:

- S-1: Mission possible (redefining the mission statement)
- S-2: Not business as usual (reexamining the business plan)

S-1: Mission Possible

At the off-site location, start by distributing your existing mission statement, business plan, marketing plan, and tactical plan. The first three documents are more strategic in nature. They represent overviews, or long-term destinations of your company. The last document is your "to-do" list to help you carry out your overall mission. Based on these documents and conversations among senior brass, figure out how you currently define "Point A." During this stage, you must reexamine all your current documents to see which ones remain intact and which ones need further refinement. Remember, you have gathered at this off-site location to determine what you need to take your business to the next level.

First, you must ensure that the purpose of the mission statement is still as valid as the day you created it. Otherwise, now is the time to refine it. Many practitioners have initially created a mission statement, but then, as their practice developed, they have strayed from it as a result of where their business is coming from. Now, after they go back to it, they see it is really different from their overall objective. Therefore, the purpose of the mission statement is to set a goal that you want to achieve. The goal should be specific and directed. It should be focused on a singular strategy. One advisor's mission statement is:

> *To develop a $100 million money management practice servicing only high-net-worth individuals with investable assets of at least $1 million.*

In this statement, the specific mission is to serve high-net-worth individuals whose asset base is at least $1 million. Identifying this high market clientele enables us to develop a game plan that is specific to the needs of this very niche marketplace. These overall concepts can come in handy to help you identify the tactical strategies needed, such as niche advertising, seminar presentations, and so forth, toward achieving this goal (more on this later in the chapter).

Another advisor has as a mission statement:

> *To be the premier leader assisting educational personnel in making sound financial choices.*

This advisor's desire is to work solely with college professors and other educators with their 403(b) plans and other investment options.

A third advisor states:

To provide comprehensive and modular financial planning services for physicians.

This advisor only wants to work with doctors.
A fourth advisor has a more expanded mission:

To provide one-stop shopping for clients, whereby we can work directly, or through affiliates, within all areas of financial services.

A key point is this: None of the four mission statements presented here is the "right" way of doing business. As stated before, it goes back to what you want to accomplish in your practice. Many advisors I have spoken with say their revised mission statement and resulting game plan are completely different from when they first started their practice. At the beginning, their client base was less specific. Most of these advisors would take anyone who walked in the door. As they have become more successful throughout the years, and as time has become scarcer, they have become pickier in their choice of clients. Therefore, they keep narrowing the list and refocusing their client base to come up with the specific characteristics of the refined target market. Remember, the mission statement will help define what business you are in and help you focus on what business you want to pursue, which is Point B.

S-2: Not Business as Usual

After re-evaluating and re-designing the mission statement, detail that information in a comprehensive business plan. The business plan formalizes what you want your business to accomplish. The business plan is the road map toward accomplishing specific objectives laid out by the business. Therefore, having the off-site group think through where the business should ultimately be is an extremely important concept at this stage.

Be detailed, number-oriented, and to the point. Have long-term objectives (five years or more) along with short-term objectives (one year). Assign a dollar amount to the objective and an appropriate time frame. Be specific. You do not want to be vague; otherwise, you are unlikely to achieve success.

My 10-point business plan consists of:

1. Executive Summary—a short and sweet version of what you are trying to accomplish
2. Company description
3. Mission statement
4. Service and product offerings
5. Target markets identified
6. Marketing and sales strategy
7. Landscape—operating in the current environment
8. Senior management
9. Financial data
10. Point B: The exit strategy

See Appendix 7-2 for a sample business plan. In fact, ask your peers for a copy of their business plans. See the types of objectives each firm has laid out. Remember, there is so much business out there that there is room for all of us to coexist. Where the business plan ultimately goes will have a direct correlation to the types of clients you wish to work with in the future.

ANALYSIS

Now that you have a strong overview of where you are going, the next section takes a hard look at your infrastructure to determine whether you have the proper tools in place to determine your starting point and advance to the next level.

I add it up this way:

- A-1: Assessing where your practice is today
- A-2: Analyzing your clientele (Rattiner's Analysis of Client Evaluation)
- A-3: Examining the infrastructure
- A-4: Determining what you want to be when you grow up
- A-5: Directions to get to Point B from Point A

A-1: Assessing Where Your Practice Is Today

I don't know about you, but I find it difficult to manage in the short amount of time the huge amount of work I am responsible for. At some point, we need to accept the trade-off. With limited time, the question becomes "what should we focus and concentrate on?" It is better to define your practice as a specific thing, rather than being all things to all people. Unless, of course, if you operate as a financial services supermarket and try to compartmentalize and specialize in different functions and have qualified people run each function.

Therefore, write down the types of services you provide and the specific list of clients you provide them for. Put that information on a spreadsheet. We will complete it later.

A-2: Analyzing Your Clientele

When I started becoming busy, I knew I needed a more specific game plan in place to evaluate what I had and determine what I wanted to keep. It wasn't that I was turning clients away. Theoretically, I still have a problem with that. Rather, with so little available time and much in the way of obligations, my viewpoint is that life is too short to work with clients you do not want to work with in areas that are no longer of interest. I had to make some hard decisions. That is when I decided to prioritize my objectives, do the things I wanted to do, and work with those people who are enjoyable to me. That is when I created Rattiner's Analysis of Client Evaluation (RACE).

Rattiner's Analysis of Client Evaluation (RACE)

This package helps you separate your existing clientele into "the good, the bad, and the ugly." You should categorize them (see RACE under "MAP" below) and focus on those who help you accomplish your "starting point," as described above.

Ranking Your Clientele: Win, Place, and No Show

At this juncture, begin the process of developing a revised client-based list. One of the best ways to do this is to see whom you are currently servicing. From that list, identify how many of each type of client you see and determine whether you enjoy working with them. You may have many of a specific type of client you do not really enjoy working with. These clients may have been added one by one over the years and, before you knew it, you had a large number of them.

A-3: Examining the Infrastructure

No analysis can be complete without determining whether you have the appropriate resources in place to carry out your "starting point." If the infrastructure is not present, you need to make it compatible to the "starting point" so the objectives become doable.

The infrastructure is comprised of:

- Staffing
- Technology
- Regulatory issues
- Internal workings, such as office space requirements, sharing of information, covering of positions

Staffing

As a coach for many of my kids' athletic teams, the one thing I have learned is that you are only as good as the players you have on the team! As a manager for some of my previous employers, the same thing holds true. I cannot begin to emphasize the importance of building a winning team. A winning team consists of players who want to contribute as specialists in their positions. Each staff member must be a team player and know and understand his or her role. In essence, each must be a position player, someone who knows the position inside out and can substitute for another staff member during absences, extended leaves, or firings.

You begin by hiring specific people who can fill a need. Unlike the pros in the NFL or NBA drafts, where they select the best available athlete, you should select employees who can contribute toward a specific goal or overcoming a particular deficiency within the organization. This way you are bringing in people who understand their roles within the company. And the best way to work with employees, as with clients, is to manage their expectations. If the employee knows what to expect ahead of time, with regard to job responsibility, promotions, acting, and committing on behalf of the company, that employee will be much happier. Therefore, hire new staff based on what they can contribute to that position. Your ultimate goal is to have versatile role players who excel at their chosen position and can fill in where needed.

Technology

With clients demanding more information and advisors needing to cover all bases, technology is increasingly becoming one of the more important as well as possibly the most expensive assets of the firm. Networking is critical for the success of any firm because, as a team, all information must be shared. Any person in my office can access any file or any printer from any computer. And by the time a system is in place, it must be updated or it can become antiquated very quickly. Hire a "technology consultant" to take care of any hardware and software issues that arise. I have one. His name is Stewart Goldfarb. I'd be lost without him. With limited time, you cannot be all things to your business. And what I have learned from the past is that I would rather pay somebody to perform a task and free me up to work on the things I like, usually at a higher billable rate. You need to know what you can delegate and what you should directly work on. Have the technology person design the networking system you will be using. Describe to that person what it is you are trying to accomplish and let that individual figure out your system requirements. You need to make sure you get a system that can be updated both easily and quickly for future growth. It is easier to have someone who is a specialist handle all these issues so you can maintain your billable hours.

Your Phone System.   Probably the best thing you can do is make yourself reachable anywhere and any time. I have a phone number that goes wherever I go. If I leave town, which is quite often the case, I can have all calls forwarded to me without my clients really knowing where I am. From a client perspective, the main concern is that I am reachable all the time. As long as I call my clients back right away (part of my policy is to return phone calls within 24 hours if I cannot be reached immediately), they are happy and satisfied. With technology the way it is now, that can be made possible easily and inexpensively.

You also need to become a paperless office. Everything on the network is backed up daily. There is no need to keep tax returns or financial plans from yesteryear if you can retrieve them via your backup support. This allows for greater efficiency and helps you focus on keeping the things you need. Ultimately, you want to be able to access those files from anywhere—from another computer, from home, or even from out of town.

Software.   Many experienced planners, including myself, have gone through thousands upon thousands of dollars trying to find the right software. New programs keep entering the marketplace that may need specific hardware adjustments. The volume of software is also quite extensive. Financial planning, portfolio management, investment optimization, mutual fund analysis, needs analysis, investment performance reporting, tax preparation, client contact, and client education are just some of the types of programs I use. I have not developed any of my own programs. A brief list of programs that work for me includes Lumen Financial Planning Professional, Morningstar Principia Plus, Frontier Analytics, Lacerte Tax Software, and Kettley Client Education. I feel fortunate that the programs I use accomplish most of the tasks I set out to do for my clients.

Interoffice setup.   Assign a number to all permanent documents and subsections of documents and keep them in the master file for ease of use by staff. In other words, each component that our firm is responsible to complete on behalf of a client should have its own self-contained assigned number. For example, one of the things I pride myself on is providing my clients with a free gift that costs me about $30. It is Quicken. I provide a template for them with assigned numbers for each category. Income and expense are broken down into subcategories and then listed alphabetically. Each subtopic is assigned a specific account number. Some clients may use all, some, or none of the accounts. In any event, when the client e-mails or sends me the disk every month, any staff person in my office can immediately enter the information into the database because all clients are treated in the same way. This is called "systematizing the process," where the entire process works well for whoever is responsible for entering the data. And it works out better for me personally, since now I do not have to spend my time entering client data and charging a fee for such work. Rather, I can focus on what I like to do best, the planning element. Clients meet with me by phone or through a telephone appointment to review their financials. Any adjustments are made, when necessary. Clients enjoy the added involvement because they see that they have direct input into the situation.

Any forms you use, such as for data gathering, tax return preparation, budgeting, investment allocation, and so forth, should be standardized to provide your staff with the best opportunity to learn the system and to ensure that all clients are treated in the same way.

Regulatory

At this juncture, you are probably well established in the area of regulatory concerns. You probably already know that there are two categories of securities regulatory issues: advice and product. Insurance regulations are conducted similarly by states. A brief review is provided here.

Brokerage.   In the advice arena, you must pass the following National Association of Securities Dealers (NASD) exams: the Series 65 exam to become a registered investment advisor, and usually a Series 63 on blue sky law (depending on the state). In lieu of taking two exams, you can take a Series 66. Some states may even require you to take the Series 7 exam (see below). If you manage assets, where you register depends on the amount involved. If you manage under $25 million, then you would register with your state of business. If you manage more than $30 million, you register with the SEC. If you manage between $25 and $30 million, you have the option of registering with either. This was done to provide a *de minimus* range to allow for market fluctuations so that reps would not have to constantly change their registration.

On the product side, if you wish to sell mutual funds, variable annuities, and variable life insurance, you need a Series 6. If you wish to sell the three products just mentioned and also stocks, bonds, and options, you need to pass a Series 7 exam. Again, you may also need the Series 63 exam.

Insurance. If you want to sell life, health, fixed annuity, and disability insurance, you generally need a license that enables you to do all of the above. Usually, this is called the "life and health" license. If you want to sell variable annuities as well, you need at least a Series 6 NASD license (discussed above). If you want to sell homeowners, automobile, and umbrella insurance, you would need a "property and casualty" license. Finally, since insurance licensing is state controlled, as compared to NASD licensing, which is federally controlled, you need to obtain a license in each state where you do insurance business. In theory, you could need 50 state insurance licenses.

CPAs and registration. Let me mention something important with respect to organizational setup. It is strongly advisable, especially for Certified Public Accounting (CPA) firms, to form a separate entity to handle the expansion of your existing accounting business or create a new business (apart from the CPA's other businesses). For example, if a CPA firm branches into the investment advisory business, the separate entity enables the two practices to be organized and run as separate and distinct entities from one another. In the event the CPA firm's advisory business is subject to audit, the CPA's traditional accounting and tax firm clientele will not be subject to the audit. In other words, by forming two separate entities, rather than the one stand-alone, only Registered Investment Advisor (RIA) clientele would be subject to SEC or state exam audits. This also ensures that these accounting clients are not subjected to RIA inquiries.

The CPA firm should form the second entity, but it does not have to be physically located in a separate space. For example, Keri CPA firm decides to form Keri Advisory Services. Both firms are located in the same office space. However, a dedicated phone line and separate business cards will accompany Keri Advisory Services. In other words, Keri's CPA and Keri Advisory Services are wearing different hats for business depending on the functions they are performing for clients.

Internal workings includes office space requirements, sharing of information, covering of positions, and creating an office procedures manual. These types of dealings must be well thought out in advance.

Office space requirements. It is important to secure office space based on where you see your mission going and how rapidly expansion is anticipated. For example, my office space includes several other offices that I rent out. As the firm becomes larger, it has the option of taking over the rented space, minimizing the likelihood of a future move because we outgrow our space. Now would be a good time to renegotiate on office space since the office marketplace in many cities is drying up. It may be advisable to lock into long-term leases now, or even buy an office condominium or small building because of the favorable interest-rate environment.

Sharing of information. This topic deals with how well the team works together. All information that comes into the firm should be subject to a detailed organizational process to alert every staff member as to where critical information is kept. This may include creating a centralized client filing system or central database, and even alerting other personnel of the receipt of certain client information.

Covering of information. It is imperative that every person in the office be able to fill in for someone else. On scheduled days off, a job-sharing arrangement should be put in place to ensure that staff can fill in during a pinch, sick leave, or even termination. This scheduled "covering" or fill-in should occur once per month. All of the information necessary for the fill-in staff should be documented in an office procedures manual.

Office Procedures Manual

This is your official office bible. It should be used as the one central reference source where all firm information is stored, and staff members can see what each other's jobs are. It should also contain other key information, such as account numbers, codes, and how to deal with all firm clients as well as key contact information for clients, staff, and so forth. Each client or alliance should be described in a separate paragraph to alert the reader as to what is done for a particular individual or entity. For companies, it should also mention the key contact personnel your firm should have at the client's office. Remember, the goal here is for any staff person who has absolutely no history with the client to know what is done for that particular client, and who to access there, so that the job can continue being done properly by anyone at your office. The manual should be updated monthly.

This manual should specify:

Firm Information
- Description of the firm
- Philosophy of the firm
- Business Plan
- Marketing Plan
- Staff members' office and home contact information
- Summary description of each staff member's job responsibility
- Job description for each staff member

Client Information
- Listing of all firm clientele
- All contact information for firm clientele
- Description of major issues for each client
- Specific procedures and issues for each client listed separately

Nonclient Information
- Listing of key account numbers and codes, such as for FedEx, Airborne, or UPS

A-4: Determining What You Want to Be When You Grow Up

Having put your thoughts down on paper and having been in the business for a while, you now have a clearer understanding of what it is you want to work on, who you want to work with, and how you want to get paid for that service. This is sort of like a second homecoming. This second chance enables you to see what was hit and what was missed, and make changes to your liking. In one way, I equate it with post-mortem estate planning, where we can help our clients make up for planning strategies after death that may have been overlooked or not done properly during their lifetimes. The success of our practice demands that every once in a while, we need to stop and smell the roses, or make sure the roses are still capable of growing into the future.

Just as in financial planning for our clients, there is no substitute for uncovering all the facts, having everything out in the open, and then making an informed decision. Essentially, we have done all of our homework and now we are in the best position to move forward. At this point, all the discussions should be summarized, analyzed, and interpreted to match the mission statement.

A-5: Directions to Get to Point B from Point A

Now that we know where we are and have clearly defined where we need to be to accomplish our mission, the next step is to connect the dots in order to determine how to get to Point B from Point A. All the necessary steps are laid out in front of us, which should help make our journey that much easier. Again, there is no one way to accomplish this. It is solely a matter of what is right for your business. Pick a way with a light at the end of the tunnel so you can see the road. Drive through the tunnel with your lights on and a reliable map to determine where you are going.

MAP

Map out your course of action. You are still looking at the big picture, the macro-level, now. Ask the group "Where do you intend for the business to be in the future?" Start with projections for one, three, and five years. Longer plans do not make much sense because the nature of this business is changing too rapidly. Look back at where you were five years ago. In fact, the nature of your business has probably changed as well. Many practitioners I have interviewed said that five years ago they were considering the big change in their business model from commission-based to fee-based compensation. Others have told me that their initial goal was to gather assets. Whatever it was or is going forward, your objective is to figure out how to work best on what you want within your designated time allotment so you can work smarter, not harder.

The four steps to map out your future are:

M-1: Determine which services your company performs

M-2: Begin by reviewing your client list

M-3: Weigh all the areas—objective quantification

M-4: Revise your marketing plan

Map   221

M-1: Determine Which Services Your Company Performs

This is a good test to see whether you are working in areas identified in your business plan. You may be performing services for some clients that you are not doing for others, either intentionally or not. After listing these services, you may find that there is an entire area of services you have not been performing for any clients. Remember, your overall business plan determines the future direction of the company. M-1 is a tactical approach to ensure that you are carrying these plans out in accordance with your macro-level objectives.

Begin by listing the services and/or functions you perform. Give your strongest area (the one you practice most in) higher scores and decrease by one all the others you care to get involved with. Start with ten and work your way down. Each service and/or function should have its own (separate) score and should not share the same score with any other one listed.

Exhibit 6-1 shows how one advisor would score his or her practice.

Exhibit 6-1   How One Advisor Scores His Practice

10. Investment advisory services—money under management
 9. Financial planning—comprehensive approach
 8. Financial planning—modular (i.e., retirement, estate, education, income tax, investment)
 7. Specialized planning—modular (i.e., divorce, closely held business, business succession planning)
 6. Seminar circuit
 5. Transaction approach—commission-based product sales
 4. Hourly consultation
 3. Paying gigs unrelated to core practice (i.e., book or article writing)
 2. Nonpaying professional gigs (i.e., trade or membership committee assignments)
 1. Nonpaying personal gigs (i.e., involvement with civic or charitable, or social functions)

The services that you have just identified are the ones you want to continue working on in priority order. Services you do not want to perform should not be included in any final listing. Remember, you are streamlining your business to work in those chosen areas with those clients you wish to help. Time is short. Life is too precious to be doing things you have no real heart for continuing.

M-2: Begin by Reviewing Your Client List

Over the years, you have accumulated many different clients. If you are like most financial planners, early on, the core requirement was living and breathing. Over the years, you became somewhat more selective, and over the last few years, you have worked solely from referrals. Now it is time for the ultimate cleanup. It is time to go back into the client database and reexamine and reevaluate your clients because much has happened since the beginning. Chances are you may not be servicing them as well as you could, simply because there are too many of them. Or there are many clients with whom you do not connect anymore and of whom you would love nothing more than to rid yourself. So your next objective is to list all clients and categorize them. Included on the list should be the following: Name, services performed, annual revenue generated, and either an A, B, or C, as discussed below.

Assign a ranking to each client. Rank from No. 1 (being the highest) through the end of your client list. Then divide the total number of clients into approximately equal groups denoted by (A, B, and C). Your "A" list are clients you love. These are the ones you genuinely care about, you have become friends with, want to see succeed, and so forth. Your "B" clients are clients you like, but it is probably more of a business relationship than anything else. You enjoy their company, but it is business as usual. They would probably be best described as friendly acquaintances. The bottom line is that you enjoy them, but not as much as the clients on your A list. Your "C" clients are ones who do not give you any true joy, since these people are there for no apparent reason other than that they probably started with you and you needed as many clients as possible early on. These are clients you do not look forward to in your quarterly or annual meetings, and who probably hassle you or your staff at some point during the year. These are clients your staff would gladly like to see removed from the client

Map   223

database. As I keep repeating, life is too short to waste your time servicing clients you truly do not enjoy.

With each client grouping divided similarly among A, B, and C, you now need to determine how much time you have to work with your clients. Begin eliminating from the list those clients with whom you do not wish to continue a relationship. Determine whether you want to keep only your A clients or those categorized as A and B. In all likelihood, you will end up removing your C clients. Chances are you will probably end up removing as much as one-third of your client base. At first, it will seem like a lot, because your revenue will drop considerably. You may begin to have doubts, but you need to stay focused and commit to your long-term objectives. Think of it this way. If you were at one time a commission-based planner and then converted to a fee-based or asset management system, there were some pretty significant sacrifices you had to make to change your philosophy of working with clients. You took the initial hit and then, over time, perhaps relatively quickly, you successfully made the change and ended up making more money over the long haul. That is what you need to do here. Be truthful to yourself. If you do not want to work with these clients, then they deserve a C and need to get the boot.

This is a hard step for any financial planner. Many of these clients gravitated to you when you were first starting out. Now that your practice is on a different level, perhaps you are not best suited to continue your relationship because the nature of your business has changed. Or maybe some of these clients are big pains and not worth the hassle. The old cliché that 20 percent of your clients cause 80 percent of the problems for your office probably holds true in your situation. There are fund managers, employers, and planners who have a rotating system whereby every year they evaluate their clients and remove the bottom 10 percent from their database. That type of rotation allows for greater consistency and efficiency in your workings with clients. Since this is a tough move for you, you need to be careful and deliberate in your attempt to keep those clients who will ultimately end up helping you to achieve your goal. Do not be rash and hasty in coming to decisions. Plot them out over two months to ensure that you have considered the full impact and not left anything out in your evaluation.

You may also want to have a backup plan. That is, after the final cuts are made, you do not want to leave your ex-clients high and dry. Arrange with several financial planners in your geographical area to take on some of the clients you want to remove. Be upfront with them. Tell them who these clients are, what portion of your practice they represent, and why you are reevaluating your clients. Tell them that they did not make the cut. Some of these financial planners may be up for the chance of working with them. After all, every client does need the services of a financial planner.

M-3: Weigh All the Areas

We will start with the listing we have identified in M-1. We have assigned a hypothetical point value for each service identified in M-1, and calculated a composite score for each listing (see Exhibit 6-2).

As you know, not all financial planning subject areas are created equal. Certainly you do not equally enjoy all areas. Therefore, you have to determine which of these areas you enjoy working in most. This will help you align with clients who have strong needs in those areas. Selecting services and functions you wish to continue working in will help make it an easier transition in deciding which clients you want to continue working with and which clients should be nixed.

To help figure out which areas make the most sense to continue working on, assign specific point values to each area to help you quantitatively measure this objective. Those areas you want to work in will receive a higher point value. Point values will be recorded as 3, 2, or 1. "3" represents the highest level. These are the A services and functions. B will represent the next level and be assigned a "2." C represents the lowest level and for that assign a "1." Next, assign the ranking with a composite score. In this example, what you would most like to perform is investment advisory services. This service was given a 10 ranking and will now be assigned a 3-point value. Multiplying these rankings gives a composite score of 30. That is the top score you can achieve. Continue to do this with the other services. Complete this task for each of the services, tally them up, and list them in priority order with the higher scores coming before the lower ones. Those scores ranking highest represent the significant tasks we wish to continue. Not all scores will be divided evenly or even in order of 3, 2, and 1. Rather, the services represent the importance of the task, and the point

Map   225

Exhibit 6-2   Composite Score for Each Service Identified in M-1

Service	Point Value Assigned	Score
10. Investment advisory services— money under management	3	30
9. Financial planning— comprehensive approach	3	27
8. Financial planning—modular (i.e., retirement, estate, education, income tax, investment)	3	24
7. Specialized planning—modular (i.e., divorce, closely held business, business succession planning)	3	21
6. Seminar circuit	2	12
5. Transaction approach—commission- based product sales	1	5
4. Hourly consultation	2	8
3. Paying gigs unrelated to your core practice (i.e., book or article writing)	1	3
2. Nonpaying professional gigs (i.e., trade or membership committee assignments)	2	4
1. Nonpaying personal gigs (i.e., involvement with civic or charitable, or social functions)	2	2

value represents what we enjoy doing. Therefore, it is quite possible to have a lower ranked service assigned a higher point value and thus a higher composite point score.

As shown in Exhibit 6-3, even though No. 5, transaction approach, is ranked as a preferred service as compared to No. 4, hourly consultation, the No. 4 hourly consultation received a total

Exhibit 6-3   Service/Composite Score from M-3 Chart

5. Transaction approach—commission-based product sales	1	5
4. Hourly consultation	2	8
3. Paying gigs unrelated to your core practice (i.e., book or article writing)	1	3
2. Nonpaying professional gigs (i.e., trade or membership committee assignments)	2	4

composite score of 8 versus a 5 for No. 5 transaction approach. Thus, in the final assessment, No. 4, hourly consultation, ranks higher than No. 5, transaction approach, in determining what services to continue performing for clients. The same holds true for the next two service categories listed. No. 2, non-paying gigs, is ranked as a preferred service as compared to No. 3, paying gigs. No. 2 received a score of 4, compared to No. 3, which received a score of 3. In our final assessment, No. 2, non-paying gigs, ranks higher than No. 3, paying gigs, in determining what services to continue performing for clients.

Once this task is completed, work your client rankings (see "Evaluation," below) into this process to determine the ultimate scores.

Start with the listing identified in M-1. Then determine a point value and score to see how it will play out.

Analyze the Results

You have just determined a reasonable cutoff to see which services make the grade. As I stated before, you cannot be all things to all clients. Pick the areas you work in then prioritize them, and then factor in your enjoyableness for each. Your objective is to make them both work for you.

Look for results with a minimum score of 21. Basically, it is encompassing your top four areas (10, 9, 8, 7) at your top individ-

Map   227

ual score (3). This way you can focus on the top three areas that fulfill you and your firm the most. This will enable you to have a greater concentration and specialty, where you will truly be known as the experts in your chosen fields.

M-4: Revise Your Marketing Plan

Now that you have agreed on a direction in which to take the business that is in agreement with your mission statement and business plan, you need to develop a tactical approach to make it happen. That is where the marketing plan comes in. A marketing plan is a tactical road map that takes you to Point B from Point A. It is a detailed and descriptive method to attract and retain clients. It spells out all the steps and assigns a dollar amount and time frame to each. It quantifies the success of your objectives so you can measure them periodically.

You should come to realize that traditional sources and game plans of marketing do not always work the best. For those practitioners who are most successful in this area, the one common trait I have observed is that they think *outside* the box. They do not follow the common protocol. Rather, they see what they want to achieve and then strive to hit it, many times by taking unconventional steps to lead them to this Promised Land. They have decided it is no fun or not profitable to be ordinary when carrying out the ultimate tactical operation for growing the business.

Top 10 Practitioners Who Think "Outside the Box"

One practitioner I know is based in Phoenix and is doing this as a second career. He was an airline pilot for Eastern Airlines for almost 20 years. After Eastern's bankruptcy in 1989, he wanted to dedicate his professional life to helping those airline personnel with whom he grew extremely close to ensure that they had adequate money to retire. So he developed his own financial planning practice specializing in helping airline personnel. In fact, those are the only clients he takes on. It grew so successful, he opened a branch office in Denver because many of those pilots now work for United Airlines and live in Denver. The moral of this story is that just because you have come into financial planning from an entirely different vocation does not mean that you have to go cold turkey and forget your roots. You may be able to adopt a marketing plan that emphasizes your past, which you probably still somewhat enjoy, and incorporate that into your marketing strategy going forward.

Another practitioner I know was a traditional CPA. He worked in accounting, auditing, and taxes for 20 years. He was sick and tired of doing draining work with clients, then turning them over to a broker who spent one-tenth the time with them and made 10 times the money. He said to me, "What's wrong with this picture?" I met him during one of my California CPA Education Foundation classes. He was sitting in my Introduction to Personal Financial Planning class. We went to lunch, he explained his situation to me, and I gave him advice on how he could convert his existing clientele into financial planning and investment advisory clients and market these new service to future clients. Today, when I see him during speaking engagements for the California CPA Education Foundation, he is proud to report to me that not only has he given up his traditional practice, but he is making about five times the amount of money he previously did as a traditional CPA. He is enjoying his business more since he feels that he is directly helping people in advance (rather than reporting the facts after the fact), and he is able to call his CPA friends during tax season as he is playing golf with a client and discussing strategy. Now that's success!

A third practitioner decided that with the way of the world becoming specialization, he too would become one in the financial advisory field. He truly enjoyed investing and everything that went along with it. He took it upon himself to become known as the investment guru in his local area. He decided to change his business cards to read "investment planning consultant." He contacted local newspapers and offered to write for them for free. In fact, he would write anywhere for free. He wrote some articles in professional journals as a way of legitimizing his claim to his peers. When prospects approached him, he would reiterate his investment positions, his extensive knowledge of investing, and his knowledge of clients in this area. Today, he manages over $100 million and works only in this field. He farms out other areas to affiliates who then serve the remainder of his clients' needs.

A fourth practitioner taught in the public school system in Denver for many years. During her tenure in the system, she was

Map   229

not comfortable with the advice she or any other teachers were receiving. She was unsure of where to turn to invest her money and had little faith in the person who was providing this advice to her and her peers. She thought she could do a better job than this individual. After she retired from teaching, she did just that. She developed and refined a financial planning practice that worked on assisting other educators with their 403(b) investment decisions, as well as a host of other investment opportunities.

A fifth practitioner stated that he loved to speak in front of a crowd, any crowd. If there were people in the room, it was his calling. So he decided to do just that. He made arrangements with many restaurants in town to keep fishbowls on the counter to allow restaurant customers who dropped in their business cards to win a free lunch. He plastered about 20 of these fishbowls around town. He would work out an arrangement with the restaurant in advance to hold a customized lunch for the winners in that particular restaurant, inviting about 15. Every day, he would hold a luncheon seminar in some restaurant around town from 11:30 am to 1:00 pm. Of the prospects who showed up each time, he was able to turn about two into clients. It was an expensive ordeal, but this was his calling. He would set up appointments before and after the seminars. His office was in the southern part of town, so his clients there would meet him in his office, and the clients from the north would meet him for coffee or at their homes.

A sixth practitioner targeted new homeowners in an area. He would use a direct mail campaign to caution the prospect about the urgency of meeting with him to do tax returns and/or financial plans. He would work off new tax laws, or just specific information relevant to homeowners, such as deductibility of primary or secondary residences, primary or secondary indebtedness, or rental properties, and whether they belong on Schedule E (rental property schedule) or Schedule A, 1031 tax-free exchanges, and so forth. He would send his assistant to the county clerk's office to get a listing of those people who had bought homes recently and use that as a marketing list. She would then devise a master list of several thousand well-thought out and targeted prospects. He told me his response rate was close to 5 percent, 1 to 2 percent being common for direct mail.

A seventh practitioner teams up with an attorney, a CPA, a stockbroker, an insurance agent, and an actuary/pension consultant. They call themselves the "Traveling Advisors" and their claim to fame is that they have something for everyone. This group of six (five advisors, along with the financial planner) advertises in local newspapers emphasizing certain topics and then sending the appropriate advisors to speak on these topics. All speak equally, and any prospect can meet with any of them. While certain advisors, the lawyer and accountant must do the work in their own specialties, they keep a running total and split their revenues equally at year-end. All prospects-turned-clients are considered clients of the Traveling Advisors. They have a huge database and work as a team to market to these newly formed clients for referrals in any of the areas. There are two ways this group markets. One is through a general newsletter sent to clients and prospects each month. In every newsletter, each advisor has a one-paragraph biography and two advisors write feature-length stories. Each advisor gets an opportunity to write several stories a year. The second marketing strategy showcases each advisor in his or her specialty. The group pays for two of these letters a year. Since there are six of them, it works out evenly. For example, the lawyer has a letter on wills, the CPA for tax season, the actuary/pension to the small business owners on the list, the stockbroker to clients with $250,000 and more of investable assets, and the insurance broker on property and casualty. He then catches them with property and casualty (P&C) and focuses on life and disability after they have become clients. So there's something for everyone!

An eighth practitioner had been burned when she got divorced and was miserable and poor. She vowed that other women would not dig themselves into the hole she found herself in. So she decided to help those women and became a divorce specialist who works primarily with older women and their finances. Having been in the same position herself, she knows the group she works with and can use appropriate methods to potentially reduce or eliminate the likelihood that these women will find themselves virtually penniless after a divorce. She works with several divorce attorneys who do not want to get into the details of the financial side of the divorce and often rely upon her for this necessary information.

A ninth practitioner takes a holistic approach to financial planning, doing what many companies today are calling "life cycle analysis" or "life planning." He looks at every aspect of a client's life, not just the financial side. He looks at what makes the indi-

Map   231

vidual unique, he gravitates toward family history, history and feelings about money, tries to get behind and understand the psychological side of the client, in addition to going over the financial aspect. Even though the practitioner is not a psychologist, he feels that by asking the right questions, he can uncover deep feelings that lead the client to act in a certain manner concerning finances. This practitioner feels that all areas are interrelated and that the only way he can do an adequate job for clients is to know everything about them. His recommendations are therefore appropriate to all aspects of the client's personality.

A tenth practitioner works with doctors. His philosophy is simple. His slogan is "You know how to make it; we can show you how to keep it!" Many doctors are notorious for thinking they know everything—especially when it comes to handling their own finances. For several years, I was the financial speaker at the American Academy of Dermatologists Annual Convention. It was fun. The doctors were really good people. They seemed to listen, but they really didn't. They definitely had a misconception. Many of the doctors in attendance figured that they did not need financial planners because they read all of the consumer financial publications in the marketplace. After all, these publications can be found in their waiting rooms. "If it works for them, then it can work for me!" one doctor exclaimed. Many others came to me after the sessions saying they had made inappropriate investments and had very little to show for it. Some even stated that they were too poor to retire! Ugh! Can you imagine that? Obviously, here is a situation where the income earners are making significant sums of money only to see it fly away. And these doctors are working to age 65 and beyond simply because they do not have a financial planner checking their nest egg.

As you can see from these ten practitioners, the importance of developing a marketing plan cannot be overstated. Many planners I know have not developed a formal marketing plan because they still operate under the client philosophy of "if they have money, then we'll take 'em!" But from a practical standpoint, we do not want to be all things to all people, and we want to develop key criteria to use in differentiating our practice from someone else's practice.

The bottom line is that you need a definitive course of action to get to Point B from Point A. Again, it is contingent on the services described above, the joy of performing each of those services, which results in the composite score we just calculated.

Whatever type of business you are involved with, make sure you follow through on the marketing plan. It works in the many different facets of financial planning.

The Marketing of Financial Planning Fast Track™ (FPFT™)

One success that I have had with marketing is the Financial Planning Fast Track (FPFT) program I initiated under the direct supervision of the Metropolitan State College of Denver's approved CFP™ certificate program. I have taught for 12 years in educational programs leading up to earning the CFP™ designation. I have taught for New York University, the College for Financial Planning (at its Community College of Denver affiliate), and at Metropolitan State College of Denver. Over the years, I have heard many complaints from students expressing their frustration over having to take a series of educational course offerings over a two-year period. Many stated that the commitment was too long. Others stated that they lost interest and focus during that time. As a result, they pay tuition fees in full, start the program, but never complete it.

I started thinking outside the box. I said "Wouldn't it be great if I could somehow develop an alternative delivery system to satisfy the CFP Board educational requirement with a more focused and shorter time frame educational program?" And that is when FPFT came into being. I knew we had to satisfy the 30-hour-per-class educational requirement, that we had to use the same books as the traditional course, and that we had to make sure the students were doing so much work in so little time. So we decided to offer these programs in four full-day increments. Each of the four days was eight hours apiece and totaled 32 hours of classroom time. We separate each of the sessions by five to six weeks to provide students with a full opportunity to read all of the materials prior to class. Since we use American College materials, there are textbooks, audio tapes, and study guides that accompany each class.

And we met the students' expectations upfront. Remember that the main reason planners get sued is that they do not meet their clients' expectations. Expectations have even broader implications than that, and I wanted to make sure that everyone who

Map 233

signed up for this program knew what to expect. The difficulty level was higher than that of the traditional program, primarily because the students have a limited amount of time to do the work, and it must be done in advance of attending. Each day, the student gets tested on the prior preparation and also on the in-class materials. Each of the four tests is averaged out to determine a final grade. Students must pass all six courses in order to earn their certificate from the Metropolitan State College of Denver, so they can then qualify to take the CFP™ Certification Examination.

This delivery system worked, especially for planners already in the business who wanted those three letters next to their names, and for companies that wanted to upgrade their field forces to operate at the highest level.

My Specialty as an Insurance Expert

My earlier success stemmed from a conscious decision about how I wanted my financial planning career to go. While I was getting started and was working as the technical manager in the American Institute of Certified Public Accountants' (AICPA) Personal Financial Planning Division, I made the decision early on that if I wanted to get noticed and known as an expert, I needed to pick one discipline and know it extremely well. And I did. I chose insurance planning, primarily because of my background in a management executive program at a large New York–based insurance company. I did this by writing articles for several journals and trade association magazines, and began teaching the old CFP™ 2: Risk Management and Insurance section for New York University (NYU) for the CFP™ educational program. That success within insurance enabled me to branch out into other specialties, notably income tax and overall personal financial planning.

The press asked me specific technical questions, and even more important, came to know me and my relationship with the industry. From this, a monthly CPA newsletter hired me as the editor and I began attaining many editor and writing jobs, which allowed me to acquire the knowledge I needed within the industry to make myself more well-rounded. And from there, the projects became larger. All clients like to see their planner's name in print. Although most never read the articles, they know the advice must be technically sound when they see it in print.

My marketing plan for JR Financial Group, Inc., consists of:

- Executive summary
- Market analysis and objectives
- Developing marketing targets—niche marketing
- Using the 4p's to develop the marketing plan
- Creating strategic alliances
- Marketing budget
- Action plan
- Monitoring plan

See Appendix 7-2 for a copy of the JR Financial Group, Inc., marketing plan.

EVALUATION

We determined that with so little time and so many clients we were going to prioritize our client list by assessing the importance of each client with respect to the overall objective of the business. This weighting of the client is done in the evaluation stage.

At this stage, we quantify some of the decisions we have made to determine what course of action might best service our firm. We look at a variety of factors (as shown in Exhibit 6-4) and provide a

Exhibit 6-4   Factors Responsible for Success of Practice

E-1: Client name
E-2: Type of service
E-3: Annual revenues
E-4: How acquired by firm
E-5: Referral generator
E-6: Workability
E-7: Rank

point value for their relative importance to the development and success of our practice, and then take steps to ensure that clients with the highest scores are ones that remain, while the others graduate from our service.

The spreadsheet in Exhibit 6-5 shows how the rankings should be positioned.

Use the sample scoreboard in Exhibit 6-5 when evaluating your clients. Each client should be scored for all categories. Then categorize your clients by overall score and keep your strongest areas first, those with the highest score, and then decrease by one. Assign rankings to each category. Compare the scores under each category. You will be scoring categories II through VI. A maximum point value of 50 can be assigned.

E-1: Client Name

Put in alphabetical order to ensure no client is unintentionally omitted. This list represents all clients of the firm. Include those with an ongoing relationship as well as those who engaged you for a specific project, since they may decide to revisit you in the future.

E-2: Type of Service

List a code number from the services noted above under M-1. Any services you provide that are not included on the list should be factored into this category. Any ones on the list that you do not provide should be removed.

Exhibit 6-5   Positioning of Rankings of Factors

Client Name (1)	Type of Service (2)	Annual Revenues (3)	How Acquired by Firm (4)	Referral Generator (5)	Work-ability (6)	Rank (7)

E-3: Annual Revenues

Determine how much revenue these clients will continue generating for the firm annually in the future. Remember, it does not matter how much revenue they have generated thus far. This is a prospective model designed to free up time in the future by making the most of what you have today. This is a future growth plan based on client projections. If the prospects appear to diminish or even disappear, you need to score them as such. We are taking the approach that there will be insufficient free time to include everyone in the final cut.

Score this category as:

$20,000+ scores a 10
$15,000+ scores a 9
$10,000+ scores an 8
$7,500+ scores a 7
$5,000+ scores a 6
$4,000+ scores a 5
$3,000+ scores a 4
$2,000+ scores a 3
$1,000+ scores a 2
Every client below that scores a 0

Note: if your revenue structure is different from what we have suggested, use your real numbers.

Analyzing the Results

These results can also be tied to your firm's overall business objectives and tailored to meet your firm's needs. Basically, figure out what your firm's targeted revenues should be and include a 20 percent bottom line profit. Ideally, you would want to have as many clients as possible score between 6 through 10, which means each client is billable for at least $5,000. Then follow through with the multiple for each client multiplied by the category to derive a gross revenue number. Add them all up to determine your firmwide gross revenue, which should equal your business plan projections. For example, let us assume the following:

Score	Category	Number of Clients	Gross Revenue
10	$20,000+	9	180,000
9	$15,000	7	105,000
8	$10,000	10	100,000
7	$ 7,500	12	90,000
6	$ 5,000	24	120,000
			595,000
			(Tie into business plan projections.)

You will use the individual scores from 10 through 0 in the final ranking of your clients to determine which ones you are more likely to keep with your firm.

E-4: How Acquired by Firm

This category addresses how you and the client got together. Was the client referred or solicited? Did the client attend a seminar you gave? Was he or she a walk-in? Many of these clients could have come to you when you were doing business in a manner you no longer utilize today. It could have been early in your career when the first priority was living and breathing. Others may have come in as a result of an entirely different system you had in place at that time. This is an important point, because the way you initially met them may help determine whether you continue to stay on as their financial advisor. Other clients may have been a safer bet, perhaps generated through a referral. Still others may have been price-shopping or, even worse, performance-shopping; these clients were obtained through seminars, solicitations, or walk-ins, and you no longer have the cheapest game in town.

Score this category as:

Referral:	10
Holdover from a previous owner:	8
Seminar:	6
Solicited:	4
Walk-in:	2

E-5: Referral Generator

What is the likelihood that this client can generate future referrals, leads, and other opportunities for business, such as introducing you to co-workers, alliances, business associates, community activists, friends and relatives, and so forth? Clients who can assist you in bringing in business should be scored higher than other types. Remember, at this stage of your career, you want to aggressively generate your business primarily through referrals and leave other types of methods on the back burner. The basic question you should ask yourself is "Who does this person know, and how will that work for me?" If these clients can be centers of influence, they probably are worth keeping. If not, again, you need to figure out the future direction of the business and select clients who will help you achieve that objective.

Score this category as:

Very Likely	10
Likely	8
Possibly	5
Probably Not	2
No	0

E-6: Workability

If ever there was a subjective category, this is it. How do you feel when you are with specific clients? Do you enjoy their company? Are they pleasant? Do they require much handholding? Do they complain, threaten, or hassle you or your staff? At this point you should send around client surveys to your staff. Quantify the scores and ask for written explanations of things that you and other staff members should know. It is important that all your staff members buy into this concept. Having unhappy staff dealing with unsatisfied clients leads to a huge internal dilemma and inadequate handling of the firm's other clients. Remember, life is too short to deal with problem clients. It is time for a reminder of the old adage: 80 percent of the clients generate 20 percent of the business and 20 percent of the clients generate 80 percent of the problems. Eliminate those clients who you feel are not conducive to growing your practice to the next level.

Score this category as:

Enjoy immensely	10
Fun to be around	8
Acceptable	5
More of a nuisance than anything	2
You want out	0

E-7: Rank

Add up your clients' scores. Rank them from highest score to lowest. Separate the categories of clients depending on score range as:

45+ are A clients
35+ are B clients
10+ are C clients
<10 are D clients

Remember, life is too short to deal with any client who scores below "B." Definitely keep your "A" clients, possibly your "B" if time permits, and remove all the others. Also remember to work through this exercise on an annual basis to ensure that your firm is where it wants to be at all times.

How Do You Remove All the Others?

There are several ways to handle this. One method is to graduate them! Tell them they have successfully completed your planning program and that you cannot add any additional value to the relationship for the fees they are paying. Second, provide a referral list of possible planners who are looking to accept new clients. However, do not hand them the clients blindly. Print out a score sheet from the client and review with them to see if this is someone they may be able to work with. Believe it or not, there are some planners up to the challenge of working with difficult clients. Third, recommend software where they can handle all of their issues directly. Whatever you do, make sure you have an exit strategy in place. It is not professional to leave any client high and dry.

7

The Model Financial Planning Practice

76 POINTERS TO RUNNING A SUCCESSFUL FINANCIAL PLANNING PRACTICE

How would you describe the model practice? Or, even better, is there a model practice? I would say the answer depends on what it is you are doing for the client. Clearly, there is no one right way to practice. Many planners I know operate their practices completely differently. They are firm and passionate in their beliefs, yet they will vary when performing similar services for their clients. And it works for all of them in their own particular situations and geographic regions of the country.

To create your own model practice, you should start out writing down just what it is you wish to accomplish. Figure out which clientele you are serving and why. Know exactly what they are requesting. State the reasons for your client meetings. Ask yourself, if it were me on the other side of the conference table, what would I like to get out of this entire relationship?

Consider adopting the Rattiner Practice Model (RPM), a model of 76 pointers to running a successful financial planning practice, when constructing your own practice.

THE TEN COMMANDMENTS FOR CLIENT-CENTERED RELATIONSHIPS

1. You should adhere to the practice standards published by the CFP Board of Standards as a guide for doing the right thing. These standards represent a minimum level of acceptable practice and should be used as a starting point in delivering financial planning services. As of January 2002, 10 standards have been released. You can keep up to date with new standards by visiting the CFP Board web site at *www.cfp-board.org*. See the Appendix for the complete set of standards as of the date of publication.

2. You should follow a structured approach to the financial planning process. By focusing on client concerns through the use of comprehensive methods leading to the satisfaction of your clients' objectives, and the ultimate recommendations to address these concerns, you will have covered the entire gamut of client issues. The PIPRIM© approach (please see Chapter 4) is a logical and organized way to make that happen.

3. You should express the value and the benefits to clients of participating in a financial planning engagement. Tell them it is not about product. It is about process and what you walk away with! I tell my clients point blank, "I do not know how to pick specific stocks; I do not know which way the market is headed; and I do not know where the economy is going; but I am your guy!" Most say, "Rattiner, you're not much of a salesperson, are you?" And I say, "You're right, but that is not what this is about."

   I respond by saying "I can help you stay focused and remain on course. I can help you sleep better at night knowing that we have an established game plan for the achievement of your financial objectives." I then go on to tell the client "I am never going to lead the league in return, but through my approach, we will be competitive with returns, and more important, devise a wealth management strategy to help you achieve your goals. Now is that what you want, Mr. and Mrs. Client?"

With a core index strategy and a select active strategy, we are hedging our bets on the downside and limiting them on the upside, while remaining in a good position to take advantage of market movements. Remember, your purpose in undertaking this engagement with your clients is to not sell products, but to satisfy needs.

4. You should be realistic. Tell it the way it is! The reality is that not everything will be accomplished by the client due to limited resources. You need to say "No way!" when your client asks you whether something is attainable and you believe, based on the current circumstances and examination of the current data, that the client's objectives will not happen as envisioned. Your clients will have nothing but respect for you.

5. Your clients need to know that you will be there for them, always. For example, if I am on the phone with a client, I will not have my assistant interrupt me, nor will I answer my cell phone under any circumstances, unless it is a true emergency. It is important for my clients to understand that when they are in the office meeting with me to discuss their finances, everything else takes a backseat. I tell my clients that my service is continuous. I am here for them to answer all questions and address their concerns. In essence, this "personal coaching" aspect will ensure that they have the necessary assistance and drive to do the things they want, when they want.

6. Your clients need to understand your method of compensation. You need to disclose the source if you receive moneys from product sales. Whatever method you select, your clients have to know the reasons why you are operating in that manner and you must assure them that it will not be a hindrance to the service you provide.

7. You should listen to the client, and their concerns. Set the tone early and often. Hammer home your dedication throughout the entire process. They are coming to see you for a reason. You need to respond by restating everything they say and phrasing it in a positive manner that ensures complete follow-up and responsibility on their part.

8. You should avoid conflicts of interest at all costs. I make a point to back away from any possible situation in which my integrity and objectivity are questioned.

9. You should develop an "action to-do" list that outlines the responsibilities of all parties involved and the dates by which the tasks will be completed during the financial planning engagement. Spell out your role, your client's role, and possibly other professionals' roles in achieving your client's objectives.

10. If you make a mistake with the client, own up to it. Admit it, rectify it, and move on!

The next sections refer to specific technical responsibilities you should meet during the financial planning engagement, in the areas of insurance planning, investment planning, retirement planning, and estate planning. You can find the income tax planning model at the end of Chapter 5. The following practice model is set up as an audit checklist to ensure that you are operating within the model practice.

INSURANCE REPRESENTS THE CENTER
OF THE UNIVERSE: COVER ALL YOUR BASES!
(MODEL NO. 11 TO NO. 17)

11. When reviewing your client's life insurance policy:
    a) Separate long-term needs from short-term needs.
    b) Recalculate needs regularly.
    c) Review ratings of existing carriers.
    d) Review reasons why current insurance was purchased.
    e) Determine how original needs have changed and identify new needs.
    f) Review beneficiary designations.
    g) Review policy riders and options.
    h) Review each policy's features.
    i) Compare client's current health if debating whether to switch policies.
    j) If it is a term policy, evaluate conversion and renewability features and feasibility.

k) If it is a permanent cash value policy, evaluate the true cost of insurance with the value received.

l) Determine if it makes sense to gift one of the client's life insurance policies.

m) Determine whether it makes sense to name a charity as a revocable or irrevocable beneficiary and establish a wealth replacement trust.

n) Determine whether it makes sense to establish a charitable trust to own the life insurance on the client.

o) Evaluate the effect of current life insurance ownership on its value in the estate.

p) Determine if any incidents of ownership exist for insurance that is intended to be outside the estate.

q) Determine if beneficiary designations of any policies owned outside the estate will cause inclusion within the estate.

12. When reviewing your client's health (a) and disability (b–h) policies:

a) Inquire whether your client opted for the best type of medical coverage based on his or her family situation.

b) Determine the monthly disability needed.

c) Determine whether sufficient coverage exists under the client's current policy, or if the existing coverage was purchased many years ago when the client was earning a lower salary.

d) Determine whether the policy provides a definition of "own occupation."

e) Determine whether the policy is noncancellable and guaranteed renewable.

f) Determine whether a provision for residual and partial disability exists.

g) Determine whether a guaranteed insurability rider or COLA rider has been added.

h) Determine whether the elimination period is appropriate.

13. When reviewing long-term care insurance:
   a) Identify qualification triggers for benefit eligibility. The use of activities of daily living (ADLs) and/or physician referrals is preferred.
   b) Compare existing policy triggers to current products. Consider replacement of policies requiring prior hospitalization.
   c) Determine levels of care provided. Avoid policies that do not cover all levels of inpatient care. Evaluate client's needs regarding home care versus inpatient care.
   d) Review elimination period and relate to other resources for coverage.
   e) Review benefit level relative to current costs and other available income.
   f) Review benefit period relative to family history of client.
   g) Compare premium histories of guaranteed renewable policies.

14. When reviewing homeowners insurance coverage:
   a) Ensure whether coverage is adequate to replace dwelling only. The replacement cost and the value may be two very different numbers.
   b) Is the proper form of insurance in place? A homeowners policy on a property currently being rented out is not acceptable.
   c) Determine the last time the client reviewed the cost of the coverage.
   d) Determine whether the client has replacement cost coverage or actual cash value (ACV) coverage.
   e) Determine whether the policy contains an inflation-adjustment rider.
   f) Determine whether personal property coverage is adequate based on assets owned.

g) Determine whether replacement cost protection on personal property exists.

h) Determine whether your client understands the limitations on high value items.

i) Determine whether your client has floaters for all high value personal property.

j) determine whether an HO 15 (Homeowner 15) rider exists.

k) Determine if disaster coverage is necessary and appropriate.

15. When reviewing your client's liability coverage:

a) Determine whether current policies include adequate coverage for the client.

b) Determine whether current coverage is enough to qualify the client to obtain an umbrella policy.

c) With the client's current circumstances, determine whether the client's umbrella policy is sufficient and cost-efficient.

d) Determine whether the client has any high-risk assets, such as a swimming pool, that would warrant additional or special coverage.

16. When reviewing your client's auto policy:

a) Consider whether state-mandated levels are met and whether they are adequate.

b) Consider the deductible relative to other assets.

c) Determine whether it would be appropriate to remove collision coverage on older vehicles.

d) Determine whether all owned vehicles are included on the policy.

17. When reviewing business insurance:

a) Determine whether coverage is appropriate.

b) Determine whether insurance agents have been performing an adequate job of discovering all the pertinent exposures.

INVESTMENT PLANNING: CREATING WEALTH (MODEL NO. 18 TO NO. 42)

The following are all phrased as reminder questions.

18. Did you discuss your client's expectations about the scope and nature of the investment planning services to be delivered?

19. Did you explain the tradeoff between risk and return, the concept of real return, and the asset allocation process?

20. Did you convert the client's financial planning goals and objectives into relevant investment planning goals and objectives?

21. Did you identify planning time horizons for each separate investment goal to be funded?

22. Did you explain unsystematic and systematic risk?

23. Did you identify the risks inherent in each asset currently owned by the client?

24. Did you identify before tax-deferral opportunities the client may not be using to the maximum extent, such as 401(k) plans?

25. Did you discuss the difference between yield and total return?

26. Did you determine the tax issues that are important to the client and that may affect the selection of investment products?

27. Did you explain in simple terms the basic concepts of the Capital Asset Pricing Model, the Efficient Market Hypothesis, and Modern Portfolio Theory?

28. Did you help your client develop an investment policy statement?

29. Did you develop a risk profile of the client and spouse that will serve as a guide to the types of investment products that can be recommended to the client?

30. Did you determine the rate of return required for each client's portfolio based on the analysis completed for each separate funding need?

31. Did you develop an asset allocation strategy to reallocate the client's existing portfolio into one that can achieve the client's goals?

32. Did you determine if tax-exempt bonds are appropriate considering the client's marginal tax bracket?

33. Did you determine if Treasury securities might appeal to the client due to their relative safety and the exemption from state income taxation?

34. Did you determine whether a Section 529 plan or an education IRA would be appropriate savings vehicles for the children's education planning?

35. Did you examine the client's investment holdings in employer qualified plans to determine if the client has too large a concentration of total assets in the employer's securities?

36. Did you determine how much of a percentage loss of total portfolio value in a bear market or market correction might upset the client, and discuss the strategies for portfolio hedging that may be possible?

37. Did you discuss the tax treatment of mutual fund distributions and the necessity to retain mutual fund statements until the fund is completely liquidated?

38. Did you explain the concept of correlation and how the asset classes selected for the portfolio are designed to diversify the portfolio so as to minimize the probability that all asset classes in the portfolio will decline simultaneously?

39. Did you discuss the benefits of using a dollar-cost averaging strategy to implement the investment product decisions?

40. Did you use yield curves to help guide the optimal maturity of fixed-income asset classes?

41. Did you examine the cost structure (front-end fees, back-end fees, management fees, etc.) of the mutual funds to determine if the cost burden is exorbitant?

42. Did you determine the appropriateness of various benchmarks of portfolio performance for all or a portion of an investment portfolio?

RETIREMENT PLANNING (MODEL NO. 43 TO NO. 53)

43. If the client's savings program will not result in a sufficient amount to fund his or her retirement lifestyle, there are basically four courses of action:

    a) save more,

    b) earn more (a higher investment return on the retirement savings fund),

    c) retire later, or

    d) retire in a more modest lifestyle.

44. Wherever possible, the client should be saving through a tax-deferred vehicle such as a qualified plan, or personal retirement plan, such as an IRA, SEP, or SIMPLE.

45. In determining the client's retirement savings needs, use appropriate assumptions for investment rate of return, inflation rate, years until retirement, and years during retirement.

46. Retirement plan funds should be maintained in tax-deferred accounts to maximize the benefits of tax deferral. Urge the client to consider alternate sources of funds needed during the preretirement period, so that retirement plan balances will not be eroded.

47. Review beneficiary designations on all retirement plan accounts to ensure that they are consistent with the client's goals.

48. Keep retirement planning in view as short-term decisions are being made regarding the use of income and assets.

49. Review the client's retirement projections periodically; revise the analysis periodically, and in the event of material changes in the client's situation (such as change of employment, divorce/marriage, or death of spouse).

50. As the client approaches retirement, plan to incorporate the stretch (multi-general) IRA to enable the retirement funds to grow tax deferred as long as possible.

51. Fully analyze any projections made by other professionals when projecting a pension maximization or other recommendation.

52. Monitor the client's investment return; compare it to assumptions that were used to build the retirement fund. If the client's investments are not realizing the expected return, the client may need to shift the investment allocation or modify the retirement lifestyle.

53. Monitor the client's expenses compared to projections; modifications in lifestyle may be necessary.

ESTATE PLANNING ISSUES (MODEL NO. 54 TO NO. 76)

54. In considering any gift or estate strategy, analyze the basis aspects of any particular property being planned for use in the strategy.

55. Where spousal transfers are involved, always check the citizenship of the transferee spouse.

56. Where necessary, be willing to pay a small tax to achieve an important personal objective.

57. Recommend a will even in situations where the plan in place will avoid probate completely.

58. Encourage the use of a durable power of attorney and the medical proxies available under state law.

59. Strongly recommend filing a will and other estate documents for safekeeping with the appropriate court.

60. Among retirees consider all charitable giving techniques that would enhance current income.

61. Review all indications of domicile and try to consolidate domicile as much as possible.

62. Avoid presenting clients with probate and revocable trusts as an either-or proposition.

63. Use joint ownership arrangements sparingly as an estate planning technique.

64. Estimate estate liquidity needs and identify sources of liquidity.

65. If life insurance is to be purchased as a source of liquidity, avoid even initial ownership by the insured.

66. Discourage clients from using joint, mutual, or reciprocal wills, and/or joint trusts.

67. Compile a family tree for the client, clarifying relationships and identifying critical dates (e.g., marriages, births, deaths, gifts, etc.).

68. Construct a net worth statement for the client, extrapolating from that the degree of planning appropriate.

69. Identify items that would be classified as income in respect of a decedent in a prospective gross estate, and attempt to determine how best to handle those items.

70. Make sure the client understands the planning limits imposed by spousal rights in community property states and common law states.

71. Determine and present to the client the estate plan that the client currently has (even if it is all intestacy).

72. Do not allow the generation-skipping transfer tax to discourage clients from making transfers to grandchildren or others until the exemption is fully utilized.

73. Consider carefully what plans are in place for the disposition of pension plan benefits and whether different dispositions should be explored.

74. Assess the adequacy of provisions for minors and dependents, and make recommendations as needed.

75. Where there is a closely held business interest, determine definitively how the succession in interest is to be achieved, whether by a buy-sell agreement or through another technique.

76. Survey the post-mortem elections that may be available to the particular estate and adopt strategies that will preserve the availability of these elections.

Use these action items as part of your personal financial planning audit checklist to ensure that you have not omitted any critical issues and to help you shape your model financial planning practice.

APPENDIX 7-1: CFP BOARD PRACTICE STANDARDS

Ten Practice Standards have been approved by the Board of Governors and all are in effect as of January 1, 2002. These standards, which were approved in May of 2001, supersede all standards in effect prior to January 1, 2002.

Practice Standard 100-1

Establishing and Defining the Relationship with the Client

Defining the Scope of the Engagement

The financial planning practitioner and the client shall mutually define the scope of the engagement before any financial planning service is provided.

Practice Standard 200-1

Gathering Client Data

Determining a Client's Personal and Financial Goals, Needs, and Priorities

The financial planning practitioner and the client shall mutually define the client's personal and financial goals, needs, and priorities that are relevant to the scope of the engagement before any recommendation is made and/or implemented.

Practice Standard 200-2

Gathering Client Data

Obtaining Quantitative Information and Documents

The financial planning practitioner shall obtain sufficient quantitative information and documents about a client relevant to the scope of the engagement before any recommendation is made and/or implemented.

Practice Standard 300-1

Analyzing and Evaluating the Client's Financial Status

Analyzing and Evaluating the Client's Information

The financial planning practitioner shall analyze the information to gain an understanding of the client's financial situation and then evaluate to what extent the client's goals, needs, and priorities can be met by the client's resources and current course of action.

Practice Standard 400-1

Developing and Presenting the Financial Planning Recommendation(s)

Identifying and Evaluating Financial Planning Alternative(s)

The financial planning practitioner shall consider sufficient and relevant alternatives to the client's current course of action in an effort to reasonably meet the client's goals, needs, and priorities.

Practice Standard 400-2

Developing and Presenting the Financial Planning Recommendation(s)

Developing the Financial Planning Recommendation(s)

The financial planning practitioner shall develop the recommendation(s) based on the selected alternative(s) and the current course of action in an effort to reasonably meet the client's goals, needs, and priorities.

Practice Standard 400-3

Developing and Presenting the Financial Planning Recommendation(s)

Presenting the Financial Planning Recommendation(s)

The financial planning practitioner shall communicate the recommendation(s) in a manner and to an extent reasonably necessary to assist the client in making an informed decision.

Practice Standard 500-1

Implementing the Financial Planning Recommendations

Agreeing on Implementation Responsibilities

The financial planning practitioner and the client shall mutually agree on the implementation responsibilities consistent with the scope of the engagement.

Practice Standard 500-2

Implementing the Financial Planning Recommendations

Selecting Products and Services for Implementation

The financial planning practitioner shall select appropriate products and services that are consistent with the client's goals, needs, and priorities.

Practice Standard 600-1

Monitoring

Defining Monitoring Responsibilities

The financial planning practitioner and client shall mutually define monitoring responsibilities.

Financial Planning Practice Standards copyright© 1998-2001 Certified Financial Planner Board of Standards, Inc.

CFP™, CERTIFIED FINANCIAL PLANNER™ are marks owned by the Certified Financial Planner Board of Standards, Inc. These marks are awarded to individuals who successfully complete the CFP Board's initial and ongoing certification requirements.

APPENDIX 7-2: JR FINANCIAL GROUP (JRFG) BUSINESS PLAN

JR Financial Group (JRFG), (the Firm) is a financial information company specializing in disseminating knowledge to advisors and consumers.

The Advisor Side

The Firm dispenses information to advisors to help them become more knowledgeable on financial planning issues so they can practice financial planning better with their clients. The Firm accomplishes this by providing training activities directly to advisors, and by writing industry wide technical, marketing, and practice management information for advisors to purchase.

On the training side, the Firm achieves this through:

- the creation, design and implementation of Financial Planning Fast Track™ (FPFT™), which provides a "boot camp" approach for those financial services professionals desiring to receive the requisite information necessary as determined by the CFP Board of Standards, in order to take the CFP™ Certification Examination through an alternative format (distribution channel);
- personal financial planning (PFP) company-specific certification;
- specific CPA industry PFP information on how CPAs can start in the business;
- practice management and marketing information on how advisors can take their practices to the next level.

On the writing side, the Firm does this by writing:

- and editing a high-end journal called *Personal Financial Planning Monthly (PFPM)*, which is an industrywide trade publication earmarked for financial planners, CPAs, attorneys and other industry technical specialists;
- a monthly column on advanced planning issues for *Financial Planning Magazine;*

- several pieces for a web-based delivery system for S&P Fund Advisor, on issues relating to mutual funds; and

- advanced advisor case studies through Horsesmouth.com;

- authoring various published books, including *Rattiner's Financial Planners' Bible*, through John Wiley & Sons; *Getting Started in Financial Planning*, through Bloomberg Press; *Adding PFP to Your Practice*, through the American Management Association; *Practicing Financial Planning* through Mittra and Associates; and the *PFP Library*, through Harcourt Brace/Aspen Publications. The Firm is also writing the *Financial Planner's Answer Book*, to be published by Aspen Publications in 2003.

The Consumer Side

The Firm provides educational seminars to consumers through its subsidiary, Financial Planning Institute, LLC., to raise awareness of financial planning issues. Consumers benefit through this delivery system by directly receiving the same information professional advisors receive, but tailored to their level and specific needs. Thus, consumers avoid receiving this information from brokerage and/or insurance intermediaries (middleman) whose primary goal is to sell them products and services.

The Firm accomplishes this task by providing a series of four two-hour seminars in various subject areas in its training room. Seminars are spread over a two-month period whereby the instructors personally get a chance to know the attendees. Various seminars are running concurrently to enable consumers to sign up for more than one and to provide them with regular access to the seminars instructors.

For those attendees needing further assistance in their financial endeavors on techniques learned throughout the seminar series, the Firm has a variety of packaged services and products to fulfill those needs. It provides personal financial coaching, financial planning, income tax preparation and insurance and investment products to consumers who need the help towards accomplishing their many financial goals. The Firm helps systematize their concerns into an orderly and cohesive fashion.

The Firm provides ongoing communication to its clients by:

- sending out monthly newsletters to its regular clients and prospects
- providing a chatroom for consumer questions
- posting general information for seminars to its long-standing clients

The Firm contracts out with various insurance and investment companies and is in the process of selecting a money management partner.

Executive Summary

Company description. JR Financial Group, Inc. (JRFG) is a Colorado-based company providing financial information services to advisors and consumers. 100 percent of the company's stock is owned by Jeff Rattiner, its president.

Mission statement. JRFG's mission is twofold: to provide financial planning information to financial advisors practicing in the marketplace so they may further their knowledge when dealing with their clients, and to consumers who need to have an understanding of basic knowledge in order to accomplish their financial objectives. In essence, the Firm trains the trainers and educates consumers directly.

Products and services.

The Advisor Side

JRFG provides an alternative to the traditional CFP™ educational system; a very rigid and structured boot camp, complete with comprehensive study materials including its own specially designed handouts, to financial advisors who desire to accelerate the typical time commitment into six months, instead of the typical two year period.

Target markets. JRFG targets financial advisors who currently work in the financial services industry and desire the CFP™ designation so they can advance to the top of the profession.

Marketing and sales strategy. JRFG plans to advertise in various trade publications to recruit individual financial advisors and to write proposals to financial services professionals to establish training sessions at various company headquarters.

JRFG also plans to "franchise" the concept under the direct supervision of the Metropolitan State College of Denver by selecting qualified regional individuals to recruit a potential territory for offering FPFT to companies and unaffiliated individual advisors. Recruiters have been hired for the Northeast, the Midwest, and the South. Currently, the Firm is looking for a recruiter for the Far West (California region). Qualified instructors will be given course training in Denver before they are eligible to provide FPFT training. The overall goal is to have three programs running per year per territory (15 in total) in accordance with the exam testing cycle in these five regions of the country. The Firm also wants to make it super convenient for enrollees to take classes on an ongoing basis if they miss their regularly scheduled class.

Competitive advantages and distinctions. JRFG's chief advantage is through its high-powered, energy-packed teaching delivery system, which is provided by Jeffrey H. Rattiner, CPA, CFP™, MBA, a recognized leader in the industry. The Firm expects to capitalize from his "brand name" in the marketplace.

Management. President Jeff Rattiner has been a practicing financial planner for over 20 years. He specializes in working with both financial advisors and consumers.

Organization Structure. The Firm has hired a technical curriculum developer, whose responsibility is to design, develop and maintain course curriculum and a test question databank for the various advisor-oriented projects. His responsibilities also extend to book and journal technical article writing, student program support, and author recruitment

Operations. JRFG conducts its business at its location at 6410 South Quebec Street, Englewood, CO 80111-4628; (tel): 720-529-1888.

The Consumer Side

JRFG provides:

- fee-based comprehensive and modular financial planning services for an hourly ($100 per hour) and/or flat fee ($800 per plan)

- commission-based alternatives for middle-to-upper end individuals, on a load basis
- income tax preparation and planning services
- "retainer types services, personal financial coaching, and ongoing support" to clients who are paid up with the Firm

Financial plans generally take eight hours to complete. Jeff Rattiner and Jake Koebrich are licensed to receive insurance and securities commissions from sales of recommended products.

Target markets. JRFG targets the greater Denver metropolitan area. Greater Denver has a population base of over two million persons. Potential target markets include Greater Phoenix and San Diego.

Marketing and sales strategy. JRFG aims to differentiate itself from other financial planning firms by taking a pure education and knowledge-based approach when working with clients so that they may achieve a reasonable comfort level throughout the financial planning and investment processes.

The Firm wants to grow the Denver practice (see financials) to a self-sufficient operating system (whereby the principal is not involved in the day-to-day operation of the consumer practice) and then copy it to various regions of the country. The Firm will attempt to do this by franchising this education and knowledge based model to potential regional partners once every three years. These regional firms will pay a franchise royalty for the rights to use company branding identification, receive training and power marketing, use seminar materials and receive home-office support. The overall goal is to change the national standard of providing financial information to consumers to help them make better-informed decisions.

Competitors and market distribution. There are many other providers of fee and/or commission based financial planning services in the Greater Denver metropolitan area, but very few, if any, take a 100% knowledge based approach towards soliciting potential clients.

Competitive advantages and distinctions. JRFG's chief advantage is through its knowledge-based delivery system by having Jeffrey H. Rattiner, CPA, CFP™, MBA, a recognized leader in the industry, provide most of the training to financial advisors and consumers. The Firm expects to capitalize from his "brand name" in the marketplace.

Management. President Jeff Rattiner has been a practicing financial planner for over 20 years. He specializes in working with both financial advisors and consumers.

Organization Structure. The Firm has hired a financial planner, Jake Koebrich, whose responsibility is to design, develop and maintain education information seminars for consumers. His responsibilities also extend to the personal coaching of these clients, including developing, implementing and monitoring financial plans, preparation of income tax returns and tax planning, product selection and implementation, and recruiting other reps to work under the brand name and design. His other responsibilities include maintaining the firm wide administrative and technological infrastructure so the Firm may operate in an efficient and seamless manner.

Operations. JRFG conducts its business at its location at 6410 South Quebec Street, Englewood, CO 80111-4628; (tel) 720-529-1888.

The Future

Financial Numbers. Annual revenue projections for the current year are $200,000. In 2003, we expect revenue to surpass $400,000. In 2004, we expect revenue to exceed $500,000.

Long-term goals. JRFG's long-term goals are to open offices in Phoenix in 2005 and San Diego in 2008 running the same type of consumer operation in those locations.

JRFG hopes to bring in two partners to run the additional two offices (at fair market value of gross billings).

Company Description

Company mission. JR Financial Group, Inc. (JRFG) has as its mission to provide a financial knowledge-based approach to capturing its marketplace of advisors and consumers. JRFG's mission is to provide live training to advisors nationwide and to provide education seminars to consumers locally.

Legal status. JRFG is a Denver, Colorado based company whereby 100 percent of the company' stock is owned by Jeff Rattiner. JRFG is a Subchapter S corporation.

Industry Analysis

JRFG is extremely well positioned to take advantage of the significant opportunities presented by the dissemination of financial knowledge to advisors and consumers. Having been published through the authoring of five books, and a continued editor, columnist, featured author and trainer for the largest publishers and most circulated magazines and journals, Jeffrey H. Rattiner is widely known and accepted as a guru on all financial planning topics. The Firm wants to capitalize on the branding of Jeff Rattiner in each of those areas as the "guy who trains the trainers" or the leaders of the financial services community. JRFG does not see many other financial information-based knowledge-oriented financial planning firms taking this "knowledge approach" towards working with high net worth individuals. The Firm believes that consumers will jump at the chance to be educated directly from the person who educates advisors who offer these same types of services directly to clients, thereby eliminating the need for the intermediary, the financial broker or insurance agent.

Barriers to entry. With the commoditization of financial planning services and products, which means that many planners are selling the same products and offering the same services without distinguishing themselves from their competition, profit margins may be coming down in the future. Consumers are demanding more free services from their advisors. Advances in technology also make it harder since many financial service organizations offer free calculator software and other helpful tidbits on their web sites.

Current environment. The current environment supports additional financial planners entering this marketplace. With 260 million people living in the United States, [and 50 percent of them (or 130 million households to service)] and approximately 100,000 licensed or registered financial planners to service them (excluding the 150,000 additional self-proclaimed planners), there are many consumers that will need JRFG's help in bettering their financial lives. In Denver, those numbers are two million people and approximately 1,000 CFP™ licensees. Focusing on the middle market (which is where the majority of these people fall) provides an opportunity to work with many clients.

Long term opportunities. Long-term prospects appear excellent for the reasons stated above. More consumers are working with licensed financial planners and understand the importance of planning ahead for their future.

Target Market

The Advisor Side

JRFG targets existing financial advisors who do not have a financial planning designation.

The Consumer Side

JRFG targets households in the greater Denver area that fit the following profile:

- Age: 30–75
- Income Range $60,000+
- Net Worth $100,000+
- Occupation: Consumers who have a steady job, are in retirement or are self-sufficient
- Location: Metro Denver

Marketing Plan and Sales Strategy

The Advisor Side

JRFG plans to use the following marketing mediums:

- Regional directors
- Trade journals
- Website
- Referrals from enrolled and prior students
- Corporate advertising

The Consumer Side

To educate its client base and explain its services, JRFG plans to use the following marketing mediums:

- Public relations (through its professional side)
- Brochures
- E-mail Newsletters

Operations

JRFG conducts its physical business at its location at 6410 South Quebec Street, Englewood, CO 80111-4628. The training center is also located in the same building.

Management and Organization

President Jeff Rattiner has been a practicing financial planner for over 20 years. He specializes in working with middle-income families and their concerns. He is a graduate of City University of New York. With a BBA degree in marketing management, and of Hofstra University with an MBA degree in Certified Public Accounting.

Long-Term Development and Exit Plan

JRFG will grow steadily over the next ten years. By 2012, JRFG plans to have five offices with each office operating as a turnkey system which would not require the day-today operation and management services of Jeffrey H. Rattiner. The Firm plans to franchise the delivery system for providing advisor financial planning training through qualified financial instructors, so Jeff Rattiner will not have to be involved in much of the future teaching.

A primary major goal of the Firm will be to have a business it could sell, or a secondary goal would be to incorporate any of Jeff's children to continue in its operation.

Strategy for achieving goals. JRFG will consider opening additional consumer franchise offices in various locations throughout the United States at the rate of one every three years.

Risks. The greatest risks of expansion are the chance that JRFG becomes too decentralized in its operation and management of the Company.

Financial Numbers

Income statement. The following is a projection of JRFG cash flow for the next three years.

	2003	2004	2005
INCOME			
Gross revenue	$400,000	$450,000	$500,000
OPERATING EXPENSES			
Salaries and wages	$150,000	$175,000	$200,000
Employee benefits	$30,000	$33,000	$36,000
Payroll taxes	$30,000	$35,000	$40,000
Professional services	$5,000	$5,000	$5,000
Mortgage	$36,000	$36,000	$36,000
Web development	$2,000	$3,000	$4,000
Depreciation and amortization	$3,000	$3,000	$3,000
Insurance	$2,000	$2,500	$3,000
Utilities	$4,000	$4,400	$4,800
Postage and supplies	$1,000	$1,100	$1,200
Marketing and advertising	$10,000	$12,000	$15,000
Travel	$12,000	$15,000	$18,000
Entertainment	$3,000	$3,000	$4,000
Bad debts and doubtful accounts	$3,000	$4,000	$5,000
Total operating expenses	$295,000	$332,000	$375,000
Net income before taxes	$105,000	$118,000	$125,000
Provision for income taxes	$35,000	$36,000	$41,000
Net income after taxes	$70,000	$82,000	$84,000

Balance Sheet

Assets
Current assets

Cash	$20,000
Accounts receivable	$10,000
Total current assets	$30,000

	2003	2004	2005
Fixed assets			
Building	$250,000		
Equipment	$10,000		
Furniture	$20,000		
Total fixed assets	$280,000		
Total Assets	**$310,000**		
Liabilities			
Accounts payable	$5,000		
Accrued payroll	$15,000		
Taxes payable	$5,000		
Long-term notes payable	$180,000		
Total liabilities	$200,000		
Net Worth			
Shareholders equity	$80,000		
Retained earnings	$30,000		
Total net worth	$110,000		
Total Liabilities and Net Worth	**$310,000**		

The Three Fundamental Rules of Working with Clients

Rule No. 1: The client's interests always come first.

Rule No. 2: If the client's interests do not appear to come first, then refer back to rule No. 1.

Rule No. 3: If the planner's interests become a little too aggressive and appear to contradict those of the client, then refer back to rule No. 1.

Resources (Keeping In Tune with the Industry)

I have been stating all along that it is impossible to practice financial planning without the help of capable resources. There is too much to know and too many people are depending on you to act alone. No matter what profession, any good professional needs to know where to turn to find the answers to technical problems, what-if scenarios, practical assistance, external resources, and the like. This chapter provides you with a list of specific tools with contact information to help your practice become more efficient and continue to operate at a higher level.

BELONG: JOIN A PROFESSIONAL MEMBERSHIP GROUP

If you want to receive the latest and greatest, you need to join a professional membership group. There are many of them out there that will follow the path you have identified throughout this book. Several are listed below. Contact them by phone or e-mail for more information.

American Institute of Certified Public Accountants (AICPA), Personal Financial Planning (PFP) Division

This organization represents CPAs who specialize in financial planning. Membership requirements include having a valid CPA license and being a member of the AICPA in good standing. The AICPA has its own designation, the Personal Financial Specialist (PFS). You can attain that designation now through a point system, in lieu of taking the PFS exam, by completing an application on the AICPA's web site. Member benefits include receiving a bimonthly division newsletter called *The Planner*, an annual PFP Practice Handbook, technical practice aids, discounts to the AICPA PFP Technical Conference, money saving tools, and the ability to purchase consumer brochures. It also has an Investment Advisory Service Center for CPAs who wish to provide money management services, expand educational materials, and work closely with the state CPA societies. For more information, call (888) 777-7077 or visit their web site at *www.aicpa.org*.

Association for Investment Management and Research (AIMR)

The Association for Investment Management and Research (AIMR) is an international, nonprofit organization of more than 50,000 investment practitioners and educators in over 100 countries.

Founded in January 1990, AIMR was created from the merger of the Financial Analysts Federation (FAF) and the Institute of Chartered Financial Analysts (ICFA). The FAF was originally established in 1947 as a service organization for investment professionals in its societies and chapters. The ICFA was founded in 1959 to examine candidates and award the Chartered Financial Analyst (CFA) designation.

AIMR's mission is to serve its members and investors as a global leader in educating and examining investment managers and analysts and sustaining high standards of professional conduct. AIMR's membership is global in scope, and its activities are worldwide.

The Research Foundation of AIMR sponsors practitioner-oriented research through funding and publishing a diverse assortment of monographs, tutorials, and research papers to broaden investment professionals' knowledge and understanding of their field.

AIMR offers services in three broad categories: Education through seminars and publications; Professional Conduct and Ethics; and Standards of Practice and Advocacy.

AIMR's members are employed as securities analysts, portfolio managers, strategists, consultants, educators, and other investment specialists. These professionals practice in a variety of fields, including investment counseling and management, banking, insurance, and investment banking and brokerage firms.

For more information, call (800) 247-8132 or visit their web site at *www.aimr.org.*

Financial Planning Association (FPA)

The Financial Planning Association is the membership organization for the financial planning community. It was created when the ICFP and the International Association for Financial Planning (IAFP) unified on January 1, 2000. Members include individuals and companies who have contributed to building the financial planning profession and all those who champion the financial planning process. FPA members are dedicated to supporting the financial planning process in order to help people achieve their goals and dreams. The FPA believes that everyone needs objective advice to make smart financial decisions and that when seeking the advice of a financial planner, the planner should be a CFP™ certificant.

A nationwide network of local chapters is the backbone of the FPA. Each one promotes the advancement of knowledge in financial planning, supporting programs, and projects that enable members to better serve their clients.

The FPA's official publication is the *Journal of Financial Planning.* This award-winning publication features prominent writers who cover all aspects of financial planning, including news that shapes the community. Also, the FPA has a web presence at *www.fpanet.org.* FPA's web presence includes articles, forums, online networking, and substantive information of interest to those who support the financial planning process.

The FPA offers services and resources designed to help the public understand the importance of the financial planning process and the value of objective advice from a CFP™ professional. Resources include issue-based campaigns designed to educate consumers about specific personal finance issues, a service to connect consumers with local CFP™ professionals, web-based consumer information, and brochures. Consumers can visit *www.fpanet.org* to access this information. They can also call (800) 282-PLAN. This organization represents financial planners who have an interest in planning as well as CFP™ licensees.

FPA offers a variety of conferences, publications, and other member benefits. It's the closest organization in terms of representing traditional financial planners. For more information, please call (800) 322-4237 or visit its web site at *www.fpanet.org*.

Investment Management Consultants Association (IMCA)

IMCA's mission is to ensure quality service to the public by developing and encouraging high standards in the investment consulting profession. Its role has been to broaden the public's understanding of investment management consulting and to promote and protect the interests of the profession. It also provides forums for ongoing education and information sharing among members. A common purpose among its members is the establishment of a support network that makes its members more knowledgeable professionals. For more information about IMCA, or to become a member, call (303) 770-3377 or visit its web site at *www.imca.org*.

National Association of Personal Financial Advisors (NAPFA)

NAPFA—the National Association of Personal Financial Advisors—is a professional association of comprehensive, fee-only financial planners in the United States. NAPFA has over 750 members and affiliates in 45 states, who provide consumers and institutions with comprehensive and objective financial advice on a fee-only basis. NAPFA members keep the best interests of the client in mind: Neither the advisors nor any related parties receive compensation contingent on the purchase or sale of a financial product.

Members must agree to a code of ethics and fiduciary oath, have a bachelor's degree, specialized education or training, adhere to continuing education requirements, have three years of experience, offer comprehensive financial planning services, and submit a comprehensive financial plan. Members receive the *NAPFA Advisor* and *Newslink*. NAPFA holds an annual conference.

For more information, call (800) 366-2732 or visit its web site at *www.napfa.org.*

FINANCIAL PLANNING SOFTWARE PROGRAMS

Most planners I know have "been there, done that" when it comes to evaluating potential software products they think might give them a unique edge. However, you will find out that not all software is alike. Most of the planners I know have had experience with many of the different software programs in the marketplace. After all that, they still do not like any software for all its features; they like certain parts of some and not of others. Many planners I know go so far as to develop their own programs through a spreadsheet analysis. In your exploration, you will find many fine features and even more unnecessary features. For features you are unlikely to use, it does not pay to spend the extra money.

Go through the list and select the programs that offer the greatest possibility for your practice. Then have your assistant call the vendors and request a demo on each one you are interested in. After you receive all the demos, go to an offsite location with your computer consultant and try each one out in an apples-to-apples comparison. Have a list of questions (from this book) or other issues you are concerned with and put it on a spreadsheet. Report the results in spreadsheet format, labeling pros and cons of each program. Then narrow it down by ranking them in priority order.

The following software programs are listed for informational purposes only. Neither the author nor the publisher endorse any of these products.

Financial Planning Programs

Program: *BNA Income Tax Planner*
Developer: BNA Software
Phone Number: (800) 372-1033
Web Site: *www.bnasoftware.com*

Program: *BNA Estate Tax Planner*
Developer: BNA Software
Phone Number: (800) 372-1033
Web Site: *www.bnasoftware.com*

Program: *Brokers Ally Financial Planner*
Developer: Scherrer Resources
Phone Number: (215) 542-5710
Web Site: *brokersally.com*
E-mail: *support@sri.com*

Program: *Cheshire Financial Planning Suite*
Developer: Cheshire
Phone Number: (800) 734-6734
Web Site: *www.cheshire.com*
E-mail: *eric@cheshire.com*

Program: *Crescendo Estate Planned Gifts Software*
Developer: Crescendo Interactive
Phone Number: (800) 858-9154
Web Site: *www.crescendosoft.com*
E-mail: *cresardis@hotmail.com*

Program: *Easy Money for Windows*
Developer: Money Tree Software
Phone Number: (541) 929-2140
Web Site: *www.moneytree.com*
E-mail: *mike@moneytree.com*

Program: *Expert Series*
Developer: Sterling Wentworth
Phone Number: (801) 955-6100
Web Site: *www.sterwent.com*
E-mail: *cgardner@sterwent.com*

Program: *ExecPlan 4.11*
Developer: Sawhney Systems, Inc.
Phone Number: (800) 850-8444
Web Site: *www.sawhney.com/home.html*
E-mail: *robertf@sawhney.com*

Program: *Financial Planning*
Developer: AdvisoryWorld.com
Phone Number: (800) 480-3888
Web Site: *www.advisorworld.com*
E-mail: *pwilson@advisorworld.com*

Program: *Financial Planning Prof*
Developer: Lumen Systems, Inc.
Phone Number: (800) 233-3461
Web Site: *www.lumensystems.com*

Program: *Financeware.com*
Developer: FinanceConverter
Phone Number: (877) 883-7526
Web Site: *www.Financeware.com*
E-mail: *feedback@financeware.com*

Program: *Finpack 2000*
Developer: FDP Corp.
Phone Number: (800) 337-2677
Web Site: *www.fdpcorp.com*
E-mail: *patti@fdpcorp.com*

Program: *FPLAN Professional Advisor*
Developer: First Financial Software
Phone Number: (800) 719-8761
Web Site: *www.Fplan.com*
E-mail: *jason@fplan.com*

Program: *InsMark Illustration*
Developer: InsMark Inc.
Phone Number: (925) 543-0500
Web Site: *www.insmark.com*

Program: *LGW Turnkey Web Solution*
Developer: Life Goals.com Corp.
Phone Number: (888) 326-0006 x229
Web Site: *www.lifegoals.com/turnkey2/intro.asp*
E-mail: *sales@lifegoals.com*

Program: *M-Plan*
Developer: Mobius Group, Inc.
Phone Number: (800) 662-4874
Web Site: *www.Mobiusg.com*
E-mail: *sales@mobiusg.com*

Program: *MasterPlan for Windows V4*
Developer: Master Plan Financial Software
Phone Number: (800) 229-5080
Web Site: *www.masterplanner.com*
E-mail: *sales@masterplanner.com*

Program: *Methuselah 2000*
Developer: Unger Software
Phone Number: (888) 864-3776
Web Site: *www.ungersoft.com*
E-mail: *sales@ungersoft.com*

Program: *Profiles+*
Developer: Financial Profiles
Phone Number: (800) 237-6335
Web Site: *www.profiles.com*
E-mail: *sales@profiles.com*

Program: *PFP Notebook*
Developer: Brentmark Software
Phone Number: (800) 879-6665
Web Site: *www.brentmark.com*
E-mail: *jane@brentmark.com*

Program: *X Financial Planning Software*
Developer: LifeGoals.com
Phone Number: (888) 326-0006 x225
Web Site: *www.lifegoals.com*
E-mail: *sales@lifegoals.com*

Mutual Fund Information Programs

Program: *Investment Survey (Expanded)*
Developer: Value Line, Inc.
Phone Number: (212) 907-1681
Web Site: *www.valueline.com*
E-mail: *cjambe@valueline.com*

Program: *Investment View*
Developer: Weisenberger, A Thomson Financial Co.
Phone Number: (888) 371-4575
Web Site: *www.wiesenberger.com*
E-mail: *Kathleen.marmon@tfn.com*

Program: *Investor Square*
Developer: Manhattan Analytics
Phone Number: (800) 251-3863
Web Site: *InvestorSquare.com*
E-mail: *jacobr@advisorsquare.com*

Program: *Monocle II*
Developer: Monocle Systems
Phone Number: (512) 263-1191
Web Site: *www.monoclesystems.com*

Program: *Mutual Fund Survey*
Developer: Value Line, Inc.
Phone Number: (212) 907-1681
Web Site: *www.valueline.com*
E-mail: *cjambe@valueline.com*

Program: *Principia Pro v4.0*
Developer: Morningstar
Phone Number: (800) 735-0700
Web Site: *www.morningstar.com*
E-mail: *chris.boroff@morningstar.com*

Program: *Steele Mutual Fund Expert*
Developer: Steele Systems
Phone Number: (800) 678-3863
Web Site: *www.mutualfundexpert.com*
E-mail: *custserv@steelesystems.com*

Wealth Management Analysis/Performance Reporting Packages

Program: *Axys*
Developer: Advent Software
Phone Number: (800) 685-7688
Web Site: *www.advent.com*
E-mail: *kgolden@advent.com*

Program: *Asset Allocation Planner*
Developer: Cheshire Software
Phone Number: (800) 734-6734

Determines optimal portfolio based on client's risk tolerance and investment time frame. Contains historical data back to 1973 including efficient frontier curves and calculates rate of return and standard deviation for portfolios.

Web Site: *www.cheshire.com*
E-mail: *eric@cheshire.com*

Program: *Broker's Ally for Windows*
Developer: Scherrer Resources
Phone Number: (215) 542-5710
Web Site: *www.brokersally.com*
E-mail: *support@sri.com*

Program: *Broker's Notebook*
Developer: Reuters
Phone Number: (800) 521-2475

Program: Blueprint
Developer: CDA/Weinsenberger
Phone Number: (888) 371-4575
Web Site: *www.wiesenberger.com*
E-mail: *Kathleen.marmon@tfn.com*

Program: *Captool Professional Investor*
Developer: Captools Co.
Phone Number: (800) 826-8082
Web Site: *www.captools.com*
E-mail: *sales@captools.com*

Program: *Centerpiece5.2*
Developer: Performance Technologies, Inc.
Phone Number: (800) 528-9595
Web Site: *www.centerpiece.com*
E-mail: *sales@centerpiece.com*

Program: *Cheshire Asset Allocation Software*
Developer: Cheshire Software
Phone Number: (800) 734-6734
Web Site: *www.cheshire.com*
E-mail: *eric@cheshire.com*

Program: *dbCAMS+v2.0*
Developer: FCSI (Financial Computer Support Incorporated)
Phone Number: (877) 432-2267
Web Site: *www.dbcams.com*
E-mail: *info@dbcams.com*

Program: *Frontier Analytics*
Developer: Allocation Master
Phone Number: (858) 552-1268
Web Site: *www.allocationmaster.com*

Program: *Ibbotson Analyst*
Developer: Ibbotson Associates
Phone Number: (800) 758-3557
Web Site: *www.ibbotson.com*
E-mail: *aauerbach@ibbotson.com*

Program: *Ibbotson Encorr*
Developer: Ibbotson Associates
Phone Number: (312) 616-7363
Web Site: *www.ibbotson.com*
E-mail: *aauerbach@ibbotson.com*

Program: *Ibbotson Fund Strategist*
Developer: Ibbotson Associates
Phone Number: (800) 758-3557
Web Site: *www.ibbotson.com*
E-mail: *aauerbach@ibbotson.com*

Program: *Ibbotson Portfolio Strategist*
Developer: Ibbotson Associates
Phone Number: (800) 758-3557
Web Site: *www.ibbotson.com*
E-mail: *aauerbach@ibbotson.com*

Program: *Portfolio Tracker2.2*
Developer: RAM Technologies
Phone Number: (905) 795-9222
Web Site: *www.ramsoft.com*

Program: *Power Optimizer*
Developer: AdvisoryWorld.com
Phone Number: (800) 480-3888
Web Site: *www.advisorworld.com*
E-mail: *pwilson@advisorworld.com*

Program: *Power Plus*
Developer: AdvisoryWorld.com

Phone Number: (800) 480-3888
Web Site: *www.advisorworld.com*
E-mail: *pwilson@advisorworld.com*

Program: *ProSource Premier*
Developer: National Datamax
Phone Number: (888) 673-4180
Web Site: *www.nationaldatamax.com*

Program: *Ramcap*
Developer: AdvisoryWorld.com
Phone Number: (800) 480-3888
Web Site: *www.advisorworld.com*
E-mail: *pwilson@advisorworld.com*

Program: *Ramcap Plus*
Developer: AdvisoryWorld.com
Phone Number: (800) 480-3888
Web Site: *www.advisorworld.com*
E-mail: *pwilson@advisorworld.com*

Program: *Virtual Advisor*
Developer: Advisor Software
Phone Number: (800) 738-6369
Web Site: *www.advisorsw.com*

Technical Programs

Program: 2002 ERISA Facts
Developer: National Underwriter
Phone Number: (800) 543-0874

Program: 2002 Field Guide
Developer: National Underwriter
Phone Number: (800) 543-0874

Program: 2002 Tax Facts
Developer: National Underwriter
Phone Number: (800) 543-0874

Program: Financial Planner's Library
Developer: Aspen
Phone Number: (888) 551-7127

Client Contact Packages

Program: *Client Data Systems for Windows*
Developer: E-Z Data
Phone Number: (800) 777-9188
Web Site: *www.ez-data.com*

Program: *Client Info Plus*
Developer: Mountech Soft
Phone Number: (888) 668-6832
Web Site: *www.mountech.com*
E-mail: *dain@mountech.com*

Program: *Peak 98*
Developer: Springwater Soft
Phone Number: (315) 431-9868
Web Site: *www.springwatersoftware.com*
E-mail: *sales@springwater.com*

Program: *Text Library Systems*
Developer: Financial Planning Consultants
Phone Number: (800) 666-1656
Web Site: *www.financialsoftware.com*
E-mail: *Hannah@financialsoftware.com*

Client Relationship Programs

Program: *Back Room Technician*
Developer: Kettley Pub
Phone Number: (800) 777-3162

Program: *Financial Planning Omniscience*
Developer: FP Publications
Phone Number: (505) 269-2955

Program: *Moneymax*
Developer: Financial Psychology Corp
Phone Number: (800) 735-7935
Web Site: *www.moneymax.org*
E-mail: *kniber@kathleengurney.com*

FINANCIAL PLANNING PUBLICATIONS

Books

You should get into the habit of keeping your library stocked with professional books that can be used as resources to provide you with timely and thorough information. Several of the ones I am familiar with are listed below.

Marketing

- *Values-Based Selling* by Bill Bachrach (Aim High Publishing, 1998)
- *Fundamentals of Insurance for Financial Planning* by Burton Beam, Jr. (The American College, 2000)
- *Endless Referrals* by Bob Burg (McGraw-Hill, 1994)
- *The Guide to Financial Public Relations* by Larry Chambers (St. Lucie Press, 1999)
- *Mastering the Game* by Kerry Johnson (Louis and Ford, 1987)
- *Effortless Marketing for Financial Advisors* by Steven Moeller (American Business Visions, 1999)

Practice Management

- *Getting Started as a Financial Planner* by Jeffrey H. Rattiner (Bloomberg Press, 2000)
- *Adding Financial Planning to Your Practice* by Jeffrey H. Rattiner (American Management Association, 2000)
- *Creating Equity: Building a Hugely Successful Asset Management Business* by John Bowen, Jr. (SDC Publishing, 1997)
- *Deena Katz on Practice Management*, by Denna Katz (Bloomberg Press, 1999)
- *The Financial Services Revolution* by Clifford E. Kirsch (Irwin, 1997)
- *Fundamentals of Financial Planning* by Robert M. Crowe and Charles E. Hughes (The American College, 1993)
- *The E-Myth Revisited* by Michael E. Gerber (Harper Collins, 1995)
- *Flashpoint: Measuring the Art of Economic Abundance* by Mark E. Matson (McGriff Publishing, 1999)

- *The Financial Advisor's Toolbox* by Ed McCarthy (McGraw Hill, 1997)
- *Protecting Your Practice* by Katherine Vessenes (Bloomberg Press, 1997)
- *Best Practices for Financial Advisors* by Mary Rowland (Bloomberg Press, 1997)

Reference Books and Manuals—Technical Topics

All of the following provide an in-depth look covering a particular subject matter. The books in the first section cover all areas of financial planning. Some are textbooks while others are reference resource guides.

Personal Financial Planning and Related Topics

- *The Financial Planning Answer Book* by Jeffrey H. Rattiner (Aspen Publishing, early 2003 release)
- *Personal Financial Planning Portfolio Library* by D. Larry Fowler, William Mears and Jeffrey H. Rattiner (Aspen Publishing, 2000)
- *Practicing Financial Planning* by Sid Mittra and Jeffrey H. Rattiner (Mittra & Associates, 2000)
- *Personal Financial Planning* by Practitioners Publishing Company (Practitioners Publishing Company, 2001)
- *Tools and Techniques of Financial Planning* by Steven R. Leimberg (National Underwriter, 2001)

Investment Planning

- *The Management of Investment Decisions* by Donald B. Trone, William R. Allbright and Philip R. Taylor (Irwin, 1996)
- *The Prudent Investor's Guide to Beating the Market* by John Bowen, Jr. (Irwin Publishing, 1996)
- *Wealth Management Index* by Ross Levin (Irwin, 1997)
- *Investment Policy* by Charles Ellis (Business One/Irwin, 1993)
- *Wealth Management: Guide to Investing and Managing Client Assets* by Harold R. Evensky (Irwin, 1997)
- *The New Common Sense Guide to Mutual Funds* (Bloomberg Press, 1998)

- *Stocks in the Long Run* by Jeremy Siegel (Irwin, 1994)
- *Asset Allocation: Balancing Financial Risk* by Roger Gibson (Irwin, 1996)
- *Stocks, Bonds, Bills, Inflation* by Ibbotson & Associates (Ibbotson & Associates, 2002)
- *Investments* by Charles P. Jones (Wiley, 1998)
- *Investments* by Herbert Mayo (Dryden, 6th edition, 2000)

Income Tax Planning

- *Federal Tax Handbook* by Research Institute of America (Research Institute of America, 2002)

Retirement Planning

- *Planning for Retirement Needs* by Kenn Beam Tacchino and David A. Littell (The American College)
- *Social Security Manual* by National Underwriter (National Underwriter, 2002)
- *Pension Answer Book* by Panel Publishers (Aspen Publishing, 2002)
- *Estate and Retirement Answer Book* by Panel Publishing (Aspen Publishing, 2002)
- *IRA Answer Book* by Panel Publishing (Aspen Publishing, 2002)
- *Social Security: The Inside Story* by Andy Landis (Mount Vernon Press, 1993)
- *Tools and Techniques of Employee Benefit and Retirement Planning* by Stephen R. Leimberg (National Underwriter, 2002)

Insurance Planning

- *Fundamentals of Risk and Insurance* by Emmett Vaughn (Wiley, 1998)
- *McGill's Life Insurance* by Ed Graves (The American College, 1994)

Estate Planning

- *Fundamentals of Estate Planning* by Constance J. Fontaine (The American College, 2002)
- *Preserving Family Wealth* by Richard Duff (Berkley Books, 1995)
- *Tools and Techniques of Estate Planning* by Stephen R. Leimberg (National Underwriter)

Divorce Planning

- *The Financial Advisor's Guide to Divorce Settlements* by Carol Ann Wilson (Irwin, 1996)

Education Planning

- *A Professional's Guide to College Planning* by Raymond D. Loewe (National Underwriter, 1998)

Time Value of Money and Cash Flow Issues

- *An Introduction to Cash Flow Analysis* by Robert J. Donahue (The Regent School Press, 1998)

Journals

All of the following provide in-depth technical topics that shake the industry.

- Aspen's *Personal Financial Planning Monthly* (800-243-0876)
- FPA's *Journal of Financial Planning* (800-322-4237)
- American College's *Journal of Financial Service Professionals* (800-392-6900)
- Institutional Investor's *Journal of Investing* (212-224-3185)
- *Trusts & Estates* (770-955-2500)

Magazines

All of the following are the standards of the industry:

- *Financial Planning* (212-765-5311)
- *Investment Advisor* (732-389-8700)
- *Asset Management* (732-389-8700)
- *Investment News* (313-446-0450)
- *Wealth Manager* (609-279-3000)
- *Financial Advisor* (732-450-8866)
- *Personal Financial Planning Monthly* (800-243-0876)

9

The Twenty-First Century Practice the Way I'd Like to See It

STRUCTURING YOUR SMALL FINANCIAL PLANNING FIRM TO REAP THE BENEFITS OF LARGER FIRMS

So far I have spoken about what you can do to advance your practice to the next level. I've provided marketing tips, practice management ideas, and a quantitative framework for bringing it all together. I have even covered specific strategies, such as using Form 1040 as a method for attracting and retaining clients. But I have not spoken about what I would like to see in our profession moving forward, over the next 10 years or so.

In developing my thoughts on this topic over the past 12 years, I have had the privilege to listen to many small practitioners voice their concerns to me. Small practitioners often believe that they are at an unfair disadvantage and that they cannot compete against the larger wirehouses, independents, banks, and insurance companies. They feel that in this era of mega-mergers and other consolidations, the only way for them to compete is to become specialists in one area and know that area extremely well. They must become niche players who fit a particular role, boutique firms. In my mind there is nothing wrong with that, but they feel that they are at a serious disadvantage, since larger firms can provide stronger advice simply because they have the resources (both manpower and cash) to do it. Although our conversations come from many directions and involve practitioners with varying types of practices, the conversations always end up rallying around one key issue.

Perhaps the biggest question I get during these one-on-one sessions is:

> Where can a small practitioner like me go to get good technical financial planning advice? I have several clients that need so-and-so and I feel uncomfortable making recommendations in areas I do not typically come across and do not practice regularly in. I cannot find anyone who truly understands the issue and more importantly, that I can rely upon with total confidence.

To me, this type of statement basically says, "who can I trust when receiving heavy duty technical information? I feel at a loss because I cannot operate in the same manner the big financial service organizations currently do." The more I have thought about it, the more I would interpret these statements to say, how can the small practitioner attain this information and assure its adequacy? Maybe it's time that our profession design a new model displaying a twenty-first century financial planning practice.

THE WAY I SEE IT

If many small practitioners have concerns about technical issues that they provide in the form of advice for their clients, and the majority of them do not have the resources to attract top talent themselves or retain independent technicians, then let us form a loose federation of financial planning firms. Independents would join forces to provide ancillary technical services they cannot do individually like the larger firms simply because of economies of scale. This partnering in no way affects the running of the practitioner's individual practice. Practitioners are still the sole owners of their firms and their operating structures remain the same. Rather, the creation of a federation enables those smaller firms to compete in a manner with their larger counterparts in ways not dreamed of, until now. Together smaller firms will see that the whole (of many different financial planning firms) is greater than its individual parts! In other words, by joining forces, these conglomerates would not compete for business, but rather supplement each other to operate at a higher technical level and provide the makings of big institutional powerhouses.

HOW COULD WE STRUCTURE SOMETHING LIKE THIS?

We need a powerful local financial planning firm to step up to the plate to begin putting this all together. Once that happens, many other firms will do the same. A firm that is nationally respected, operates ethically, and is in touch with the small practitioner would contact enough firms to join about 10 other firms to form this arrangement. I am not talking about setting up just one firm operating in this environment. Multiple arrangements involving many qualified practitioners would take place.

For discussion purposes, the hypothetical firm that elects to pursue this strategy, which we will call "LetsGetTogether Inc.," would send out a mailer to a select listing of financial planning firms across different geographic regions. Lists can be purchased from the many national financial planning publications and/or membership organizations. Planners that serve on national or local trade or membership association committees would be able to identify select committee members who have firms that complement their own and who would make sense to partner with.

The letter would go something like this:

Dear Fellow Practitioner:

With the ever-increasing change in our profession and the demand to be constantly current in everything we do, it has become tough to go through it alone. While we are all professionals who always do what is best for the client, it is becoming apparent and ever more difficult to become a complete one-stop technical superstation to answer all our clients questions on demand. As such, I'm calling on all of you to help us form the "Federation of Financial Planning Practitioners" (FFPP). The FFPP would be a central clearinghouse for those practitioners who need immediate answers to clients technical concerns. The FFPP would be set up similarly to national accounting firms who want an international presence and end up aligning with other overseas firms to provide a "give-and-take" concerning client issues, referrals, and advice. These accounting firms appear bigger than they really are, have a presence in varying marketplaces, and possess the ability to operate at the highest level.

Our firm is trying to associate with financial planning firms that hold expertise in a variety of technical subject areas. We want to become part of a 10 firm loose affiliation in which we can all rely on each other for technical expertise. Each firm would have dedicated personnel any of us can contact to answer client technical questions in a timely fashion. We would not operate jointly, in unison, or as a single entity. Rather, we would depend on one another for technical assistance and support. Our goal is to join a composite of firms that has an expertise in all areas of financial planning.

If your firm is interested, please contact Mr. John Doe at (303) 555-1212. We look forward to exploring future possibilities with you.

Sincerely,

I. M. Ready
President

If your firm wants to pursue this strategy, the FFPP can be structured in one of two ways.

Option No. 1: Have each firm contribute a technical specialty to the FFPP. Firms that are experts in any of the financial planning technical disciplines, such as insurance, investments, income tax, retirement, estate tax, divorce, charitable giving, small business, education, and so on would provide a technical specialist to the group for the other member firm participants, to address technical issues that arise in each of these areas. A qualified staff person from each participating firm would be responsible to address the concerns to any of the member firms that need assistance in that firm's specialty area within a 48-hour turnaround. These qualified technicians would be salaried employees of the host firm. Each firm would be responsible just to pay the salary of the person representing their firm in the FFPP. For example, if there were 10 specialty topics that were identified by the member firms, then 10 financial planning firms would join ranks as a loosely joined federation of firms designed to assist each other in the alliance. Each firm would specialize in a different topical area. This approach will lend itself to advancing each of the 10 firms to a higher playing field. The overall goal would be to be able to answer any client question with much assurance within a relatively short time period.

Each firm would continue to operate as an independent financial planning firm. There would be no organizational difference in the manner in which the firm continues to operate, and no revenue sharing arrangements with the member firms. There would be no joint board of directors or uniform operating policy. Rather, each firm would be able to leverage the expertise of known technical specialty firms and contribute to the overall well-being of the profession. Each firm would be able to leverage the other firms to ensure overall competence in each of the major financial planning disciplines.

Option No. 2: Have each firm contribute a certain amount of retainer dollars each month to an independent outfit (FFPP), which would be responsible for hiring a team of technicians to address member questions with a 48-hour turnaround. These specialists would be experienced and well-versed in the one subject area they represent. They would come from industry and have anywhere from 10 to 30 years practical experience. Questions and issues can be discussed by phone, e-mail, fax, or even live, and all members would be able to provide "key advice on demand in all technical areas within a quick turnaround time." This approach would lend itself to having more than 10 firms participating (as described in the option No. 1 approach) so economies of scale can be met by participating member firms.

For example, if 10 specialists were hired at $75,000 each, a total of $750,000 would be needed here. Assuming miscellaneous operating costs of $250,000 (for the overall executive director's position, an executive (office) assistant, telephone and other electronic charges, and office space at a remote location), a total of $1 million dollars would be needed each year. If we can have 500 firms (that sounds like a lot, but remember, there are over 500,000 self proclaimed and credentialed financial planners in the marketplace) contributing $2,000 each, per year ($166 per month), 250 firms contributing $4,000 per year ($332 per month), or even 100 firms at $10,000 per year ($833 per month) hardly an ungodly sum, then a true service would be provided to those practitioners. Think about it. If your firm wanted to hire a specialist, they would surely have to pay more than the amounts mentioned above to do it. Even if that person was solely on retainer. This approach enables the small practitioner to have access to some of the best and brightest minds in the business.

This organizational structure would not be like a membership association, such as the Financial Planning Association (FPA). The FPA does an exceptional job of providing member benefits and locating various sources of providers of information for its members and possibly developing some of its own materials for those purposes as well. However, in my scenario, the FFPP would have live, in-house salaried employees whose sole responsibility would be to field questions and concerns from its member public. In essence, it would be a telephone bank of people, much like mutual fund companies have "call people" ready to answer questions from customers on its mutual fund accounts on demand.

THE REALITY

Think about it. Wouldn't you feel comfortable with a team of experts that can bail you out of complex critical issues simply with just one phone call or piece of correspondence? These alliances would enable small practitioners to reap the benefits of large firms who specialize in financial planning issues without the significant cost and personnel necessary to compete at the higher levels. If we are all in the same boat together, would it not make sense for all of us to come together for the common good of our clientele and the profession? Maintaining an excellent and technically superior back office presence enhances each of our roles with our clients. Remember, as I keep saying throughout the book, there is more than enough money in the field for all of us to earn a very healthy and comfortable living and do the right thing for the client.

Index